Sabotaged

Dreams of Utopia in Texas

JAMES PRATT

University of Nebraska Press | Lincoln

Library of Congress Cataloging-in-Publication Data
Names: Pratt, James, 1927– author.
Title: Sabotaged: dreams of utopia in Texas /
James Pratt.
Description: Lincoln: University of Nebraska
Press, [2020] | Includes bibliographical references
and index. | Summary: "'Sabotaged' is the account
of French, Swiss, and Belgian intellectuals who
followed Victor Considerant to Texas in 1855 in a
quixotic attempt to fulfill their dreams of a new life
in a utopia"—Provided by publisher.
Identifiers: LCCN 2019021372
ISBN 9781496207920 (cloth)
ISBN 9781496220127 (epub)
ISBN 9781496220141 (pdf)
ISBN 9781496220134 (mobi)
Subjects: LCSH: Considerant, Victor, 1808–1893. |
Fourier, Charles, 1772–1837—Influence. | Utopias—
Texas—History. | Utopian socialism—Texas—
History. | Collective settlements—Texas—History. |
La Réunion (Tex.)—History.
Classification: LCC HX655.T4 P73 2020 | DDC
307.77092 [B]—dc23
LC record available at https://lccn.loc.gov/2019021372

Set in ITC New Baskerville by Laura Ebbeka.

Frontispiece:
Auguste Savardan in 1852, age fifty-nine. Savardan
Collection (de Lesseps).

To the memory of Peggy Harrison,
my ninth-grade English teacher,
who taught this Texan not to
say "git," "gist," and "fur" and
who taught me to write.

Contents

Illustrations

Preface

Who would have thought that early settlers of the Three Forks of the Trinity River included European intellectuals bent on establishing a socialist utopia near the hamlet of Dallas, Texas? Surprisingly, I found La Réunion, an 1855 Fourierist colony on the banks of the Trinity River three miles west of this hamlet. The colony was peopled by immigrant French, Swiss, and Belgians, and they left many records. Thus, by accident I was lured into a hunt for scattered materials that had never been listed in established library resources. As I accumulated writings, they revealed links to mid-nineteenth-century social history between the Southwest and the world.

My quest has been arduous and exhilarating. I found living descendants of the nineteenth-century colonists. I came to see Dr. Auguste Savardan, one of the French leaders of La Réunion, as the hero of the La Réunion venture. I discovered the Countess O. de Lesseps, his descendant, who invited me to visit Savardan's family château in Sarthe, France, which overlooked the village where he had served as mayor. My research came alive before me. Savardan's materials were conserved in his library just as he left them. At the bottom of a Louis XII stairway hung his portrait. On the wall of the main salon hung the large painting of his wife and daughter that played its part in our story. Neatly shelved in his library were his bound books and images of Fourierist dreams of a new society. The countess served lunch on his still-intact china. The cedars of Lebanon that he planted still grow as giants framing the parterre of his garden.

I found in the Hôtel de Soubise and the École Normale Supérieure in Paris the papers of La Réunion leader Victor Considerant and the European American Society of Colonization in Texas (Société de colonisation européo-américaine au Texas), the parent stock company that raised funds for La Réunion. A French great-great-granddaughter of another major leader of the movement had written a thesis on her ancestor. A Texan granddaughter had translated materials from her immigrant forebear. A member of the defunct Familistère de Guise (Social Palace at Guise) kindly gave me records from that related organization, the brainchild of La Réunion's chief investor. In the Franche-Comté (now the Bourgogne-Franche-Comté), a librarian in Salins and a grandson of Fourierist leader Clarisse Vigoureux in Besançon supplied data. As a child one leader had seen his father, a commandant of the National Guard during the first revolution, lead in the town square revolutionary ceremonies that replaced religion. Others had been in Napoleon's army. The French Sûreté Nationale had records of these Republicans who had fled to Texas or been placed under house arrest for opposing Napoleon III as he carried out his 1851 coup d'état.

Fourierists from other failed communities came to La Réunion for a second try at utopian living. After the demise in 1847 of Brook Farm, West Roxbury, Massachusetts, letters in various New England libraries showed attempts to continue that social experiment with ties to the Texas colony. I found other connections across France, Switzerland, and Belgium.

The utopians' story gradually emerged as the complex tale of a diverse group of Europeans who sought a new society but were forced to interact with the nineteenth-century Anglo and Native American frontier. They experienced life on ships under sail with Spanish gunboats sniffing in their Caribbean wake. They plied Buffalo Bayou between Galveston Bay and Houston—so narrow a channel that two ships could not pass as they brushed blooming magnolias. They walked for three weeks across empty Texas, were frustrated and baffled by the Texas legislature in session, and had to buy their stolen horses back from Chief Ned, a famous Delaware Indian living in Texas. They were buffeted by the rising political winds of abolition, by the Know-Nothing Party's suspicion of foreigners, and by the rabid southern editor of an Austin newspaper who would rather have seen Texas "a howling desert" than peopled with the likes of one of these Fourierists, who was a Universalist minister and an alumnus of Brook Farm.

La Réunion colonists' lives inspired my research into and my record-ing of the facts of this last major American attempt by adepts of Charles Fourier to reconstruct the whole of society as a utopia. The entire cast is listed in the appendix. I warn readers that a lot of people and places appear in the story, and each is real. There are no composite characters.

Scenes written to heighten the reader's interest are grounded in con-temporary accounts. For example, in chapter 1 I have created the dialogue between Savardan and his cook and the story of Savardan finding the abandoned babies; as mayor, he was directly responsible for foundlings abandoned at city hall. Finally, some "dialogue" that makes the story more readable lacks direct citations but is written in the style of the times. Thus, consider me as your trusted narrator, bringing to you the story embedded in reams of material gathered over years of research. The appendix is a compilation of individuals and places connected to the La Réunion venture either directly or peripherally.

Acknowledgments

I am indebted to numerous people for their generosity in helping me research and write this piece of history over some thirty-five years. The list below does not begin to truly acknowledge their numbers or kindnesses.

First and foremost, for counsel and continuing support, I thank John Crain, director of the Dallas Historical Society and later officer of the Summerlee Foundation. He obtained major gifts from the Caruth Foundation and Fikes Foundation and some project support from the Dallas Historical Society, all located in Dallas, Texas. John Crain went with me and my daughter Alexandra Pratt to a farm hamlet north of Dallas to meet Maximilien Reverchon's great-granddaughter Marie Caillet, starting my accumulation of data about the La Réunion colony.

For suggestions and final editing, I thank Joanne Henderson Pratt, without whose help I would never have finished this project and achieved publication. Barbara Miercourt and Susan Tungate provided valuable editorial input. Mme Marguerite Trapp provided continuing support in translating French manuscript letters over many years. Alexandra Pratt, Bernard Lapeyre, and Michael Cordillot also helped with translations.

Peter Agnew provided advice on organization and general support for four years while finishing his dissertation at Southern Methodist University in Dallas, Texas. Ben Huseman in the smu DeGolyer Library provided this same support. Jeremy Adams, Jonathan Beecher, Carl Guameri, and Michael Cordillot gave scholarly advice. Orialice Strait and Lois Agnew provided administrative support. Jean Claude DuBos as well as Gaston Bordet and Thomas Bouchet supported my work and offered guidance through their publication, *Cahiers Charles Fourier*.

My mother, Margaret Barret Pratt, was the founder of the local history and genealogy department of the Dallas Public Library. Her professionalism and unstinting help to earlier researchers earned many friends for this project before I even thought of it; for example, she helped track down Polish archive content on Kalixt Wolski. Lois Hudgins, Lucile Boykin, Marvin Stone, Carol Roark, Frances Bell, Lloyd Bochstock, and others aided research on the project. The Dallas Scottish Rite library provided information regarding the early Dallas hamlet. Peggy Riddle and numerous personnel of the Dallas Historical Society provided help. Everett DeGolyer Jr. and James Phillips at the DeGolyer Library at Southern Methodist University in Dallas initially guided me. In the Abernathy Library of American Literature at Middlebury College, Middlebury, Vermont, I found papers of John Allen. In the Mordecai Papers at the University of North Carolina, Chapel Hill, were those of his wife, Ellen Lazarus Allen. I found more Universalist papers at the Massachusetts Historical Society, at the Andover-Harvard Theological Library, and at the Houghton and Widener Libraries in Cambridge, Massachusetts. In Red Bank, New Jersey, I found the papers of the North American Phalanx, which led me to the University of Syracuse, which has papers of Albert Brisbane. In the late 1950s the main catalog of the Library of Congress had no index listing for La Réunion, but a kind reader in West Texas directed me to find Amédée Simonin's important diary of his trip to Texas in the library's manuscript collection.

Mme Wendy Mill and Ian Frazer spent a year gathering materials in France and Belgium. In France, Besançon librarian Jean Claude DuBos, descendant of colonist Julie Considerant, insisted that my wife and I stay in his home while we were researching in that city. A librarian in Salins showed me burial locations. The librarians at the Hôtel de Soubise were very helpful, and at the Hôtel de Rohan I found François Jean Cantagrel's Réunion archive. They also identified student work of the Réunion leaders and data on their army life in Metz at the École Normale Supérieure. Henri Labrouste's great library reading room in the Bibliothèque nationale provided several publications of Dr. Auguste Savardan.

I am particularly indebted to Mlle Myriam Lodeweyckx, librarian in the Center for American Studies, Brussels, who granted me great hospitality in organizing my time in Belgium, even to offering me stack privileges in her library during closed hours. Mme John Bartier helped with her husband's Bibliothèque Maçonnique. Mme Nicole Demaret, conservator of the Musée de Folklore, and Mme Laurette Locatelli in Tournai found the witty poet and later town hero Adolphe Leray, who stated that he left La Réunion "with only a carrot." M. Rabau, former leader of the Familistère de Guise, gave me a generous gift of materials on Jean-Baptiste André Godin. Herr Klaus Linow in Zurich identified some twenty-five Swiss who contributed to the project before, during, and after La Réunion.

Mme la Comtesse O. de Lesseps, descendant of Auguste Savardan, invited me to spend a day in her family château in La Chapelle-Gaugain, Sarthe. She and her family have preserved the history, artifacts, and milieu of generations back to Louis XI, including Savardan's leather-bound library and his index of it, his portrait as a young man and that of his wife and stepdaughter, illustrations of the ideal Familistère, the elegant etching portrait of Charles Fourier, and his burial place. Gabrielle Cadier-Rey, the descendant of Réunion leader Allyre Bureau (the first sketch artist of La Réunion), introduced me to her mother. Her thesis on Bureau led me to explore colonist travel routes in Texas. Judy Davison provided information for Randoll Davison. David V. Trout provided information for V. E. Gibbens, who discovered the first travel journal of La Réunion colonists searching for land in North Texas. M. Bruno Verlet alerted me to the French in Texas Symposium at the University of Texas at Austin. Mlle Marie Caillet provided the Julien Reverchon travel diary and family data, as well as his recorded hunting bag on first arrival at La Réunion. Judge Newton Fitzhugh gave important advice on the mores of the early Dallas hamlet in slave-owning times and gave me his early Texas histories.

Laura Wilson shared the key cell phone number that led to the University of Nebraska Press. Alisa Plant at the press enthusiastically accepted the manuscript and with her assistant, Courtney Ochsner, shepherded *Sabotaged* into publication. Heartfelt thanks for the help of the highly professional staff of the press for making this project a reality.

Sabotaged

Introduction

Charles Fourier's Philosophy in Brief

French philosopher Charles Fourier, who lived from 1772 to 1837, formulated a concept he called "passional attraction." Labeled the "Messiah of Reason," he criticized bourgeois society for having created an unnatural one. He detested industrial society. He was contemptuous of the individualism of the utilitarians. Fourier proposed a completely nonrepressive society in which basic human drives would be expressed and cultivated. He wanted a community tied together by the bonds of emotion. In Fourier's view, human nature was created by God, and society should respect that.

Fourier decried the speculation, cycles of inflation, and industrial stagnation that prevailed when the free market was reestablished after the French Revolution. He advocated elevating the status of manual labor. To the Judeo-Christian belief that work is unavoidably toilsome, Fourier responded that all work was arduous and irksome. To overcome its dehumanization, he advocated turning work into something pleasurable, desirable, and deeply satisfying physically and mentally by placing it under what he called a "phalanx," or communal association of producers recalling the ancient Greek interdependent fighting unit. His *phalanstère*, or phalanstery, built on 810 psychological types (or 1,620 if both female and male types were included), was to become a self-contained community. He championed variety and short periods for work.

Fourier pointed out many kinds of oppression, later expanded upon in modern education theory, the movement for the emancipation of women, and even personnel management. He argued that the family was partly responsible for the subjugation of women because it turned people inward to spouse and children rather than outward to society.

Fourier recognized twelve fundamental passions: the five senses, four passions of the soul (friendship, love, ambition, and parenthood), and three "distributive" passions. The latter consisted first in the love of variety. He held Christianity in contempt because it made people feel guilty when they pursued their natural desire for variety in work or sex. Society should strive to eliminate all tedious or unpleasant jobs. Adam Smith was wrong in his liberal political economy because it created stunted and repressed human beings.

Rivalry and conspiracy were the second distributive passion he addressed. In Fourier's vision, productive phalanx teams would compete with one another, satisfying a natural urge. The harmful aspects of production would not be reproduced, because the phalanxes would keep the overall good of society in mind rather than encouraging individual profit in the market.

He defined the third distributive passion as two or more different varieties of passions combined. Fourier was an ardent advocate of sexual liberation and a staunch defender of sexual preferences, ideas that were not accepted by religion or society and that were suppressed even by some of his followers, including his self-appointed disciple Victor Considerant, who organized Fourier's thoughts in a three-volume dialectic and who would lead the establishment of La Réunion on the banks of the Trinity River in Texas in 1855.

This is the account of French, Swiss, and Belgian intellectuals and frustrated individuals who followed Considerant to Texas, driven to fulfill their dreams of a new life in a utopia.

1

The Doctor's Community

Two babies wrapped in a bloody rag lay on the steps in front of the village hall door. Mayor Auguste Savardan stopped and hitched his horse. When he opened the bundle, one child moved. The smaller one, the one with the umbilical cord still draped loosely around its neck, did not. The mayor, also a doctor, felt for a pulse. Finding one in each baby, he rewrapped the bundle, sighing. He carried them inside the hall and laid them on the warm bricks near the faded coals of yesterday's fire.

He sat thinking for several minutes. As usual, he would need to find a wet nurse for these twins. They were the fifth or sixth foundlings within the month. To complicate matters further, it was Sunday. The woman he usually turned this problem over to would be attending mass at this hour.

Picking up the bundle, he did not go into the nearby church but unhitched the gelding and loosened the reins, urging the horse toward his home, Château Gaugain, which dominated the village of La Chapelle-Gaugain. Inside the wall, he drove the horse around the north side of the château and hitched the gelding's reins to a ring in the limestone wall. He carried the tiny forms into the warm kitchen, calling the cook to quickly prepare a pot of warm water. He cradled the almost lifeless smaller infant in the water and massaged the tiny chest. He requested the cook to bathe the other baby.

Why the doctor worried with the endless stream of infants that God really didn't want perplexed the cook.[1] Without looking away from the baby in his hands, Dr. Savardan said, "Be sure you wash your hands thoroughly." "I don't like all that dirty, bloody water on the counter next to the goose I am plucking for dinner," the cook replied, thinking that the lives of these little bastards should just as well be put in the ground. She assumed they weren't sanctioned in a marriage. She didn't really want to touch them. The doctor glanced sharply at her. "Do it anyway. These babies need us." His tone left no room for defiance.

Later, Dr. Savardan again inspected the babies. Seeing that they had survived the cold, he and the cook rewrapped them in dry, clean cloths. He took them in his carriage back down the ramp and into the countryside. Jacques Blot's wife was probably lactating.

There had to be a better answer for the lives of these abandoned foundlings. The convent in La Flèche, eighteen miles away where the doctor's four aunts lived, took some of the babies, but there were so many. The parish of only seven hundred people had to rely on women in farm families to suckle them. The few babies that survived became extra work hands, a reward to those families. The foundlings could look forward to a life without education, a life of ignorance and servitude.[2]

To Dr. Savardan, known throughout the community as a kind man, albeit a nonbeliever, a religious convent was not an answer. Savardan wanted families to be in charge of education. He hated seeing boys and girls separated in asylums under the hand of a religion he considered oppressive. As early as the age of three he had questioned the logic of church practices after he wandered into a Communion ceremony. Later, the bishop said to the local priest, "Since this good man has charity, but not faith, do not discuss religion with him; just make sure you pray for him."[3]

After he became mayor in 1836 at the age of forty-four, Dr. Savardan was stunned by the poverty, ignorance, and lack of resources available to solve community problems, including this abandonment of so many newborns.

With the discipline he had acquired in medical training, he attacked the problem wholly, counting available resources. He began with a detailed census of the area surrounding the village of La Chapelle-Gaugain, which was located a short distance from the Loire Valley. He even counted beehives.

As he analyzed the numbers, he thought about the possibilities of combined resources in all aspects of income production and education. When he read the ideas of Charles Fourier, he embraced that philosopher's dictum to combine talent, resources, and labor to reorganize

1. Auguste Savardan as a young man, age about twenty-six.
Savardan Collection (de Lesseps).

society.[4] Fourier's chief disciple was the charismatic Victor Considerant. Savardan was influenced by him as well. After thoughtful consideration of all the options, Dr. Savardan decided to turn his château into an asylum for foundlings. He had been elated when the Council General of the Seine, in its last session of 1847, "voted unanimously to make La Chapelle-Gaugain a model community with a rural asylum for foundlings and a farm school.[5] But that had not yet happened.

2

A Better Site for a *Phalanstère*

In this community of indifference, Dr. Savardan decided to appeal to a group that stood for social betterment, the École Sociétaire in Paris, founded to carry out the precepts of Charles Fourier. Savardan wrote to the École, asking for support for his project. Allyre Bureau, administrator of the Paris office, responded on behalf of the exiled leader, Victor Considerant. Bureau replied that, sadly, the school could not offer support until old debts had been paid. Bureau could not say when that might be or how much money might be offered.

In an effort to move his project forward, Dr. Savardan wrote a tract to be published by the École pleading for his infant asylum.[1] Another year passed with no action, so he wrote a pamphlet refuting point by point the objections to his proposal for an asylum and a more efficient farm.[2]

He had become particularly interested in promoting the newly invented mechanical bailer as a way of increasing productivity. With a horse, one man, and three children, the machine could produce fifty bushels of grain daily. A rumor spread that Dr. Savardan had a machine that would cut the necks of workers.[3] Fortunately, Savardan's neck was saved by the "good people" of La Chapelle-Gaugain, who came with their pitchforks to defend him from a drunken mob terrified of his machine.

After twelve years in office Dr. Savardan was deposed as mayor in April 1848 over a dispute with the bureaucrats about keeping accurate records of foundling births. He had testified to a birth in the village register on March 22. That angered the bureaucrats, who looked bad when the mayor did not automatically attest to the correctness of the registers they presented to him every three months. Dr. Savardan wanted accurate counts; the bureaucrats wanted beautifully inscribed enrollment records that reflected well on them. Inaccuracy was unimportant. The bureaucrats won.

In 1849 Savardan published under the banner of the École Sociétaire his *Défense des enfants trouvés et de leur asile rural* ("Observations soumises à MM. les membres de la Commission départementale de la Seine"). In this tract the doctor, railing against conditions for found-lings and their 50 percent mortality rate before reaching age twenty-one, challenged the bureaucrats to abide by their commitment, made in 1847 proposals created prior to the February Revolution, to help foundlings by setting up his proposed asylum for four hundred children.

Savardan's passion for bringing about a phalanstery was resolute. Finally, "certain honorable phalansterians downriver at Nantes," those whom the École Sociétaire in Paris had estranged, proposed a subscrip-tion for the establishment of a rural home for foundlings. Désiré Laver-dant and Dr. Savardan were willing to be directors of the home, the first man for education and the second for administration.

The two began to raise funds for turning their château in La Chapelle-Gaugain into a rural school for orphans. Since Savardan and his brother-in-law Adolphe, baron de La Fontaine-Solar, had purchased the château, a national property, in 1832, he had worked assiduously to improve it as a farm. Savardan had been appalled by the rural ignorance, outmoded farming practices and machinery, bad hygiene, lack of education, and those infants left on the municipal doorstep.

Savardan worked on many fronts, at first building irrigation ditches to harness springs, allowing his château lands to yield more and better produce.[4] He became an inspector of rural asylums for foundlings in several political departments, all the way to the Nord on the channel coast, finding and attacking atrocious conditions where children were treated as slaves and encouraged to thievery and even to robbery.[5]

In 1850 Savardan sponsored a communal bakery in a village near La Chapelle-Gaugain to improve the quality and cost of bread, thereby making himself highly unpopular with those previously in control. He insisted on better education and, as a long-term investment to fund it, planted a timber crop of chestnut trees.[6]

Following the precepts of Charles Fourier, Savardan established a mutual insurance company to protect small investors.[7] But "in 1850, as the Second Republic's rhetorical vapor disappeared before the hard,

2. Auguste Savardan and his wife. Savardan Collection (de Lesseps).

inexorable realities of money, power, and state violence, a great cooling down occurred."[8] Savardan's ideas were disquieting to the Catholic Church, which taught that the only book peasants needed to read was the Bible. Fourier and his followers were understood as threats to the church. Dr. Savardan was forced to leave his sick wife for an internment in jail, to which the departmental commission condemned him under the charge of conducting "subversive demagoguery." He found consolation in the conspicuous examples of past martyred heroes—Socrates's hemlock, Jesus's cross, Galileo's prison, and in so "many other tortures," as he put it, "produced by ignorance."[9]

In 1851 Dr. Savardan and his friend Laverdant, freed from political confinement, decided to raise funds for the reestablishment of a phalansterian colony at Condé sur Vesgre, eighty kilometers east of Paris. One had been established there in 1832, but by 1851 it was for sale after the land went into bankruptcy. Before the two could gather all the funds needed to buy it, Condé's property was again sold. Laverdant, a committed churchman, eventually parted company with Savardan over his lack of faith.

Still, Dr. Savardan remained committed to establishing an infants' asylum. He again turned his attention to creating the asylum in his largely empty château. The château would work well for the purpose. The second and third floors were lined with many bedrooms, and the kitchen and first-floor common rooms were generous. There was a commodious attic. A large kitchen not far from an enormous round dovecote supplied protein to the kitchen, as well as copious fertilizer for the farm produce and the great slate-roofed barn for animals. Its adjacent area specifically for geese near the kitchen provided another.

In December 1851 Charles-Louis Napoléon mounted a coup d'état, proclaiming himself Emperor Napoleon III. As the emperor consolidated power, Savardan, the former mayor and army surgeon aide-major, was placed under house arrest for fifty-two days in March 1852.

Then Francophile Albert Brisbane, a resident of New York and frequent visitor to France, set in motion a series of events that ended Dr. Savardan's hope of carrying out Fourier's precepts in France. In order to learn firsthand the beliefs of that master, Brisbane had paid Fourier for lessons twenty years earlier. At the time of the latest coup, Brisbane had been lecturing in Paris on the virtues of Fourierism. As an American he had not been arrested, but the Sûreté Nationale, the police, ordered him for the second time to leave the country.

The coup sent Brisbane to Belgium, from where he was able to convince Considerant to sail with him that fall to America at Brisbane's expense. Considerant's goal in going to America was to escape the ennui of his four years of exile for a few weeks. Brisbane's goal was to establish yet another Fourierist colony after many failed attempts in the north-eastern United States ten years before.[10] This time he would try to persuade the French Fourierists to establish a utopian community in the free land available in the American West.

In the fall of 1853 Considerant returned from America aglow with new hopes for Fourierism. He told the adepts of the philosophy that he had seen great empty reaches of land in North Texas where establishing a self-contained community, a phalanstery, would be possible. Not only was the land empty, it could be had for free from the state of Texas. He told all who would listen that the land was as beautiful as Henry VIII's park at Richmond on the Thames. It was far away from control and bad influences. The Mormons were already establishing a colony farther west. If they could do it, why not the Fourierists?

In a style addressed to European intellectuals, Considerant set about writing *Au Texas*. In the book he set forth his vision of the new Fourierist society in Texas, a land of abundance, freedom, and pleasing weather where no crops ever failed for lack of water. When he published his book in Belgium the following spring of 1854, copies were distributed by the Fourierists in France. Dr. Savardan immediately subscribed to the project. It appeared that Texas offered a place where his long-sought dream of a new Fourierist society could be achieved without the constraints he found in France.

Dr. Savardan went to Belgium at the end of December 1854 to see how serious Considerant was about the components that the doctor knew were essential for a thriving community if they were to overcome the barriers he had met in France: a common kitchen, common school, library, common carriage, common bath, common laundry, infirmary, and places to live to suit those who did not like the noise and lack of privacy in a barracks. Reassured by Considerant's vision, Savardan agreed to become a director of the group of Fourierists assembled to formally bring into existence the European American Society of Colonization in Texas, organized as a Belgian stock company. *Au Texas* was widely read across France, and numerous enthusiasts sent in funds not only to participate in the phalanx but also as investments. Money poured in, almost $400,000 by the end of the year.

3. Victor Considerant. Courtesy of The Image Works;
photograph © H. Roger-Viollet.

The plan was to establish the phalanx before the pioneers from Europe arrived at the site. They would build houses, plant gardens, and sow the fields. They would raise fine horses and stock domestic animals.

The directors sent François Cantagrel, an architect and an engineer who had been a member of the legislature with Considerant and who had also escaped to Belgium and spent four years in exile, to Texas to find a site for what would be called La Réunion. Unbeknownst to Considerant, things had changed in America since his visit.

3

First Emissaries to the Frontier

While Dr. Savardan and the investing Fourierists gathered in Paris for their first stockholders' meeting, their appointee, François Jean Cantagrel, accompanied by Edmund Roger, a young Belgian medical student, Arthur Lawrie, a young New Yorker hired as factotum and guard, and the Reverend John Allen, a Universalist minister from the United States, were standing in the prow of a skiff cutting through thick, red water of the Red River in the southwestern United States. The shadows grew long as the ferry moved southwest toward a broken line in the riverbank ahead. It was four in the afternoon. Behind them lay Indian Territory. It was Forefathers' Day, December 22, a day still being celebrated in the New World in 1854, 234 years after the first pilgrims landed in New England.[1] With arms and voice raised, Reverend Allen gave an extemporaneous speech, expounding on the landing of the Pilgrims. New Yorker Albert Brisbane had introduced Reverend Allen to Considerant as an ardent member of the failed Brook Farm, the Transcendental utopian community turned phalanx in Roxbury, Massachusetts. He was so dedicated to Fourierism that he had named his now four-year-old son Victor Considerant Allen.[2]

But these four pilgrims saw no New England rocky, gray-granite coast shrouded in mist as they approached a low, red-sand bluff decked with bare, scarlet-tipped willows in front of unclothed hardwoods, hazy and silhouetted in the soft, late-day sun. It was the border of Texas.[3]

The group's aim was to acquire land and prepare a place to receive new pilgrims from Europe, pilgrims intent on escaping not only religion but also civilization. As followers of the philosophy of Charles Fourier, two of these men believed that Associationism, or the Combined Order, would succeed the present social order of isolation, incoherence, and conflict and that it would sweep from "our earth Repugnant Industry, Tyranny of Capital, Chattel Slavery and all forms of bondage and oppression of the human race." They were convinced that society had to be totally reconstituted to erase its evils. They spoke disparagingly of a corrupted civilization and *civilisés*. Under the power of Fourier-inspired thought, all individual evils would vanish. After many false tries, their European American Society of Colonization in Texas would finally prove Fourier's theory.

Like the earlier Pilgrims, who had realized their hopes after they saw the gray western shore of a seemingly empty land, these men hoped for free land and even dreamed of land with vacated buildings—the abandoned log fort they knew about on the edge of a settled area—to use as a receiving station for colonists. It was called Worth, a fort decommissioned fifteen months before after the Plains Indians had been forced farther west by army dragoons patrolling from a string of defenses that ran south from the Red River.[4]

Fueled by his hopes for a utopian community in this land, Reverend Allen drew inspiration that December day from the earlier Pilgrims in New England. Reverend Allen was not a tall man. The forty-year-old minister was endowed with "a noble brow" and prodigious energy. His enthusiasm blinded viewers to his plain features and unruly dark brown hair, "which asserted its rights in spite of brush and comb, and would not lie gracefully down over his brow, and it added to the look of determination there was on the little man's countenance, shown by the lines in his face and rigid and spare muscles, a 'hold on' expression which so coincided with his character."[5] He had prepared for this mission for seven years, since that day in 1847 when he had left failing Brook Farm. His dedication to Fourierist ideals had been intensified by meeting Victor Considerant eighteen months ago, when he and Brisbane visited Considerant's home.

Trusting in and believing good of everyone, Reverend Allen had never varied from the time when the recorder of the Newton and Watertown Universalist Societies in Massachusetts marked in his minutes book his incredulity with three exclamation points after young Reverend Allen offered to preach two Sabbaths for "ought save his meat and drink."[6] A peripatetic zealousness for reform was still magnified in Reverend Allen.

Though conservatives might have thought his preaching of Fourierism mixed with Christianity bordered on blasphemy, his earnestness was never in doubt. It was what had impelled him to Texas, a state in the Union for only nine years that offered great empty reaches of land but that also was permissive in many practices that were alien to the Yankee reverend's cast-iron conscience, a particular legacy from his mentor, the Reverend Sylvanus Cobb.[7]

Cobb had quit his pulpit to begin an abolitionist newspaper when the subject of slavery was still nascent in the New England conscience. Reverend Allen, too, had resigned from his first church when, ten days after the congregation agreed that he would be allowed to preach on the unpopular subject of abolition four times during the year, they changed their minds. Reverend Allen later said he was fired by the congregation.[8] In 1841, three years after this act of conscience, a Mississippi newspaper, reacting to Allen's occasional sermons on abolition, called him "a blackleg of the blackest kind."[9]

Reverend Allen's extemporizing this Forefathers' Day grew out of much experience. He had entered the ministry just after the Panic of 1837, influenced by this event, which brought to a head the need for social, political, and economic reform throughout the young republic. He served as minister in five New England Universalist churches, but the idealistic core of this man gradually rejected the status quo.[10] As early as 1843 his name headed a list of those advocating a ten-hour maximum workday in a workingman's protective union, yet ironically, on December 22, 1854, he was planning to work far longer hours in Texas.[11]

As Reverend Allen was crossing the Red River, he thought of his second wife, Ellen, who was waiting in Patriot, Indiana, with their six-week-old baby and two older children to join him "in association."[12] Going to Texas was but the latest of his attempts to restore the ethos of Brook Farm, where he had spent twenty-six months living "in association" after abandoning his preaching in conservative pulpits.[13] At Brook Farm nine years ago he had been one of a younger group who volunteered to raise money after it became evident that the farm was failing. Going about New England and upstate New York on frequent circuits, he had sought subscriptions to the *Harbinger*, a weekly magazine published at the farm that discussed social problems, and lectured on Fourier's doctrines.[14] After a fire at Brook Farm first chilled hopes for success at that phalanx, Reverend Allen wrote to a fellow Brook Farmer that he was good for nothing out of association.[15] After Brook Farm closed in 1847, Allen was anointed by W. H. Channing and the Religious Union of Associationists to evangelize in the Midwest.[16] Perhaps partly out of nostalgia for their life together at Brook Farm, a year later he married Ellen Lazarus.

From Maine to Indiana, Allen's career had touched the major reform movements from the late 1830s until now, 1854: temperance, abolition, workingmen's protection, and Fourierism.

As the Red River rushed around the skiff, Reverend Allen recalled the moment eighteen months earlier when he and Considerant sat with Brisbane on the Allens' porch in Patriot, a village on the banks of the Ohio, backed by a crescent of farmland isolated by round green hills. While they sat there together watching a paddle wheeler disappear downriver on the swelling springtime waters, Brisbane told him he was escorting Considerant to a possible site for his utopian community. This new opportunity for association made Reverend Allen offer to take up lecturing again. "When you find the site, I will sell everything and be ready in eight days to follow," Reverend Allen had replied to Considerant. "What's more, I will take up lecturing again to seek participants and investors for the enterprise."[17] That pledge gained credibility with Considerant when Ellen brought out their son, four-year-old Victor Considerant Allen, for the Frenchman to admire.[18] Walking along the Ohio riverbank, Reverend Allen showed Considerant vineyards he had planted.[19] Perhaps vineyards could be planted in the community Considerant envisioned.

As the four drifted on the river that December day, Reverend Allen was painfully aware that he was unable to deliver on his fundraising promise to Considerant. His lecturing in Indiana and Ohio on the future colony had produced almost nothing. Although well known as a lecturer on Associationism, he was almost totally ignored by the press of 1854.[20] Midwesterners did not bite on the Fourierist idea; it no longer captured the American imagination, largely due to the many failed experiments

4. François Cantagrel. Savardan Collection (de Lesseps).

in the previous decade. The last association of those formed in the 1840s on the East Coast, the North American Phalanx of New Jersey, was about to fail. Allen had been able to pry dollars out of only one investor, his brother-in-law, and in fact borrowed money himself to make the trip to Texas with the others to find land.[21]

To make up for his own lack of cash to invest in the new enterprise, Allen had arranged for five hundred cuttings from his vineyards to be crated and accompanied by his twelve-year-old son, Fred. Fred had watched from the dock as these four men embarked for Texas on the river paddle wheeler *Highflyer* in November 1854. Small for his age, Fred Allen carried with him the effects of smallpox, which he had suffered as an infant at Brook Farm. But Reverend Allen was confident that Fred would be vigilant as he shepherded the vines to Texas a month later.[22]

Now on the Red River, Reverend Allen stood on the ferry watching the water churn, venturing into a slave state to help begin a new community just as southern passions were hardening. To seek utopia, Allen was traveling with Considerant's emissary, François Jean Cantagrel. American English was new to this French leader of the vanguard standing on the deck while Reverend Allen spoke.[23] It was of no matter, since Cantagrel paid little attention to Reverend Allen; instead, Cantagrel analyzed the land and the potential of the river to carry market freight and worried about how far they would get that night. Cantagrel hoped to break ground in the prairie during the first ten days of January. The first wave of emigrants from Europe was coming soon. Time was short to prepare for their arrival. He had other disquieting thoughts. What if the railroads hadn't reached North Texas by the time the colony was ready for markets? It would take three weeks for oxen to arrive at Three Forks from the nearest river port. He felt many pressures. How was his wife, Josephine?

Cantagrel had been optimistic about Josephine traveling in the last term of pregnancy. If they had left in early August, they would have arrived in New York in plenty of time to be established for the birth of their second child.[24] But everything had revolved around Considerant, who had been clapped in jail in August by Belgian police suspicious about a gun order. This caused the signing of legal agreements incorporating the Texas colony to be delayed. By then it was late for Josephine to make an ocean voyage, but pressure from Considerant and Jean Godin, chief funder of La Réunion, forced the Cantagrels to leave on October 3, 1854. Twenty-two days on shipboard were too many for Josephine. She gave birth to the child the day before they docked in New York.[25]

When Cantagrel had first seen the New World harbor in the crisp October air, the last of the yellow leaves on the trees still lined Brooklyn Heights and the Battery. He took Josephine, their son, Simon, and the new baby off. Cantagrel was an orderly man, disciplined to plan ahead. This birth had been disorderly. He had been forced to stay with Josephine in New York longer than he might otherwise, delaying his contact with potential American investors for the new colonization society. Each day that passed without contacting an investor was so much water churning.

His original plan had been to follow Considerant's 1853 itinerary: hurry to Cincinnati, enlist Reverend Allen to travel with Cantagrel, from there, establish a business correspondent, order a saw mill and provisions, and find men for a first building crew. Then he meant to board a boat on the Ohio River, travel down the Mississippi and up the Arkansas River to Fort Smith, Arkansas, and cross Indian Territory into Texas. He had been stuck in the Mississippi a week ago for five hours, but the delay had proven providential: not only was the Mississippi low, but there was not enough water in the Arkansas River for boats to ascend to Fort Smith following the route Considerant had taken. Reverend Allen convinced Cantagrel that they had to get off the river boat, *Norma*, at Memphis, buy horses, and ride the six hundred miles to Fort Worth.

While riding across Arkansas, Cantagrel had seen streams of wagons and riders going to Texas.[26] This dismayed him and made him nervous. On behalf of those immigrants about to leave Europe to join him, he wanted North Texas to be empty. Only vacant land could be free for the taking. Cantagrel had been in the United States for two months, yet he still wasn't on the site finding land and preparing housing.

As they crossed Arkansas and traveled into Texas, the rough-hewn villages and people they encountered, the abominable food, the emptiness, and the vast distances were revelations to this scion of French wealth. The farms, the houses, the ground—everything was unkempt. Cantagrel acquired a visceral understanding of what the challenges would be if they were to create physical order for a phalanx in the wilderness.

As authors of Fourierist tracts, he and Considerant had been part of the intellectual salons of the 1840s in Paris. As a passionate Fourierist, Cantagrel had even dedicated one of his books to Considerant.

Cofounder of a daily Paris newspaper, the *Démocratie pacifique* (Peaceful democracy), which advocated Fourierism when the movement turned political, he carved out a place for himself after the February Revolution of 1848 as a Republican Socialist member of the Chamber of Deputies. He had participated in a protest demonstration in June 1849 when the government sent troops to support the pope in Rome. Because the bourgeoisie had not followed the Republican leaders into the streets, Cantagrel, Considerant, and others had been forced to flee to Belgium. He had been condemned to deportation after trial in absentia by the High Court at Versailles.

His beard, untrimmed this week, masked his architect-engineer-lawyer countenance. But he knew how to sit a horse, as did every gentleman who was born in the years of the first Napoleon's downfall, and he could endure the American frontier.

Four years older than Reverend Allen, Cantagrel had two things in common with him: Fourierism and family. They both had just left wives with new babies and had other children. He hoped Josephine and the baby would be strong enough for Considerant and his wife to bring her and the children to him in Texas when they passed through New York in a month. Or might Ellen Allen travel with her to be met at a Texas river port? He hoped the women would be compatible. Considerant seemed to think that the American women would open their arms to the French ladies. Only time would tell.

Considerant had brought these two men on the skiff together—an American Protestant minister from a utopian community and an aristocratic French reformer. Cantagrel had concerns. Reverend Allen was a radical reformer without money, tolerant but suspicious of class, living for ideas, trained and ordained as an American Protestant minister, whereas Cantagrel was a French intellectual reformer who was conscious of his class and from a family of secure financial resources. Fourierist leaders in Europe were generally anticlerical or at least cool to organized religion.[27] He had doubts about this enthusiastic man who had produced no investors and had been introduced to Considerant by Brisbane, suspicious in itself. Cantagrel had long questioned Albert Brisbane's character.[28] Yet Brisbane had pledged $20,000 to the Texas enterprise.

The third man listening to Reverend Allen extemporize while crossing the river was Edmund Roger. He had been a member of a Fourierist
club in Belgium and spoke both German and French. He had picked up
some English but spoke with his teeth clenched and was hard to understand. His role on the expedition was to translate for the Frenchman.
Small, slovenly and unkempt, he had few talents to bring to the group,
unless someone fell sick.[29] Yet it was unclear how much knowledge the
young Belgian had acquired from his recent medical schooling. Some
questioned his healing knowledge as lacking traditional values.[30]

The Belgian Rogers had not been chosen by the Frenchman Cantagrel as his traveling companion. Both were under the sway of Victor
Considerant, who had lured them to come to this side of the world and
paired them on the journey. By the time Cantagrel and Roger had left for
America, Considerant's book had stimulated subscriptions of 650,000
francs in the enterprise.[31] That was the equivalent of 130,000 American
dollars. It was meant for land purchases to start the Fourierist dream
and to lure more American investors. The French socialists were serious. By the end of the year in France there would surely be much more
money to add to what Cantagrel carried in gold and letters of credit.

After more than twenty years of talk about a reorganized society in
France, Belgium, and Switzerland, after three failed attempts at phalanxes
in France, one near Oran in Algeria, one off the coast of Brazil, and over
thirty American trials, these men were determined to reconstitute the
whole of society in the wilderness of Texas. In contrast to Reverend Allen,
who dreamed of re-creating the reality of the Brook Farm life he had
loved, Cantagrel came partly out of desperation to prove the intellectual
dream of more than two decades of his life and partly out of boredom
as an exile from France.[32] For Roger, the trip was a romantic chance
to see the world and possibly to be near the great man Considerant,
his schoolboy idol. "Like most Frenchmen, Cantagrel knew no other
language. After deciding to try the experiment in America, he studied
English by committing to memory the whole of Heinrich Gottfried
Ollendorff's *New Method of Learning to Read, Write and Speak*. When
he left home he was confident that when it came to ordinary matters
he would be able to converse with Americans. In this, however, he was

badly mistaken. So far, hardly a soul could understand a word he said, and he could not understand a word of what Americans said to him."[33]

Finally, on the skiff that day was Arthur Lawrie, the twenty-five-year-old New Yorker who had replied to Cantagrel's advice that it was "not agreeable to listen chiefly to French."[34] He had recently come west with his parents, brothers, and a sister who had just married the Reverend Allen's brother-in-law Marx Lazarus. Thus Lawrie's brothers John and James had come to know of the French plans for Texas and decided to go with Reverend Allen to Texas. At the last minute John Lawrie had thought better of leaving Indiana, and Arthur had decided to take his place. He had farmed for a short time in upper Indiana. His was an educated family. His brother Alexander was about to go to France to continue studying painting, and before going west from New York Arthur Lawrie had taken the trouble to learn a little German. Thus he could converse a bit in more than one language with Roger.

At last the ferry skiff ground into the red sand. Slaves ran out to the skiff and uncoiled ropes, securing the skiff to trees on the low bluff.[35] Seeing the reality of slavery in Memphis and the Arkansas countryside affected Cantagrel and Reverend Allen in different ways. Reverend Allen lectured anyone about its evils from his position as a minister. While Cantagrel understood that the issue of slavery truly mattered to Reverend Allen, Cantagrel was willing to temporize when the subject did not touch him personally. Besides, he could see that Reverend Allen's expressions of disgust were less than prudent in this new land.

Coming into America as a foreigner at the end of 1854 made Cantagrel circumspect. He was growing uncomfortable traveling in the South with a loud-mouthed abolitionist Yankee. Cantagrel knew about the Know-Nothings' political movement. Antiforeign sentiment, invisible when Considerant was in the States eighteen months earlier, had blossomed because of a glut of immigrants.

The four led their horses onto firm ground and the road across the border into Texas. They rode through dense forest and burnt-over clearings, skirting ranks of wagon ruts in the fading sun. About three miles north of Clarksville, they came upon a Mrs. Epperson, who put them up for the night at her house. The next day brought rain, which would have been good if it were a sign of the end of the river drought, but it forced the travelers to lie about. Lawrie took advantage of the time to write in his diary. Reverend Allen talked to slaves in a shed where they washed the travelers' linen.

Cantagrel used the time to review the geography of America. They were at the far edge of the eastern hardwood forest. The next day they rode west. During the next three days, the forests gradually gave way to intermittent prairies. The trees grew shorter as the sky grew bigger. The soil changed from a mix of red sand clay to sandy loam and then to black waxy clay. The watercourses trickled out and dried. Only small streamlets, buried at the bottoms of their courses, ran over white limestone. The fords were narrow.

Where was the vegetation to go with the tropical climate that Considerant had promised in his book? Evergreens grew fewer and fewer as they moved west. Soon they left the pines totally behind. The golden prairie grass that replaced them reminded him of the great plain at Chartres. At night, in the dry winter air, the sky appeared almost cut in two by the Milky Way; stars fairly danced, shining far brighter than those revealed by the watery Parisian skies. But the bleak, muddy-streeted village they came upon in Texas built mostly of logs and named Paris? Mon Dieu!

Eighty miles from their goal of Fort Worth, Cantagrel and Roger speculated about whether any colonists had put to sea from Belgium or France. How would these Fourierist immigrants who were largely educated men and craftsmen fit within this frontier culture?

Several generations of frontier perseverance had bred a special practical knowledge that substituted for formal education in these Anglo settlers whom the four travelers found themselves among. These frontiersmen thrived on fierce personal self-reliance. Almost everything they possessed they made themselves from the land—food, clothing, shelter, medicine, tools, and soap. For things they could not make themselves, they bartered. Coffee, sugar, and metal might require cash, but they could be done without.

Americans had lived in this province of the buffalo and Native American for a decade or less. They were primarily yeoman farmers from the Ohio Valley who had first come over the Alleghenies to Tennessee and

Kentucky a generation before rafting down the Cumberland River to settle in Indiana or Illinois. Always looking for better land, the next generation found that its wheat seed flourished in the virgin North Texas prairies, where there were no forests to clear and no rocks to haul out of fields—the rich, black soil had only to be broken to make the first crop. It could take up to thirteen yoke of oxen to make the first break, but that was faster than clearing land of trees and rocks by hand or with a horse.

For the first five years, they lived off of wild meat shot in the creek bottoms and saved their energy for planting. From the bountiful crops grown on these prairies, they earned precious cash after carting it to the nearest port, Jefferson. With the cash they bought milled lumber to replace their log cabin walls and bought a store-bought suit or dress. But the most desired purchase was a female black slave with a child, thought to be these farmers' ladder to fortune. They were not about to give up this avenue to wealth because of the consciences of preachers, Yankees, or foreigners. But the four foreign visitors to Paris, Texas, had not yet learned these lessons.

While the four set their course to buy land for the new colony, in Antwerp six Frenchmen and six Belgians boarded the ship *Lexington* and watched the sails fill. They were headed for New Orleans and on to Texas to establish the Fourierist dream.

4

Preparations and the View from Paris

In November 1854 Dr. Savardan received a letter from Allyre Bureau, the manager of the École Sociétaire office in Paris, saying, "We would like you to lead a first group of colonists to Texas."[1] Dr. Savardan's long work in the French countryside canvassing and studying the details of community organization, rural medicine, farming practices, and the education of foundling children made him an ideal person to lead a group of people across the Atlantic to found a new phalanstery.

As he sat at his desk in his office at Château Gaugain, Dr. Savardan's mind raced: Who should go with him? What supplies were necessary for the trip? Which medicines would an entire village need? How many would live there? A thousand details filled his organized mind. He tried to recruit Catherine Bossereau, who had nursed his wife for so long. To convince her, he proposed that they also bring her twenty-eight-year-old brother, Abel. Savardan could advance their costs. Working from a list of local interested people that was prepared by the Paris office, he also agreed to lend Jacques Blot in the village the cost of the trip.

He was pleased to find listed Jean Nicolas, a doctor from the Hautes-Alpes, a man near his own age. There was also a young Belgian medical student dispatched by Considerant to accompany Cantagrel. It looked as if medical needs would be well covered.

Dr. Savardan's confidence in Allyre Bureau's honesty and commitment made it easy to plunge into organizing for the new colony.

Savardan knew Bureau had three allegiances. Since his 1832 student days in Metz when Victor Considerant had first convinced him of Fourier's wisdom, Bureau had been a follower of Considerant's passion for the renewal of society, Bureau's first allegiance. A selfless, idealistic man, he resigned his commission in the army while still a student in Artillery School not many months after Considerant had won him as a convert.

5. Allyre Bureau, age forty. Courtesy of Gabrielle Cadier-Rey.

In 1835 Bureau married Zoé Rey, his second allegiance, who had now given him five children.[2] A devoted family man, he hated to be away from them.

His third allegiance was music. He played the violin and piano. He composed operas. He had used his excellent musical skills to eke out a living at the Théâtre des Italiens, along with doing École busi-

6. Zoé Bureau. Courtesy of Gabrielle Cadier-Rey.

ness. His love of music was eclipsed as investor and emigrant interest in Texas increased at the École. Everything about the Texas project demanded his attention. And then Bureau received a letter from Considerant in exile in Brussels: "So come as soon as possible, and without announcing that you are returning to Paris in three days to your loving families, so that you are not here as souls in pain singing in a plaintive tune, 'My wife expects me, I have promised, I must leave and other nonsense.' . . . Don't repeat this to your wife, Bureau! She would scratch out my eyes!"[3]

For the five and a half years Considerant had been exiled, Dr. Savardan and the circle of leaders had become accustomed to traveling to Brussels for École Sociétaire business. They worked to keep their generation's dream of a reorganized society alive. After Considerant came back from Texas in August 1853, ennui had begun to evaporate. They all revived hope for their dream.

Still, Bureau remembered his disappointment when the French Ministry of Foreign Affairs refused to allow Considerant back into France the previous May. Responding to Considerant at a distance and having to go to Brussels upon Considerant's summons had made Bureau's own work harder.

But this Republican idealist of military bearing with chestnut hair and kind, light-brown eyes set in an oval face with a low brow and large nose was excited now that he could see more clearly what was happening this December. Fourierism appeared to be reviving in more than a few leaders' minds. Considerant's book on Texas was bringing more and more people to the École office with modest money to invest and an urge to go to Texas. Bureau surmised that Cantagrel must be in Texas buying land by now.

When Dr. Savardan came to Paris to survey the École office and meet with Bureau, he thought how different the rue de Beaune in the Faubourg Saint-Germain must be from those great free expanses of that Eden that Considerant spoke of—Texas!

A few steps off the quai Voltaire on the left bank of the Seine, the offices in the narrow rue de Beaune had an oblique view across the Seine of the soot-stained limestone wall of Henri IV's palace. When Fourierist adepts walked out of the narrow street onto the quai and across the Pont Royal, they faced the Pavillon de Flore, the western end of the long wall of the Louvre and Tuileries palaces. Two years ago, behind that wall, symbol of the state, the emperor had begun a massive building program to enlarge it yet again. In Texas there were no buildings but log cabins. So much the better, since there would be no heavy hand

of a self-proclaimed emperor to trample Republican hopes. Dr. Savardan looked with disgust on the new streets, straight and wide, being cut
through the old city so that Napoleon could move the army about more
easily to control his opponents.

The rue de Beaune, a crack of a street intersecting the walls of limestone beside which visitors to the École Sociétaire walked, was lined with
buildings five stories high. All had two rows of dormers in their man-
sard roofs. On its first floor was the bookstore, which helped support the
fortunes of the École Sociétaire. It offered a range of paperback tracts of
Fourier's writings: Victor Considerant's work, *Social Destiny*, and others,
as well as the new *Au Texas*. On the walls were posted idealized views
of humanity's vision for a reconstituted society, the phalanstery. There
were drawings illustrating a grand Versailles-like building, perfectly
symmetrical, set in a square, before a river landing. A train smoked
in the distance. This was a picture of the perfect society for the perfect
human being.

Considerant had counseled going slow in building a phalanstery
in Texas, but all those applying to go to Texas made it clear that no
one was listening to him on that point. Romantic North Texas, empty
but for a few noble savages, seemed like the perfect place to escape
from emperors and popes, the Catholic Church, old armies, and the
squalor of the Industrial Revolution. Of course they should build
a phalanstery immediately. A beautiful etching of Charles Fourier,
suitable for framing, was also for sale. Dr. Savardan had one in his
library given to him by Considerant when the *Démocratie pacifique*
had been first published.

It was not happenstance that Parisian Allyre Bureau's name was first
on the Texas stock company legal banner, Bureau, Guillon, Godin et
Cie. Other than Considerant's mother-in-law, Clarisse Vigoureux, and
her friend Just Miron, Bureau had been Considerant's earliest collaborator. He was a constant, steady advocate of social change at the center
of the movement in France. He answered letters seeking information,
interviewed candidates for Texas immigration, passed dossiers about
them to Considerant and Godin in Guise, set up accounts for the
Texas enterprise, tried to convince prospective subscribers to invest

in Texas, printed and issued stock certificates, and planned a stock-holders' meeting of the European American Colonization Society. He had supervised the finding of ships with affordable berths and enough room to take groups of colonists at the times the ships were needed in January and February. Neither the École nor the passengers could afford the cost of sitting around in dock-side hotels for long. Coordination was key to the entire project. He was already transshipping colonists' gear.

Bureau's role as the focus in Paris of the clamor to go to Texas was becoming uncomfortable to him. He did not relish judging people, their strengths and their resources, and telling many of them "no." He had confessed to Considerant his dislike in turning down so many simply because they lacked enough funds. Couldn't they advance credit for good people? Considerant had declared such an idea to be folly and advised Bureau to put it out of his mind.[4]

Within the next month another *Bulletin* about the society needed to be circulated. The École had sold enough copies of the book on Texas that there had been enough money for another printing. It came off the presses and had been circulated in November.

The École's publishing gave Bureau constant worry. The police officers of the Sûreté were keeping a close watch on the École and all the individuals involved. The scrutiny constituted a critical threat to the enterprise. Now that the emperor had tight censorship control, Republicans and Fourierists were under constant surveillance by Napoleon III's police. Bureau had reason to be concerned. He had been in four Paris prisons for five months in 1849 along with other Republicans before the High Court at Versailles had exonerated him.[5]

In almost daily letters, Considerant exhorted Bureau to carry out his many instructions; he even asked Bureau to get money and personal goods such as hammocks for Considerant and his family's crossing. Bureau had seen to it that Godin's and Cantagrel's correspondence on Texas was copied and passed to everybody. He transmitted the messages between Considerant's mother-in-law and his wife back and forth between Paris and Belgium.

Bureau had to oversee the collection of École monthly subscriptions from all over France and communicate with all those Fourierists who kept the École afloat. And of course he had to administer the staff. Allyre Bureau was the chief component of the oil that made the Fourierist machine in Europe work. If the Fourierist dream of Texas were to come to fruition, it was up to him. The load felt very heavy.

7. Jean-Baptiste André Godin.

5

Preparations and the View from Guise

The Society . . . must be set up in such a way that the exigencies of capital never contradict those of Labor and that no one can ever say that we created a new Ireland. Whatever the fertility of the land . . . capital can only draw wealth from it with the aid of strong arms and active minds. It is therefore by the well-conceived advantages it offers workers that the enterprise will succeed. The operation's real needs will be visible to the administrators. . . . Also, this will help colonists become shareholders in identifying their interests with its aims.

JEAN-BAPTISTE ANDRÉ GODIN

Dr. Savardan and Jean-Baptiste André Godin both wanted to believe Considerant's stirring words about Texas. To them, Considerant seemed a new Moses, yet both wondered if Considerant's vision was based in reality. By December 1854, when the two men met at the Paris stockholders' meeting, Godin was taut, shouting to himself, "Action! Action!" Considerant should have been back in Texas getting that free land eight months ago instead of sitting in Brussels writing tracts.

Godin had done all he could to encourage Considerant's establishment of a new Fourierist community in Texas. He had anticipated Considerant's needs for operating funds and for farm equipment for the first wave of workers, and he even had seeds and cuttings gathered on the Le Havre docks for first plantings.

Godin glanced impatiently out the window of his office in Guise toward the little river while his secretary finished his dictation. He had not let the warm room put him to sleep after coming in from the cold after lunch. He had work to do. In the distance he heard the warning clanging and a sudden roar from nearby furnaces as they melted iron for castings. Deferentially, the secretary approached his desk and asked, "Shouldn't this sentence be changed?" For a second his eyes sparked at the secretary. Yes, she was right, but Godin liked to be in total control. This timid sally frustrated him, but he kept his frustrations to himself.

Godin was self-taught, without formal education. He had gone to work in a foundry at the age of ten. Now thirty-seven, he was an industrialist. He owned his own foundry, and all of France wanted his invention, an iron stove that could heat a house without having to build a masonry firebox and chimney.[1] His growing manufacturing empire was housed in ranks of large metal sheds crammed near the Oise River on the flats of the northern edge of Guise in the province of Aisne. With railroads fully in place, it was now easy to distribute the heavy cast-iron stoves throughout the country. More and more were being sold.

He already had accumulated more wealth than he and his wife and son could ever spend. He had flirted with the idea of giving some of his interest to the workers who had helped make him rich. They needed better housing and ways to educate their children. After all, he was one of them. But his wife and her family had been scandalized at the idea of dispersing their money this way. That did not change this man's iron will: if he were to build a phalanstery, he would live with the workers.

Godin's business had made him rich, a successful capitalist, but he was also a Fourierist. Godin would have smiled if he had known the Sûreté's recent evaluation of him: an honest man, therefore dangerous and to be watched.[2] Godin was prudent. Unlike Considerant, Cantagrel, and Bureau, or even Dr. Savardan fighting his bishop, Godin had never been arrested or clapped under house arrest at the time of the coup. He knew that the emperor's minions had destroyed the presses the École Sociétaire used for its newspaper, the *Démocratie pacifique*, and machinery was very important to Godin. As a precaution, he had set up a second factory in Brussels. One never knew when a known Fourierist might be surprised by Napoleon III. It had been two years since the December coup d'état. The Socialists and Republicans were in total disarray. The emperor now had full control of the entire security apparatus. Godin, the pragmatist, wanted to be prepared.

Godin planned to go to Texas himself after the first wave of colonists established La Réunion. He had been captivated by Considerant's glowing description of Texas as an empty Eden like a royal park. A great expanse of endless land, fertile and virgin, with what he said was a beautiful climate, where the followers of Fourier would not have to contend with all the bad social habits of France. In Texas no problems were created by the Industrial Revolution. Land was cheap or maybe even free. Godin thought he might establish Fourier's "essential industries" at the colony.[3]

After more than twenty years of debate, Considerant had at last showed the will to stop theorizing and move to action. He had probably been right to wait, to insist on a proper test of Fourier's ideas before acting. Godin believed fervently in Fourier's vision of the world, where capital and labor would each contribute to "attractive" industry. Considerant's Texas book had convinced him. He regretted that he himself had no real theoretical knowledge, but he was resolved to give help.[4] After Considerant's book on Texas was published, word of mouth among Fourierists spread in approval and hope. But when Godin reflected alone he knew that some things needed clarification.

Turning his chair to stare out his office window, Godin guessed that criticism would come from the Cabetists, followers of the Icarian movement, who had started a utopian community in North Texas six years earlier in the same Three Forks area on which Considerant had focused. They had failed. There were sixty-odd people spread out on a checkerboard of half-mile squares, and only every other tract was owned by them. What had the land company been thinking? How could this arrangement foster a community of people who wanted to share everything, even wearing identical clothing through pooled labor? They didn't last the summer. Ten or eleven had even died. Considerant had found two survivors in the village of Dallas and quoted them as sources for his book *Au Texas*.[5] He intended to be sure that his Fourierist followers were better prepared. But Considerant did not appear to be headed into the kind of trap that had caught Étienne Cabet; he seemed to have thought of everything. Still, there were no statutes, even by summer! How could they sell the colony to investors without a legal framework by which to judge it?[6] Godin wrote Considerant chiding him for lack of action while all who were serious about becoming members of the colony were clamoring for direction in preparing for Texas before they left Europe.

Godin had gathered three to four kilos of seeds. Now he wondered whether they could arrive in Texas in time to be used. It had been almost another eight months since Considerant's book came off the press, and Considerant had still not left Europe to take leadership in Texas. Cantagrel had been gone nearly three months. It was true that Considerant had been arrested for a week or so in August, but afterward why did he have to write the tract *Ma justification* instead of getting on a boat?

When Godin heard about this tract, he wrote Considerant, "It is no longer possible to act on the world by writings."[7] The main thing was to get that land for the investors. If the rumor of a land boom in Texas were true, it could cause them to lose the land opportunity, making the whole project impossible. Others would not invest.

After Considerant wrote Godin answering all his worries, his doubts vanished. He would increase his contribution from the earlier one-hundredth he had suggested to Cantagrel to one-fiftieth of 4 million francs, or 80,000 francs, if the 4 million were subscribed. One-tenth should be necessary to buy land. On the strength of *Au Texas*, Godin placed funds at Considerant's disposal immediately to insure there were sufficient funds to establish their vision.[8]

6

Preparations and the View from Brussels

He seemed much younger (say 38) and smaller size than I expected . . . with a very intellectual looking face, thinned—evidently by care—his mouth half hid by very thick and long moustache—no beard or brush—as he approached where we were sitting, Dana rises introducing me to Victor Considerant, as his Phalanstérien friend and "compatriot"—Cons. grasped my hand very cordially and expressed much pleasure at seeing me. I could only in a few words express my delight at meeting the Chief of the Phalanstériens of France. . . . He seems very concerned, frequently sighs as tho' a heavy weight was pressing him down.

JAMES T. FISHER, 1848

Victor Considerant blew another smoke ring and leaned back in his chair, propping his feet on the desk. If he had been in Paris, it would have been like old times, but he was not in Paris. He sat in lawyer Adolphe Demeur's Brussels office in the rue de la Régence pondering applicant lists while a roomful of people waited outside hoping to be chosen to go with him to America. It was his recent book that had brought those people clamoring outside his office and him back into the limelight. True, the limelight was not as bright as it once had been. Seven years ago, when he spoke on Fourierism to government ministers and crowds of more than a thousand as a guest from France, he had been the European leader of Fourierism. Now he was in exile. Yet only eight months after publication, *Au Texas* was certainly bringing people to his door. After five years of sitting on the sidelines, he had managed with one book to do real work for the cause. No more fishing in the countryside with the infernal waiting in the village of Barvaux. He had people to manage in Brussels, Paris, Texas, New York, Cincinnati, Patriot, and New Orleans.

But there were immediate problems in this growing theater of operations. How was he to detach himself from a string of poor exiles?

He had to accept some of them, but too many could sink the Texas enterprise. Yes, there was the debt owed to all those good Fourierists who had supported him and the École in the past. True, it had been the modest little people sending monthly checks since the 1830s that had made the École survive. They were members of a believers' network all over France who had kept the École and later the *Démocratie pacifique* housed in the rue de Beaune. And yes, even after the emperor's censorship and the demise of the Démocratie, there had still been the sale of books and images of Fourier and the phalanstery, together with the monthly memberships, that appealed primarily to the little people who hoped for a better life. *Au Texas* had to bring investors so that land could be bought by the new stock company. They needed people of means, not just people wanting to try their luck on the other side of the world.

Still, Considerant thought to himself, it was a nice problem to have, compared to his problems in exile four years ago, after the emperor's coup d'état and plebiscite ended his hopes of the Republicans regaining power or of his returning to France.

Au Texas was now manifest in legal terms, too. Lawyer Demeur had registered the European American Society of Colonization in Texas on September 26 in Brussels. For the formal creation of the society, called legally Bureau, Bourdon, Guillon et Cie, seven of the old leaders had been present to sign the instruments with Considerant. Besides the three who gave their names to the corporation there were Godin, Just Muiron, and Tandon. Cantagrel, like Considerant, was there because he was unable to remain in France. He had escaped the emperor's net in 1849 and fled to Belgium with Considerant.

Now in January 1855 things were more or less in order for the future. Bureau would continue to head the Paris office, where the parent organization would act to further work on behalf of the whole as overall management. Cantagrel, the director and nominal chief adjutant to Considerant, had left for Texas early in October to find land and prepare housing. Godin in Guise would go later to Texas when they had agriculture organized and were ready for other industries. Muiron, the founder of Fourierism with Clarisse Vigoureux, thought younger people than he should travel; he would continue to take care of old École Sociétaire business in France.[1]

Considerant listed himself in *Au Texas* as the executive of the European American Society of Colonization in Texas. He would follow Cantagrel to establish the center of operations in Texas, with Considerant serving as executive of the administration of the society and the agricultural and industrial businesses at La Réunion. He would leave soon and be in Texas by the beginning of March 1855, certainly in time to celebrate Fourier's next birthday, though that was not soon enough for Godin.[2] Godin had nagged Considerant to go during the past summer to energize American investment and seek the empresario grant that Considerant claimed could be had from the state. They needed to start buying up discounted headright certificates for Texas land. Said Godin, "Let others organize the stock company, write the statutes, interview the candidate emigrants, organize logistics and ships. You go to Texas."

But Considerant had been resolute. Careful thought must proceed action. And it was not his fault that the idiot police had thrown him in jail incommunicado in August for nine days as a suspect in a plot against the security of the Belgian state. He had been forced to waste precious time simply because he had bought a few guns to send to friends in America. Of course, he'd had to write *Ma justification* to put an end to the fantasies spread to the world about him after that experience with the public prosecutor, regardless of how many times Godin, sitting in Guise, proclaimed that time was of the essence.

The theoretician and ego in Considerant bristled. Wasn't he the man who had inherited the mantle of Fourier and given his life to it, who had organized Fourier's words into a coherent dialectic, who had found Texas, and who was acknowledged as a gifted speaker, the father of this idea? He had to superintend these tasks. Some of them were problems.

There had been a letter from Godin saying that he himself should interview personnel for the trades that would be needed in the first wave of emigrants. But that had been complicated by Godin's not being either in Brussels or in Paris at the École headquarters. Every potential colonist could not be sent to Godin in Guise. That was impractical. Besides, some here in Belgium were proscribed by the emperor. Godin wanted to meddle in everything, even writing the statutes.[3] His writing skills were far too unpolished for that. Considerant had told Bureau in Paris *not* to let Godin write articles in the *Bulletin*; they wouldn't be able to hold up their heads in Paris if he did. Considerant saw that investors who were withholding funds needed explanatory commentary from him after they read the statutes. He had not turned that responsibility over to others but had finished it himself in October. He was finishing the final chapter now. It wouldn't be long until he could leave.

Somehow, though, they had to keep Godin in the fold. He was too committed to the project to lose. The minute he had read *Au Texas* he had put 8,000 francs at Considerant's disposal. He was their biggest contributor so far. Godin was the only rich man among the leaders, and he knew a great deal about manufacturing.

Dr. Savardan was another matter. He wanted everything at once. Yes, they would need libraries and baths and schools, but not at first. The doctor had offered to help manage details. Yes, let Dr. Savardan occupy his time with niggling details.

Practicing his skill at blowing smoke rings, Considerant smiled, thinking of his book. He was proud of it. From reactions in the summer, so sure was he of its appeal that he had underwritten the first 540,000 francs of its cost. Finally, he was now out from under the cloud of being called as a guarantor.[4] The book *was* bringing in money. Nearly 580,000 francs had been subscribed at the end of November. Now, at the first of the New Year, more than twice that amount had come in. Perhaps there would be three times in another month, much of it cash already.

Cash. He had been right to correct Bureau when he had brought up that soft-headed credit idea in October. Allowing subscriptions on credit would have been the most divisive thing imaginable. Wanting to help all those enthusiastic little people was noble, but Bureau was just too nice.

In fact, Considerant believed *Au Texas* was bringing everyone back in line. Thank God, Dr. Savardan had not kept raising money the year before last to resurrect Condé, the failed phalansterian society near Paris. Imagine, he had raised nearly enough to buy the land. Those 100,000 francs Savardan bragged of would have gotten a few hectares west of Paris, but in Texas it might buy forty thousand acres! Or if he got the land from the government for free, as he expected, then 100,000 francs would pay for a pretty piece of land, perhaps a center for operations. Would Savardan do as well this time raising funds for Texas? Everyone had tried to make associations too small; the first Condé certainly was, and Savardan's second try would have been as well.

Dr. Savardan was a problem averted. It was good that he had Bureau throw cold water on Savardan's idea of reviving Condé. Now that the emperor had won his plebiscite and was without competition, Republicans and Socialists had been either silenced or exiled, as Considerant was. Considerant would have looked foolish as a leader sitting banished in Belgium while Savardan's experiment was established at Condé ninety kilometers from Paris.

Certainly, Fourier's goal could never succeed without at least 1,600 workers and without all the trades necessary for the initial industry. That idea had been proven in all the failed communes in Citeaux, Condé, Sig, and Brazil, to say nothing of all those naive early attempts in the United States.

In Texas it would be better to deemphasize the idea of a phalanx at first. They should concentrate on buying land that would appreciate while bringing together a group of friends and allowing them to grow together gradually in association. The stock company was a business, but most of the applicants for emigration wanted another trial for a phalanx. Bureau had just reported that to the stockholders at the meeting five days earlier in Paris. The company was being forced to adjust its goals to make another trial possible. How would that work with the Americans he hoped would invest and participate? He had told Bureau to make the distinction that those people allowed to go now were pioneers and would be chosen accordingly; the advance guard would not go until the fall. He wondered if he had been wrong to let them change his original position.

Considerant turned his attention back to Dr. Savardan's list of people he was to lead to Texas the following February. They looked all right as far as their needed skills, but would they have any cash to contribute? Those ten from the Aude? An old man, a veteran of Napoleon's army? Considerant had no choice but to allow Savardan to take his three retainers from La

Chapelle-Gaugain: his dead wife's maid and the maid's brother, as well as a mason on Savardan's estate. It was people such as Jean Nicolas on Savardan's list who should be encouraged: a doctor, a substantial man of property, and one who had a well-known name, since he had made an important ancient treasure find in the 1840s in the south of France.

Here in Brussels today Considerant was seeing that there were exiles crying to go to Texas, but there were also the Belgians, Belgians with money. Haeck, who had just left with Parisian Vincent Cousin, was contributing 12,000 to 14,000 francs. Jean Goetseels had bought fifty thousand shares and had sent his seventeen-year-old stepson, Philip, with the first Belgian group. Goetseels himself would take the rest of his family in a few months. De Guelle had been willing to send his son Philippe also—or had been persuaded to—so young Philip would have a companion his own age. And Considerant needed to lure de Guelle to persuade the former deputy to invest. Cousin could handle both of the youths. Julie, always a supportive wife, had helped convince the young men's mothers to let them go. After all, Cousin would need plenty of young energy to help Cantagrel. Vincent Cousin also had funds. He would invest as soon as he settled the difficult arrangements with his father; was the father just tight?[5] Cousin, who had led the first group to sail from Anvers a week ago, would take orders from Considerant and could build.

Considerant glanced at the map of Texas on the wall. Cantagrel had to be in Texas by now, though he had been late leaving New York. Was he to the site today? Would he have bought Fort Worth? If he had not yet purchased the fort's buildings, he should have bought other land and be building shelters by now. The plan had been for Cantagrel to hire Americans to set up the receiving center. But now a cadre of builders had appeared here who wanted to go, representing a shift in Considerant's original position of hiring Americans to do the initial work at the colony. But these immigrants would certainly help Cantagrel, so Considerant had given his permission. Never mind whether this entire first immigrant group was buying stock. The first wave needed to be willing hands who knew how to design and build and who wouldn't cost the enterprise too much. If they were also committed Fourierists, it would be ideal: they would contribute labor at little cost to the company. Even exiles like Sauzeau and Colas, whether or not they were believers in Fourier, had both energy and writing skills, so Considerant included them too.[6] Cousin had assembled the dozen building craftsmen and fledgling architects who had finally gotten off on the *Uriel* on December 25. For Considerant, that was a relief. With this vanguard of builders out of the way, he could focus on the final chapter of his book and the two other groups leaving in January and February.

As everyone kept telling him, Considerant knew that he himself should be leaving, but there was still the final chapter of the book. He wanted to take it with him to New York. It didn't look as if the revised printing could be completed before he left, so Bureau in Paris would have to handle the second edition of the book. Godin in Guise was again telling him to go at once. Could he leave in two weeks? Julie's mother was to be here by then, and there was a ship on January 17.

The moment Considerant reached New York the important thing would be to get the right introductions to Texas leaders in order to acquire an empresario grant. And of course he would have to impress on the Americans how well the French had supported the project. Now that there was cash, he could send people to buy up discounted headright certificates for Texas land wherever they found them. Considerant had learned the previous fall that Texas had issued certificates with the right to a free large tract of land as a reward for serving in its 1836 revolution. Later certificates gave the right to settle on and improve smaller tracts of land. These headright certificates had become a kind of secondary currency in an economy on the frontier starved for cash.

He wondered if Brisbane in New York had finished translating *Au Texas* into English by now.[7] Would it be in circulation in the United States? Considerant had had no word recently from Brisbane. It took a month to send and get a reply. Messages between France and Texas took three months. But in two years a cable was to be laid across the Atlantic like the cable laid to send messages three years earlier between France and England. Communication speed would improve.

What would he find in America? What effect would the fire last September at the North American Phalanx in New Jersey have on a new, more full-fledged trial in Texas?[8] Would those NAP friends in association now come to Texas? How could the society take advantage of this failed American situation? Not by using it as a way station. Ships sailing directly to New Orleans or Galveston landed much closer to North Texas than to New York. The sailing ships that still plied that route were less expensive than the new steamships crossing the North Atlantic. With only water transport to pay for to Shreveport, within two hundred miles of their destination, travel costs to the region of upper Texas were much cheaper than traveling via ship and train through New York.

Had Brisbane raised money for Texas? His promise of $20,000 had been a good beginning and had helped answer French doubters. Considerant ran over his list of American Associationist friends to whom *Au Texas* had been sent, checking the names of the people to whom he would make a personal appeal if they had not subscribed. What about contributions from Horace Greeley, Marcus Spring, and Charles Sears, who led the investors in the North American Phalanx? And James Fisher, whom Considerant had visited in Boston?[9] There was also that friend of Brisbane's in Ohio, Benjamin Urner, whom Brisbane had proposed as a business agent in Cincinnati. Considerant struck through the names Charles Dana and George Ripley at the *Tribune* office in New York.[10] They didn't appear to have money.

Considerant knew Cantagrel didn't trust Brisbane. If he wasn't trustworthy, why, then, had Brisbane paid for Considerant's steamship ticket last year and taken so much trouble with him in America? He and the École had known this tall, bearded man with black intense eyes from northern New York for more than twenty years. Brisbane had been to France often, the first time to sit at the feet of Fourier as a student. True, some of the funds that the French school had lent to the American school had never been repaid, but there had been many others involved in that. Brisbane had delivered Considerant to Texas, right to a marvelous site. Brisbane's tour of America had inspired Considerant to take command of a great tract of land, as the Peters Company had done in that beautiful empty wilderness south of the Red River, an idea that turned the École's despair to hope.

Considerant took one last draw on the stub of his cigar and stubbed out the end in the ashtray on his desk. He spotted a letter from Cantagrel. One cloud had just appeared on the American horizon. Cantagrel reported in the letter from Patriot, Indiana, that Reverend Allen had found only one investor in the Midwest. Brisbane in New York had spoken with great confidence of Reverend Allen's fundraising experience at Brook Farm. Perhaps this failure only showed that he, Considerant, had been right to wait for the results in France and the right tools with which to sell the Americans. There shouldn't be anything to worry about from the Midwest. He thought of four-year-old Victor Considerant Allen in Patriot, Indiana. It was encouraging to know that someone halfway around the world would name a child for you, even if you were in exile.

Considerant took his feet off the desk and reached for another list. There was the question of interpreters to go with or to meet the emigrant ships. He read the name Alexandre Raisant. Raisant had traveled for two years in Mexico and the United States. He could manage English. He was leading the group of eight on the ship *Lexington*, which would be leaving Le Havre in a week. He would be a help both as a guide and as an interpreter. Raisant certainly didn't need to be approved by Godin sitting all the way over in Guise. True, he had been a little extreme in 1837, when he had been transported in the Raban affair; better not to advertise that involvement among potential investors. Raisant was a man of pluck and daring who got in trouble with the Sûreté for his courage. Considerant naturally admired such qualities, since they were the qualities he admired in himself.

A good thing he had run into Kalikst Wolski in New York.[11] Brisbane was right that Wolski would be a good interpreter, since he had lived in America for two years. Cousin would need help when his ship arrived in New Orleans, and Wolski was of superior intellect, flexible, and at home anywhere. Poles were like that. They cut a good figure, were ornaments in any drawing room. And Wolski would probably play down his Polish Catholic background; he wouldn't let himself stand out in Texas. He had an able engineering background, which would be useful for the colony. It had been a fine idea to seek him out and send him to the North American Phalanx in New Jersey for orientation before

8. César Daly. Archives nationales (France), 10AS34.

dispatching him to meet a ship in New Orleans, even if it had cost the society some money.

Yes, they would be well situated for interpreters. Besides Raisant, Roger, and Wolski for the first wave of groups sailing, Considerant himself would have enthusiastic and warm-hearted Daly to depend on. César Daly had promised to join him in New York. With Daly at his elbow, Considerant could take his time to learn that language that was so imprecise and full of words to memorize. Everyone said Daly's English was impeccable. And why not? His father was Irish, and he had grown up in London. His mother was of good family from the ancien régime, and he had money. He dressed so impeccably that he was compared to Beau Brummell. So what if Daly were an outsider in the best conservative circles? He was an architect, though not considered in a league with Pierre-François-Henri Labrouste. Still, Daly had worked on Chartres cathedral after the fire in 1836, and a bishop had appointed him conservator of the Albi cathedral.[12] He hadn't attended the Polytechnique, but he did have Considerant's respect as a polished speaker and as a publicist, the two subjects with which Considerant was always occupied.[13] The annual *Revue d'Architecture* was a prestigious accomplishment of Daly's. Everyone was familiar with those big leather-bound works, which had been coming out once a year for fifteen years. Daly published well-done color plates, and there was nothing else like the review in Europe.[14] They must not forget to pack the gravure images of the phalanstery that Daly had made in the 1830s; they were far superior to those of Robert Owen for Lannerk. They might help sell stock in America.

Considerant was optimistic. No more waiting in the wings, no more persona non grata in the Belgian capital. He had never trespassed his good behavior as an exile guest, not even when told to leave Brussels for the countryside. "Napoléon le petit" would not let Considerant back into France, but he had been unable to chase him out of Belgium.

His father would be proud of him. His father had been a professor of humanities at Salins. His father was a hero. When a fire erupted on campus his father had allowed the fire to consume his own home and all he owned in his efforts to preserve the college library. Now Considerant, too, would be a hero with the successful establishment of a community founded on the ideals of Fourier.

Looking in the mirror, Considerant admired his handlebar moustache. It was as grand as ever. It had grown back after he had been forced to shave it to escape to France. He was past forty-six, but he knew he cut a good figure. He was again the center of attention. Ever since he had returned from his trip to Switzerland in the middle of November, he had felt interest quicken. Yes, he was again at the center of attention. His enterprise had momentum. He was the leader still.

7

Preparations and the View from
La Chapelle-Gaugain

Dr. Savardan descended the wide staircase of beige-colored limestone at the back of the château, appraising the impending adventure of his life. He had just returned from Brussels and Paris, where he had been elected to preside at the first stockholders' meeting of the European American Society of Colonization in Texas.[1] The Fourierists in Paris were as excited as he was. More than four times the amount of funds he had raised for Condé had already come into the École Sociétaire in subscriptions for the Texas enterprise.[2] He had determined to go to Texas himself. If after a year or two it had become all he hoped, then he was resolved to come back to get his family and friends, to rescue them for good from the current miseries of European civilization.[3]

This château has ghosts, he thought. His wife's memory pervaded the place. He had come here with her twenty-eight years ago. Even the early Renaissance staircase that he was walking down—built in the time of Louis XII—had its ghost story. In the sixteenth century, a willful daughter paying for a misalliance had been immured under it.[4] Whether or not the story was true, the disproportionately large staircase easily could have entombed several daughters. And the hobgoblins of the emperor's Sûreté were real enough. The rule of absolute monarchs had always touched the lives of people living in even this remote, modest château and village in the Department of Sarthe. Since Louis-Napoléon's coup d'état two years ago last December, there was hardly a place in France for Republicans—certainly not for demoralized followers of Charles Fourier.

Was Savardan right to give up on his and Lavardant's idea of reviving Condé as a commune when they were so close to raising the rest of the money to buy back its site? It had been nearly twenty years since Condé had failed. Poor Baudet Dulary's land, which housed the phalanx, had been swallowed up in debt.[5] Savardan had dreamed of reviving it, making it a new Jerusalem—a Mecca that would be a pilgrimage goal for Fourierists.[6] They had nearly all the 100,000 francs needed for the property, but about the time Considerant came back from America advertising his experience in Texas, Condé's land had been sold again. Savardan then cast about for another site for what he called the Mother School, even considering his own estate. But that was before the publication of *Au Texas* aroused so much interest. As soon as Considerant had reappeared in Europe, Savardan had been in animated arguments with him over the idea of emigration. Yes, the emperor was a threat to Republicans, but at first, Savardan of all the Fourierists had decided against emigration because of Fourier's specific strictures against overseas experiments and also out of love for France.

He passed a battery of family portraits in the downstairs hall, hung three high on the wall. There was one of him as a young man with a diffident smile, showing a handsome open face under dark brown hair. The painting revealed an idealist, but a sturdy one from about the time of his marriage. As he entered the salon, he saw himself in one of the two tall mirrors over the opposing fireplaces. His beard, growing whiter and whiter, told him that time to act, to bring his dream to tangible reality, was running out. The relaxed mouth of the youthful image in the hall was gone, replaced by a determined line.

Was he right to follow Considerant, since the Centre did not support Condé?[7] At the château Savardan was fully in control of his life but frustrated by not being able to carry out his project for a new way of life following Fourier. Last spring when *Au Texas* was published, when he had read Considerant's words, he admitted he could be wrong. An experiment in Texas sounded more promising than reviving Condé. He ratified the proposal of a fresh start across the ocean.

This was his time to implement his vision. Born three months before the king's head had been cut off, Savardan came into the world under the Terror and the Directorate.[8] He grew up under Napoleon and as a young man felt the humiliation at Waterloo, then all the reactions of the restored monarchists of the ancien régime. He applauded the July Revolution when Lafayette embraced Louis-Philippe as a prince who was devoted to the principles of the Revolution. Then for eighteen years he watched that prince gradually alienate himself from liberal opinion until the Revolution of 1848.

Now there was another Napoleon. Savardan was at first heartened by his endorsement of the doctor's work for orphans, but Louis-Napoléon would never support a phalanx.[9] This emperor had undone the Republicans. In the spring nearly three years ago, when the president was consolidating his power before declaring himself emperor, he had placed many Republicans under house arrest, including Savardan for a month.[10] Savardan, a man trained to be a doctor, approaching his sixth decade, accustomed to and in need of control, was infuriated.

Now sixty-two, free of any great responsibilities since the death of his wife, he wanted out of a regime that threatened his freedom, that prevented the goal he had dreamed of for so long. He was more than ever resolved to attempt a reorganization of society following Charles Fourier's principles.

From the Paris stockholders' meeting the week before last, he had traveled to Brussels with Karl Burkli.[11] Burkli was a Swiss leader of the movement who planned to follow Savardan in March shepherding thirty of his fellow countrymen. Bureau and Godin also went to confer with Considerant. They all worked out the terms of a provisional constitution for the future colonies.[12] Considerant had practical answers for every objection. "The beauty of the climate, the miraculous fecundity and low price of land" made Savardan's dream of the rapid foundation of a town, of a magnificent phalansterian site, seem possible.[13] As soon as he had read the provisional constitution the previous May, he had written Considerant that he wanted to be in the first group to go.[14] He had put down 3,000 francs as an ante—not a great investment, but an expression of commitment toward the beginning expenses of a center of operations in Texas—and an additional 1,000-franc gamble to buy headrights for land. He had put up 50 francs for two people who worked on his estate, Catherine and Abel Bossereau.[15]

But there was this caution: Savardan's friend Fugère told him he would regret putting himself under Considerant's leadership. He said that Considerant was "completely incapable" of leading men or dealing in business. The doctor also would regret Considerant's temper.[16] But Savardan discounted these comments. This adventure seemed his one great chance to help realize that vision away from the control of the emperor. Since his house arrest and his wife's death, as well as the École's dislike of his project for Condé, he had been depressed. But he had worked on the organization of the new colony the previous summer and gone to Belgium in late August and again the previous week to discuss with Considerant the specifics of a social experiment in the new world.[17]

The doctor heard Considerant confirm what he had written and what Savardan wanted to hear. Soon after their arrival in Texas there would be the immediate creation on the ground of a living Fourierist society. Under the umbrella of the stock company, a separate, Fourier-inspired entity would be created. It would contain "a kitchen, a restaurant, a library, a school, an infirmary, a bath, a laundry, a store, a carriage, several houses, etc., placed at the disposal of all, by means of a contribution proportioned to the use that would be made of all these things, and finally of houses completely separated for the individuals and families who would not like the regime of the dormitory or barracks."[18] Considerant spoke of this new enterprise as having room for those who wanted to speculate in land and for those who wanted to live alone and take advantage of services that the enterprise could offer. The Texas wilderness would be a wonderful site for those of the École who wanted to carry out a Fourierist trial in sharing.

Considerant also had accepted Savardan's offer to manage the details of administration in Texas, an aspect of the enterprise that he and others of the Centre feared Considerant would not be capable of organizing well.[19] Since the École had told the doctor he should lead a group, he had thought of little else.

Bureau in Paris was now saying that 2,500 to 3,000 persons wanted to go to Texas. Exiles who had fled the emperor's police and some Belgian Fourierists had already been sent to sea on Christmas Day. Another ship would leave in a week. These two groups were leaving in time to gain a year in planting, taking great quantities of seeds, pips, and cuttings that had been contributed to the cause. Savardan's would be the third group, "chosen in view of the special work of the first installations."[20]

They were to leave in four weeks. Meanwhile, Considerant was taking a *paquebot* to New York to raise American capital and seek the support of Texas politicians in Washington. Then he would meet Savardan's pioneers when they landed in New Orleans and lead them to this wonderful field for action.

Bureau had reported the week before last at the stockholders' meeting that independently of the subscriptions raised, very conservatively, and leaving out the "maybes," emigrant applications showed that the resources that they counted on taking with them to the colony had reached the sum of 7 to 8 million francs.[21] The École was assembling various supplies and industrial equipment and canvassing for ships to transport them and Savardan's group to New Orleans. There was momentum. Everything was unfolding in a logical and orderly way with the rectitude that Savardan, as a medical doctor, insisted upon. His wide range of experience would serve the association well. He had served as a former surgeon aid-major in the army for six years, led his village as mayor for twelve years, become an inspector of primary schools and of children's work in factories, and been a former secretary of agricultural shows, and of course he had administered his wife's lands at La Chapelle-Gaugain.[22] He and Jean Nicholas from Hautes-Alpes would be responsible for medical care in Texas along with that young Belgian medical student—the one who had left with Cantagrel for Texas in the fall. Dr. Nicholas, a leftist socialist, perhaps even a communist, from Hautes-Alpes, was five years younger than Savardan and had been practicing medicine for thirty years some fifty miles southeast of Grenoble. In 1850 his village, St. Bonnet, was reputed to be the commune in Hautes-Alpes where socialists were the most numerous. Dr. Nicholas ran for office as a Republican in 1849 and shared Savardan's scientific interests.[23]

In Brussels the previous week, Savardan and the Swiss Burkli had discussed with Considerant the lists of people each would take across the ocean.[24] Savardan's list of forty-five included thirty-year-old Catherine, who had nursed his wife, and Abel, her younger brother. Not only was Catherine a good nurse to support the doctors' work, but she knew how to make a barnyard produce for the larder. She had grown up with fowl and with dairy cows and cheese making.[25] Twenty-eight-year-old

Abel was an excellent woodworker and a crack shot, and he was full of energy. Alexis Renier, thirty, a seasoned mason (and son of one) on the estate, came from that sturdy stock that had worked the château's land for generations.[26] He could fill the role of one "who exhibited the strong moral force and perseverance in conquering the obstacles and inevitable disappointments of beginnings in a new country."[27] Then there was the Boulay family, who already had one experience living overseas for two years when breaking ground for Dr. Benoît Jules Mure's trial association off the coast of Brazil. Godin approved of a thirty-three-year-old Orléans metal worker named Abel Dailly. In the Aude, Fourierist comrade Ferdinand Rouby had gathered eleven colonists whom the École wanted Savardan to take with him.[28] Dr. Nicholas promised to bring several hearty hands from the Hautes-Alpes. Young Montreuil, who had been a vote canvasser at the recent stockholders meeting and was probably a substantial investor, was coming. Mlle Gaudel, a Rouen teacher in her fifties, was close to Savardan's own age. Altogether, he would be leading nine women and three young children among the emigrants coming from widely scattered parts of France.

As Savardan continued across the herringbone parquet through the salon—the château's principal room—he saw his wife's visage in her portrait, full figure and full size, wearing a formal sky-blue satin gown ready for a ball. Her arms, white gloved, floated over him on the south wall between pairs of windows leading to the terrace. His wife's daughter, dressed in rose, stood behind her. The painting showed both women with garlands of flowers woven into their hair. This image, placed above a piano, occupied the sovereign center of the room. His wife's abstracted and rather inward gaze stared out at the large salon, its flanking side walls centered on fireplaces opposing each other. The doctor's phrenological head sat on the marble mantle of the west fireplace, reflected in the high gilt-framed mirror behind it. His wife might not approve of the head being brought into the salon amid the rococo gilded furniture, but then Savardan the widower did not entertain.

Was he giving up too much to go to the New World? The honorable prestige as past mayor of the village, the roofs of which he could see through the bare treetops lying directly below the château, which was perched on the brow of its hill? The château, not grand, commodious if not comfortable, with its rows of second-floor bedrooms running the width of the house. The big attic, full of souvenirs of the past, including copies of his books, getting dusty under sturdy, hand-hewn, mortised and pegged timber trusses holding up the heavy slate roof. The productive fields and big park behind the house to the north now returned to woods, where late Stone Age menhirs, six feet high and shrouded in ivy, stood under the trees. The little cemetery, edged in lichen-covered low stone walls, where his wife's body lay. No, he was not giving up too much. He would discard all of this old in exchange for the dream of the new, for a place where there would be no emperors to control one's social improvements—or one's life.

Opening the door beside the east fireplace of the salon, he pushed aside a thick forest-green curtain hung within the plane of the wall to find the library door. Inside the library, in its center, the round blond Empire table, inlaid in pear wood and dominating the space, was covered in orderly piles of materials about the forthcoming adventure. Over the past thirty-three years, Savardan had written books, tracts, and articles for the *Démocratie pacifique*, many of them drafted at this table, on subjects that varied from medicine to the new idea of a fire insurance association, from socialism in rural communes, to organizing medical service for the rural poor, to rural asylums for orphan children. Perhaps, he thought, he had a particular concern for orphans, as he was half one himself. His father had died when he was eleven months old.

But for the double-glazed doors giving onto the terrace and the fireplace on the inner opposite wall, the walls were covered with books; he needed a ladder to reach the upper ones. There were the tracts he had gathered and combined in leather-bound sets, so that the room had a rich brown hue from the accumulation of many such sets. Even the library side of the low door he entered from the salon and the door's twin, built symmetrically across from it, were painted with trompe l'oeil images of books to hide all bare surfaces and complete the "libraryness" of this warm, intimate room. He was pleased the room reflected his personality so well.

Walking out of the library's terrace doors into the cold air, he suddenly thought, In Texas there will be no more cold winters, according to Considerant! He looked around and fixed in his mind all the windows and doors along the terrace side of the house: dining room, entry hall, salon, library, and another room east of the library. This south side of stuccoed masonry was entirely orderly in its shuttered windows and doors, which reached to limestone belt courses. They must take with them craftsmen who could build such buildings, as he understood from Considerant that neither houses nor craftsmen existed in the North Texas wilderness. That was why he had recruited Alexis Renier, an artisan living here on the estate who would be needed in the first group of "pioneers," as Considerant called those who would lead the way to that empty Texas place.

Savardan stood at the edge of the terrace, which dropped off precipitously. Fifteen feet down was a second narrow terrace. It was supported by another high wall, which let the eye plunge into woods below. The view from the terrace atop these great walls, seen through wintry bare branches filtering the smoke from the village chimneys of La Chapelle-Gaugain, lay framed by two large cedars of Lebanon, the two he had planted twenty-five years before. The view to the south from the terrace overlooking the village gave one a lofty, airy feeling of being above the world and the lord of all he surveyed.

Savardan walked outside the library past the house and a courtyard and approached a lane running west, parallel to the side of the château's great barn. From this perspective the château appeared all roof, its long, enormous, blue-gray slate eaves sweeping low to the ground. Behind it he heard geese honking in the barnyard, tucked into the hillside. It was across a court from the kitchen, which lay in the northwestern corner of the château. Past the barn on the opposite side of the road loomed the handsome, round, limestone pigeon house under a conical slate tower, its birds producing fertilizer behind a chaste Renaissance facade. Considerant had seen great flocks of many kinds of birds rise over the summer Texas plains; the dragoons accompanying Considerant had no trouble supplying dinner from this wealth of animal life. How long could that wildlife last? Yes, Catherine would be a good choice to take with him; she had demonstrated she knew how to make a barnyard function.

He walked into the tile-floored dining room. The fruit course at dinner was served on the château's gilt-edged plates. A preserved pear presented on the white porcelain was flattered by the china's wide vermilion band. It reminded Savardan of Considerant's words that in Texas they would be in a climate so mild that bananas and citrus fruit could be had year-round.[29] He smiled. He might never again be sick with a winter cold like the one with which he had just been afflicted.[30]

He walked back into the warm library, where Fourier's visage, with its intense, stern eye, shone out of a beautiful large lithograph. The elegant portrait—a relaxed pose, with Fourier's hands crossed on the top of his cane—stood on the ledge in a corner against the lower bookshelves as a reminder of the seriousness of the great cause of reconstituting society.[31] From a shelf above the ledge Savardan picked up his box of index slips to books and letters, carefully written in his elongated, forward-slanted, fine hand.[32] These book slips matched stenciled numbers on the face of each range of bookcases. It was time to finish thinking through what of his library he would take to Texas. He had to get everything crated and started to Paris for transshipping to Le Havre within a week. He had already ordered medicines, instruments, and tools, including a locked chest to hold them—everything medical needed for the colony. Beyond medical books and his books on Fourierism, what else? The book on Madagascar? Books on the New World? Alexis de Tocqueville? Chateaubriand? The American writer James Fenimore Cooper? Cooper had lived in Paris for seven years during Savardan's youth. Everyone in France remembered Natty Bumppo. Would Texas be like that world of the Mohicans? Or would there be great fires as in Cooper's *The Prairie*?

Two woodworkers from the estate entered the room, responding to Savardan's summons. He explained that they were to make a roller and a crate to hold the painting of his wife hanging in the salon. The canvas was nearly four meters high and two wide, so removing it from its frame and then rolling it would take considerable care, he admonished. After it was rolled, it would need to be well cradled, its wooden box lined, waterproofed, and made safe for transport with him during the three months sailing over the ocean and then traveling over the prairies to North Texas.

8

Preparations and the View from New York

The Brook Farmers were overawed by his eloquence; the fervor and ferocity of a prophet lived in him. He spoke like one inspired. He had such fervid faith in supernal and eternal things that he even "talked of our meeting thirty-five thousand years hence under Saturn's ring; and we agreed to do so! Thirty-five thousand years from that very evening."

MARY ANN DWIGHT

"Forget your damned socialism and come back to tend to your own business!" Albert Brisbane sat in his cluttered study in New York City reading a just-opened telegram from his brother. Brisbane tossed it aside. Brother George could take care of whatever the problem was. Their father had been dead for nearly four years, and George was showing his irritation at always having to spend his time doing what Albert ought to do. But Albert was thinking about Texas. He had no intention of worrying about things at home in Batavia, New York. Conscious concern with the petty affairs of life did not exist for Brisbane.[1] He took little if any responsibility for the minutiae of life in Batavia because his father and George had always been there to handle things. But Brisbane never thought he had escaped the realities of the world. He was merely saving himself for more important things. He scorned "with a generous contempt to waste a thought, or to raise a finger, for the prosecution of any form of business which, for the acquisition of selfish individual wealth, should divide his time or talents with his present higher and holier mission of usefulness to his kind," as he regarded it.[2]

Like Dr. Savardan, Brisbane defined his role in the world as working for Humanity. He had finally won his dream and plea of twenty years to have the French creators of Fourierism build a practical trial of a phalanx in America. Two years earlier, when Considerant had been skeptical about coming to the United States, Brisbane had lured Considerant by paying his expenses. Considerant was the chief apostle of Charles Fourier in Europe; Brisbane was the first apostle, sometimes called the great apostle, in America. He was convinced that the human misery he had witnessed all over the world could be eliminated only by a fundamental restructuring of society.

In fact, he had begun hammering out his opinion on the way to alleviate human misery when he was only twenty-four. Even earlier he had waded into European intellectual life just as the effects of the Industrial Revolution had first trampled on ordinary humans. He sought out the leading contemporary French philosophers at the Sorbonne and heard first historian François Guizot's and then architect Victor Cousin's eclectic distillations of the past.

Cousin recommended Brisbane study Hegel, so he learned German and moved to Berlin, where he sat at the feet of the great Hegel until Brisbane began to wonder why Hegel's highest view of civilization was the one currently existing in Europe. He made friends and debated ideas with the poet Heinrich Heine. Brisbane traveled with Felix Mendelssohn, Franz Liszt, and Horatio Greenough and became acquainted with a host of other focused minds. Delving into philosophy, anatomy, and the history of art was to him part of a search for some comprehensive key to human destiny.

Brisbane's persistence was zealous. Just before, during, and after the Revolution of 1830 he had roamed Europe from Istanbul to Ireland. He gained an incredibly wide experience for a man so young. After four years he returned to Paris. He appeared more focused at the age of twenty-two. Still wed to Europe, he pushed his intellectual search further. He returned to Germany and again entered the salons of the Berlin intellectual elite.

A friend in Paris sent Brisbane a copy of a book containing the phrase "attractive industry," which ignited his imagination. He then read *Traité de l'association domestique-agricole ou attraction industrielle* (1822) by Charles Fourier. In that book he came "across an idea that [he] had never met before—the idea of *dignifying* and *rendering attractive* the manual labors of mankind." Further investigation convinced him that in Fourier's theory he "had found a hypothesis which explained what [he] had been seeking to discover—a just and wise organization of human society."[3]

All that was twenty years ago. Brisbane tossed away brother George's telegram and smiled, reminiscing how he had solved the communication problem when he had first sought out Charles Fourier. He had said to Fourier, "I am here to learn about your vision for organizing society." Fourier fixed him with his large gray eyes with their tiny, piercing pupils and said, "Read my works." Brisbane had just smiled at the man with the globe-shaped head and aquiline nose that reminded some of Dante. Brisbane saw the crack in the aging man's armor. "I will pay you to tutor me in your ideas." Fourier, in poverty, accepted Brisbane's payment for twelve lessons. But in the three years that Brisbane was in Paris, he still never saw Fourier smile.

The disciples of Fourier were another matter. The ideas that they gave him, he got free: in the group around the philosopher, Brisbane found Considerant. Brisbane, a tall man with a thick black beard, jousted mentally with the shorter, handlebar-moustached Considerant.

Considerant's passion for social change had caused him to be nicknamed Phalanstère. Considerant was trying to exorcise the confusing extravagances appended to Fourier's theories in order to write *Destinée sociale* (volume 1 of this three-volume work appeared in 1834). But Considerant was mocked by cartoonists who depicted him with a long thin tail in reference to Fourier's belief that when in harmony, humans would grow to a height of seven feet and grow a tail, a useful appendage.

They came to meet first in the rue Joquelet behind the Bourse and then on the Left Bank at number 2, rue de Beaune, "a large apartment composed of a suite of salons opening onto a fine, shady garden, upon the Quai where in pleasant weather, groups would form, in lively discussion on the topics of the hour. Nothing of the kind had ever existed before. Here was a social and intellectual center, with all the attraction that material appointments could give, thrown open to the friends of the Cause, and to thinkers of every stamp who were pleased to make it their rendezvous. Not Fourier's theories alone were discussed there, but those of every school of sociological study."[4] Brisbane had returned to the New World in 1834 with the tools to bring Fourier's message to America. From Considerant and those around him, Brisbane had acquired skills in debate and oratory, journalism and propaganda. From his father back in Batavia he had absorbed the fact of wealth acquired through speculation in land on a frontier. But in Brisbane's case, that lesson was to be used for more than the accretion of dollars. He told his European friends that he had a pure purpose in speculating in land: he was building capital to fund a practical phalansterian experiment. The trouble was, to his mind, that people did not see that they were soldiers in an army fighting for Humanity—not even his closest companion, his Italian wife, Adele, could understand.

When Brisbane returned in 1834 from his six years of indoctrination in European thinking, his aunt sent her carriage to New York to bring him and his new wife to Batavia. Almost immediately he commissioned a design for a theater in Buffalo, which opened the following year. The European influence sprinkled Franklin and Washington among Dante, Tasso, Voltaire, and Cervantes, and the stage curtain illustrated the sunset of Native American culture with the advent of the Buffalo skyline.

Brisbane lived in Batavia and Buffalo with Adele for four years before she fled back to Europe with their two children.[5] He had always loved Genesee County; the place was in his bones from when he grew up in those wonderful wild forests, most of which were gone by this time. Too bad Adele had never adjusted to it; she especially didn't like the idea of frontier. The fuss she made when he went out to look at land in Kansas! Kansas was still empty in 1838 but for some Indians, but he had to look at land in Kansas.

Albert was only following his father's example. His father had gone in the first survey party to the Holland Purchase, the frontier in New York before the new century, and speculated in land with the Indians still in the trees beyond. When Brisbane Sr. died, he left each of his sons a quarter of a million dollars built on the principle of speculation.[6]

Unfortunately, when Brisbane went to Kansas dear Adele felt compelled to pray to the Virgin and bargain for his safe return. His devout wife promised Mary the silver if he got back alive. Such a fuss. When he indeed returned alive, Adele actually gave the Catholic Church the family silver. That had raised an eyebrow in his Yankee family of Scottish Presbyterian background.

With Adele and the children gone, with Brisbane's mentor, Jean Manesca, just dead, with the force of the national depression affecting his theater investment and other speculations, and with Fourier himself dead a year, Brisbane turned from his dream of financing a phalanx back to propaganda for Fourierism. He began speaking in public about Fourierism in 1839.

In 1840, in the context of the grime of American sweat shops and the rote work of the masses before the first machines of the Industrial Revolution appeared, the propagandist Brisbane set out an ideal in his 1840 work *The Social Destiny of Man*: "We assert, and will prove, that Labor which is now *monotonous*, *repugnant*, and *degrading*, can be *ennobled*, *elevated*, and made honorable, or in other words that Industry Can Be Rendered Attractive. Let this great and productive reform be once effected and three quarters of the evils, which oppress mankind will be done away with as if by magic influence. . . . The destiny of man is to be happy on this earth, but not in our subversive society, characterized by indigence and discord."

Now in 1855, spread out before him was a large map of the United States. He was thinking over what he had learned when he took Considerant to Fort Worth a year and a half before to seek a site for a practical trial of Associationism. There had been no straight route. They had to travel for five weeks, use river transport on the Ohio, Mississippi, and Arkansas Rivers, then ride horses for six weeks across Indian Territory and North Texas.

Standing at the map this day he traced with his finger the distance from Preston on the Red River between Texas and Indian Territory to the river's junction with the Mississippi. He and Considerant had looked across at the Texas shore near Preston, with its white cliffs in the distance, which turned out to be a bold stratification of red clay and white sand. They had seen water to float barges. There had been plenty of water to support the ferry that carried them across the Red River that spring day, though not so much that slaves could not manage the skiffs while poling. He slit open an envelope and read a note from

Cantagrel written as he passed through Memphis. Cantagrel explained that there was not enough water in the Arkansas River to get him and the Reverend Allen up to Fort Smith. Surely that was a freak condition with rivers as wide as the ones Brisbane had seen. It was true that the Red River had less water than the Hudson, but certainly there had been a sufficient amount.

Brisbane pictured that beautiful, sweet-smelling Texas land along the Red River, so like a park that it was still burned on his retina. It was an ideal location for his new community. No emperor there would muzzle one and kick one out of the country, as Louis-Napoléon's police had done to Brisbane for making an innocent speech on Fourier's birthday in 1849. In Paris in December 1852, he had been aroused at four in the morning to hear the army arrest a liberal general living in the building in which Brisbane was staying. He had dressed and run out into the street and to the quai. Soldiers were bivouacked along the fall of the Tuileries Palace near the Pont Royal. All day he watched the collection of power in various quarters of the city until at the end of the day there was no chance for an opposing move by the Republicans.

The following spring, after he had watched this coup d'état the previous December, they had expelled him again. He had been surprised to hear from the Sûreté that he was important enough to have merited a police file. It recorded his actions and associates all the way back to meetings of the Saint-Simonians that he attended in 1832!

In the future, settled far away in Texas, the Association in Fourier's plan would have no hideous fourteen-hour-day sweat shops where people lived packed fifty thousand in a square mile, as Brisbane had seen in Liverpool, London, and New York.[7] Maybe he would take his son Charles out to Texas or even send him to the practical trial. It was time Charles had some frontier experience.

On the map before him, Brisbane saw that the Red River was much better for a phalanstery than the Naches, Trinity, or Brazos. One had to go all the way out of the Mississippi into the Gulf of Mexico to find the mouths of these other rivers. With water transport being the only connection between the North Texas prairies and markets, the Red River would be much more efficient in getting products out of Texas. To

Brisbane, those Texas lands along the river would give the Fourierists the place they sought, unpolluted with people spoiled by civilization.

He congratulated himself that he had taken Considerant to Texas. They had both been enthusiastic, overcome with the beauty of the magnificent valleys. It had been worth getting covered with ticks in Indian Territory and twiddling his thumbs waiting for Considerant's stomach to surmount the greasy food. Considerant said it was half cooked, but that food was no worse than he, Brisbane, had eaten in the back country of Turkey or Ireland. And this virgin land would be free of all the human miseries of those Old World places. He had sent the word to the East Coast, and Considerant to Europe, even as they explored North Texas, that Considerant had decided to attempt a phalanstery, and Brisbane agreed.[8]

Brisbane had on his desk a *Bulletin* from the Société de colonisation européo-américaine au Texas that the École Sociétaire had sent him two weeks ago, surely the first of many. This edition contained the rallying piece from the Old World parallel to his column in the *New York Tribune* a dozen years before. Brisbane had offered in 1842 to pay Horace Greeley $500 a year for a front-page column on Associationism. With the skillful placement of column words that he often paid for in various newspapers over the state, with his clear spontaneous oratory, and with pamphlet after pamphlet, he began to develop attention. In the doldrums in 1842, following the 1837 panic and its 1839 echo, his words had so struck a chord in middle-class and artisan working-class imaginations that in the course of three years more than thirty communes had sprung up, only to founder in a few weeks or months. By 1855 it was obvious that the failure of the thirty-odd experiments of the 1840s had lost him his persuasive authority, even among many socialists. He could no longer use the term "Associationism" but talked instead of "Social Progress and Reform" and "Workingmen's Protective Unions." His endless repetition of the slogans "Our Evils Are Social Not Political" and "Social Reform Only Can Eradicate Them" had been believed only briefly.[9] The results in the 1840s of his great propagandizing had been disastrous for those investing, and at this very moment of appeal for investors to support the Texas colony, the North American Phalanx in New Jersey was foundering. It was the last association still alive on the East Coast, the one on which most had been staked.

In the country at large, the social agenda was being overwhelmed by the debate on slavery and Bleeding Kansas. Brisbane had mustered a little American money to contribute to the colony. Still, he continued expounding his dream of a just society, and his extemporized speeches always drew attention.

He thought again. He had heard in November that Randolph Marcy was back from making his surveys on the upper Brazos. The army was preparing to settle the Comanches. With those Indians on a reservation, there should be no security problem along the Red River. He needed to have Ham Merrill arrange a meeting with Marcy to hear the latest on conditions in upper Texas.

Ham Merrill was a neighbor in Genesee County who lived eight miles away in Byron, not far from the Brisbanes in Batavia. Now Merrill was a major in the Dragoons. He had first told Brisbane a year and a half earlier of the lands in the country of the Three Forks and of the fort about to be decommissioned when he was its commandant.[10] Merrill's fort was sixty miles south of the lands along the Red River that had so impressed Brisbane. The fort would make a good receiving station while they readied the ultimate settlement. He and Considerant had seen no human in their first eleven days of exploration guided by a detachment from the fort's garrison.[11] With better market access, the lands to develop to further Fourier's goals were on the Red River. Considerant was about to come through New York on his way to Texas. He would reinforce the point to the leader. But now, Brisbane started a letter to the École in Paris. They also should know his opinion of the lands along the Red River.[12]

He traced on the map the sinuous line of the Red River down southeast to its end, then up the Mississippi to the mouth of the Ohio, then east to stop at Patriot, Indiana. Ellen Allen would be there waiting for the reverend to take her to Texas.[13] Brisbane remembered first meeting her in the Hive at Brook Farm nine or ten years before. Among the younger women, Ellen Lazarus had been willing to listen to him and share in his goals for Humanity, even with her independent eye. Then she had married John Allen a year after Brook Farm collapsed. Her family disliked the idea of this minister Allen, for John had no money. Still, she had an income from the estate of her parents.

While thinking of the Allens, Brisbane suddenly worried about Reverend Allen's inability to find any investors in the Midwest for the Texas colony. But in his defense, without proof of French backing, it would be difficult to convince anyone. And that proof had not come until the previous fall, about the time Reverend Allen was getting ready to go with Cantagrel to Texas. The reverend had little ammunition with which to sell the colony—just *Au Texas* in a foreign language.

Following the Ohio east, his finger on Cincinnati, Brisbane thought about Benjamin Urner. This thoughtful man of Quaker heritage had ventured to the Midwest twenty years before and had always participated in important Associationist conventions.[14] Now he was establishing an insurance business and had allowed his name to be listed as agent for the Texas colony in Cincinnati.[15]

With new proof of good backing from the Europeans, Brisbane felt better about his pledge of $20,000. Brother George would have thought it too speculative—and many too many dollars—but George did not have faith in Fourier's ideas. After all, George had not sat at Fourier's feet twenty years ago and dreamed with all the other socialists in Paris. And George did not understand the reality of the land along the Red River in the area of the Three Forks. The land was a jewel. He could always adjust the amount he gave to the stock company once he saw how the colony progressed.

And for a Fourier phalanx, this land was perfect. The words of Considerant about it in *Au Texas* were glowing. Brisbane had spent the past summer translating Considerant's words into English after he got the book in June. He liked his American title for it: *The Great West*. He might be accused of being an overzealous propagandist again, as he had been in the early 1840s, but this time he had Considerant himself coming to lead the practical effort to totally reorganize society. Considerant counseled to go slow in creating the commune but to promptly buy land as an investment for the stock company. Unlike the caution expressed in those letters from Considerant, all the other letters Brisbane received from France sounded impatient for the commune. Enthusiasm was building.

9

Finding Land

In seeking land one must be concerned with taking every necessary precaution to not reveal your hand from the beginning and to avoid the traps that, in America as everywhere else, encumber the terrain of possible business deals, and particularly those that have for a purpose the acquisition of land in a country where land is the principal, almost the only object of commerce. In the times we live in, unless one sets foot on an entirely deserted island, it is necessary to deal with the ruse and maneuver of speculation.

BULLETIN of the European American Society of Colonization in Texas

In Paris, Texas, Cantagrel, Roger, Reverend Allen, and Lawrie divided paths, with Cantagrel and Lawrie headed toward Dallas and the other two headed west. It was Cantagrel who was charged with finding land for the new colony that would realize the dreams of Dr. Savardan, Brisbane, and the others. Tired, dirty, and saddle sore from two weeks' riding, Cantagrel found a haven, a bed with sheets for the first time in weeks, at the Art Saloon, owned by Adolphe Gouhenant, on the Dallas town square.

Ignoring the warning of Bourdon of the Paris office about Gouhenant, Cantagrel, as Considerant before him, fell into Gouhenant's arms. Gouhenant was not a stranger to Cantagrel. They first met in socialist circles in Paris. It was a joy to communicate directly with this fellow countryman without the strain of listening to English. Cantagrel could dispense with Arthur Lawrie and all interpreters and restore his control of what he was being told. He felt no hostility from this man, unlike the feeling he was continually getting as a foreigner when he encountered settlers. He could have a bath and wash his hair! He could eat a meal organized by a Frenchman, free of greasy pork and cornbread. Gouhenant's hospitality allowed Cantagrel and Lawrie to sleep under sheets, a rare thing enough in these reaches, as Considerant had remarked.[1] For a few hours Cantagrel and Lawrie could renew themselves in the midst of this rude world. He wished for Josephine and Simon and the baby.

But his renewal would be short. Late that December night while they were sitting in the saloon, Gouhenant told Cantagrel, "You are much too late to acquire the site of former Fort Worth as free land. You will have to look hard to find free land of any size in Dallas County and if found, it will be in small bits. Most likely you just won't find it. If you want free land, you need to look much further west." Cantagrel nodded. Now he needed a new plan.

To find land, Cantagrel, like Considerant before him, leaned on the French speakers he found on the prairie. They were members of the 1848 Cabet colony, who by now had almost seven years' experience with the frontier. They, too, were utopians who crossed the ocean to build a new society. Cantagrel remembered the names he had read in *Au Texas.* Along with Adolphe Gouhenant's name he remembered the names of Lucien Bourgeois and one other native Frenchman in the village, Maxime Guillot.[2] Along with Guillot's wife and two or three workers Guillot had recently brought from France to work at his wagon factory, they were likely Cantagrel's only former compatriots in Dallas County.[3] They had each been interviewed by Considerant on his trip and quoted by him. As frontiersmen now, they understood Cantagrel's questions about his options in finding land. In this world, where everyone was consumed with acquiring land, he needed to find free land. He needed the new land company to show a profit, as well as to shelter utopian immigrants.

Could he still find acceptable free land, or would he have to pay for good land? No suitable land that was free remained to the east of Dallas. Even hard-to-clear bottomlands had been patented.

Cantagrel was told that he might find some unpatented wetlands in the western part of the county that would need to be drained. There would be no plots of any size still free on which to build a new community near this village. Why not settle outside Dallas, the resident Frenchmen asked. The Frenchmen pressed Dallas's transportation advantages, both water and future rail. They also pointed out land appreciating around this hoped-for future center.

If Cantagrel were willing to buy, he could find sections and half sections of grazing lands in the southwestern part of the county, they told him. There were even farming lands for sale near the river, but they would cost considerably more. Gouhenant had bragging rights on his own five trades in town lots in the past three years: everything had advanced in value.[4] As he also pointed out to Cantagrel, few people had cash, and in a cash-hungry society, one surely would find plenty of land if one paid in gold. Many of these settlers were frontiersmen who never stayed anywhere more than five years and would leap at gold.

"What about Fort Worth?" Cantagrel asked. "Go look," he was advised. To identify free land, Cantagrel needed a landsman to find it for him, but it would be hard to hire a landsman, since they had moved out toward the unallocated land. They also had too many deals for themselves and with friends. And no one spoke French. To go farther out on the frontier, Cantagrel needed a translator. Perhaps he should engage Lucien Bourgeois here in Dallas, as Considerant also had suggested.

Hence, the day after he arrived, Cantagrel walked with Gouhenant across the Dallas town square and through the dead weeds on sand trails to meet Lucien Bourgeois. Behind a palisade of tightly spaced picket saplings, Bourgeois's home bore out Considerant's description of a defense from wild critters.[5]

Like Gouhenant, Bourgeois was an Icarian who remained on the Three Forks frontier after trying the communal life of equality nearly seven years before. He had been thirty-one when he crossed the ocean, full of dreams for Icarie, one of the followers of Étienne Cabet who symbolically, if naively, marched across the Texas plains wearing their identical clothing to share and share alike. They founded their colony in southwestern Denton County. A single man at the time, Bourgeois had settled on 320 acres of public land, patented under the Peters Company just north of the Dallas/Denton County line. He wrestled the frontier long enough to break ground on the required fifteen acres, build a cabin, and secure his deed. He had survived the mental transition from the urban life of Paris to the frontier life of Texas. Now he was a fron-tiersman courting the widow Sampson and living in Dallas, where he served as the village's first tailor when he wasn't plowing.[6] He agreed to become the interpreter for Cantagrel's quest.

On Sunday morning, New Year's Eve, Cantagrel, Bourgeois, and Law-rie started west to search the lands on the upper West Fork of the Trin-ity and out to the Brazos. Their first stop was to find a surveyor-guide, known as a pilot in "Fort-town." They rode at least eight and a half hours on horseback to reach it.[7] Along the way Bourgeois explained the land, soils, and options Cantagrel would face. They felt relatively safe on this trail. It had been more than six years since the last death attributed to Indians had occurred between Dallas and the Fort.

Since it was winter and dry, they took the Long Bottom trail west from the village of Dallas instead of going north to the narrower Cal-ifornia Crossing. Below the bluff two blocks west of the courthouse square, they crossed the white rock shoals near the new bridge being built and found themselves in the lowland forest that covered the mile-wide floodplain. Through the tall cottonwoods by the river channel, they saw the effects of logging and the great, very straight cedar logs that had been dragged by oxen from south of the village for Dallas's first river bridge. It was about to be finished. Its builder, Alexander Cockrell, advertised it to be the "longest in Texas." It would be weather boarded and covered with an excellent roof when it was completed in February.[8]

Long Bottom was so dubbed because it held a due west trail through the bottomland of the Trinity. The trail lay south from the river meanders against a bluff that rose on its left side and ran for five miles.[9] Midway at a cleared piece of bottomland, the trail branched to the right toward a river crossing a mile to the north.[10] It continued southwest another three miles to cross the West Fork at Eagle Ford. Rising northwest out of the river bottom, both trails turned west as they joined the Cedar Springs and the California Crossing routes from the Elm Fork and passed through Buck-and-Breck.[11] Lawrie found the country "west of Dallas . . . most beautiful and fertile. The handsomest land [he had ever seen was] just west of Elm Fork of Trinity."[12]

Soon an immense red-gold expanse that Bourgeois called Grapevine Prairie opened to their right, unbounded to the northern horizon. Its waving, chest-high grass made the plain seem limitless. Here the invading settlers had not yet killed all the herds of grazing animals, but in some places bleached buffalo skulls and bones littered the ground, commemorating the settlers' war with nature. Bourgeois told them that the great herds passed west of Fort Worth now, though "now and then a few scattered ones wandered east as far as Grand Prairie. Wild horses, too, had for the most part retired west of the Trinity River. The settlers tried to exterminate them because of their bad example. The gentlest plow horse, getting among them, became in two days the wildest of the bunch. Some people made a business to kill wild horses and boiled the oil out of their flesh. Horse oil made the finest soap grease in the world, and it was used extensively by tanners in dressing leather."[13] To the west, Grapevine Prairie ended in a wall of straight post oaks and red oaks rising out of a thicket of undergrowth. This marked the soil change supporting the real Eastern Cross Timbers. The trail through this scrub haven for ground birds ran over a stiff, brown, sandy, clay soil, unlike the shrunken, split-open-with-cracks, black, waxy ground that lay under the golden-grassed winter prairie they had traversed.

Bourgeois told them that many remnant tribes of eastern Indians had recently inhabited these thicket timbers, hiding from the roving Plains Indians to the west and also from the invading white man behind them. Now they mostly had been driven north across the Red River.

At noon they rested at the crossing of Bear Creek, an eroded defile in the prairie that was the hardest to ford between the river at Dallas and the West Fork crossing before Fort-town. A little west of Bear Creek, as the Trinity River they skirted wound closer to their route, they saw the line of bare cottonwoods and giant white sycamores marking its channel. Before the cottonwoods was a little horseshoe-shaped pond, which was the site of Bird's Fort, the first Anglo settlement in the area and abandoned more than twelve years ago.[14] Sibley had disbanded his troops here. Sam Houston a dozen years before waited briefly here with his commissioners, upset they had not produced the Indians that he had sent his commissioners to find five months earlier so that they might smoke the pipe of peace.

In another ten miles, between Big Fossil and Little Fossil Creeks, they came to Birdville, the seat of Tarrant County government.[15] This hamlet sat on the literal frontier, the site of the westernmost organized government before El Paso and Santa Fe. But the huddle of fifty wore its political mantle uneasily. Neighbors at sixteen-month-old Fort-town did not want to abide by the county vote that had made Birdville the county seat. They schemed to undo it. "Should we seek land here?" Cantagrel asked. "No," Bourgeois said. "Why start with land that has all those trees to clear, when prairie is so much easier to break?" All the colony needed of forest was a tract for firewood, which naturally occurred in drainage draws.

From Birdville, their day's destination was visible five and a half miles to the southwest, a low eminence marked against the rim of the earth in the afternoon light. Before it, a tiny glint of light in the brown-gray winter forest marked the West Fork, more than a mile closer to them east of the fort.

Riding in the bare forest an hour later, the travelers crossed the river, only a narrow, shallow ribbon a few yards wide in the middle of its floodplain this winter day. Cantagrel wondered: with this little water, could the river float even a skiff? Soon after, they reached a disheveled area that had been the army's first summer campsite before it moved to the nearby mesa top five years before. The camp had been established to take advantage of Cold Spring. Travelers still watered themselves and their horses, as they had from time immemorial, at this known stopping place—a big spring in the side of the bluff, which now hid the fort on top.

They followed a trail up the east face of the bluff in the late afternoon light. The elegant sky promised Considerant's vision of a white fort to receive utopians. The sky overwhelmed the tableland peninsula that sloped gently south and west. At its extreme northern end, the log buildings of the decommissioned fort commanded a view of the Trinity channel at the bottom of a precipitous bluff and of the forest on both sides of the ox bows looping to the north and west.

Over the top of the forest opened a grand vista of receding ridges, blues of varying shades under a canopy of thin, pale-lavender cirrus clouds edged in cerulean to the north and gold to the west. In the sunset they saw the hills rise to the west and north and encompass the country to the east.

As he enjoyed the vast distances, so different from France, Cantagrel now understood Considerant's vision of a wilderness staging area for the new society. But how his spirits withered as he reached the mesa top and surveyed the fort before him. Could this sullied place be their utopia? Order was gone.

Fifteen and a half months after the fort's decommission, the pristine parade ground had become a jumbled mélange, rutted from wagons full of buffalo hides or pecans and puddled by tethered animals. People camped, selling goods off the back ends of wagons; one offered whiskey from a barrel. The blood and viscera of a freshly slaughtered cow attracted two pigs, while the carcass, head and hide separated, lay draped over a pile of akimbo firewood. Discarded debris littered the ground, softened by dead grass poking through it. The eight-acre garden, which Considerant had proclaimed in his book would never grow weeds, was nowhere to be seen. Indeed, there were weeds everywhere in what was now known as Fort Town (and later as Fort Worth). A general store had taken over one fort cabin. A doctor had claimed an officer's quarters. The army's whitewashed log walls, which had given the fort civility, were spattered and peeling. There may have been fifty people scattered about the area. Cantagrel's mouth tightened as he comprehended the reality of settlers having beaten the utopians to this site.

Captain Ephram Daggett, a veteran of the Mexican War, had turned the cavalry stable on the east side of the fort's quadrangle into a "hotel." The men walked into the hotel to see Santa Anna's captured silver "punch bowl," the chief decoration inside the hostelry. Daggett was among the forces that had so surprised Santa Anna in an 1847 Mexican War battle that the general had abandoned his camp gear, even his uniform. Hence, the general's wash bowl had become Daggett's punch bowl, reputedly made of five thousand silver pesos. The visitors did not revere the punch bowl as much as some did.

Outside the hotel, when Captain Daggett needed to lure business, "Doc Gounah," as Adolphe Gouhenant was called, stretched canvas to paint the incipient town's first commercial marquee. Stretched across the stable front and covering half the height of the building, he was "pictured as gracing the Captain's festive board, life-sized wild game lusciously cooked to inveigle the appetite and . . . deer running . . . bears . . . and lesser game."

On this late Saturday Cantagrel was intent on business, even after riding all day. That evening, the party met Surveyor King, who knew of a large unallocated tract on the Brazos. Cantagrel planned to start the next day. They spent the night sleeping on the hotel's thin straw pallet.

At daylight Cantagrel had second thoughts. He wanted maps, as well as words. He decided to wait for King to guide them. Instead of leaving as proposed, he spent New Year's Day and the next day making copies of surveyors' maps. King finally declined to accompany them, his excuse being that he was obliged to go to Austin. Cantagrel paused. Was King giving this foreigner Frenchman the runaround?

On Wednesday, dropping down the gentler west side of Fort-town's bluff, the three started northwest toward the land King advised them as being vacant and far from any organized government. They expected to find a man at a Mr. Snyder's place up the Belknap trail who would show them the country.

West of Fort-town, the land soon changed from the prairies to the east. It began to roll and rise and proved to be broken occasionally. The utopians followed a well-marked road beaten down and rutted by the army traveling between its old and new posts. Out of the river bottom, it became a winding trail, moving ever up to gain some seven hundred feet in height before it reached the edge of the county. They passed out of the Eastern Cross Timbers into prairies with motts, or small groves, of a tree they had not seen before, a curly-leafed, dark, evergreen oak that Bourgeois called "live oak." It dotted the red-gold grassed hills in the vicinity of Creamlevel, a hamlet of two or three cabins perched on the "hog back" between the Trinity and Brazos.[16] The travelers stayed overnight at the house of Mr. Snyder, about thirty miles from Fort-town. They could find no one to accompany them farther.

Now they were without a landsman and provisions; besides, Reverend Allen and Roger would be waiting for them in Alton. They sought Isaac Healey, a surveyor, who was supposed to be at a Mr. Forman's house.[17] He was away. After dinner at Forman's, they continued east, flushing flocks of wild turkeys, examining the rolling country toward Alton, until two hours after dark, when they found Isaac or Jim Ventioner in northwestern Tarrant County and were allowed to stay the night. Mr. Connelly, another guest, gave news of having put up Considerant and Brisbane eighteen months before.

On Friday the land smoothed as they rode farther northeast toward Alton. In the far distance, black smoke rose in a great plume in the clear air. Bourgeois explained that the prairie was probably being prepared for spring plowing by burning the grass, the first act of settlement. He also pointed out the area along a creek where Gouhenant had led him and the sixty other Icarians to begin their commune in 1848. He showed them the cemetery where they had buried eleven comrades. "So many Frenchmen dying in only three months on the prairie," thought Cantagrel. "What had they done wrong? Of what did the Fourierists have to be careful?"

Five days and no land found. Cantagrel wondered why he accepted this responsibility. Nothing was as he had envisioned it from listening to Considerant and reading his book. Alton was a county seat without information. Not only was no surveyor available in Alton, but there was no Reverend Allen or Roger waiting for them as agreed. Another frustration. Should they go north to find the missing Fourierists or wait there? The next day Cantagrel chose to ride out with Bourgeois and look at land toward the Elm Fork while Lawrie stayed to watch for the two men. Late in the afternoon Lawrie found Reverend Allen and Roger riding into town—bareback!

The two men had met with considerable bad luck, as Reverend Allen proceeded to explain. "After leaving Gainesville on our journey west into the upper Cross Timbers, we encamped, our horses tied close by the tent," Reverend Allen said. "In the night, I checked the animals. They were gone. At first light we circled the area, but not having the practiced eyes of frontiersmen, we could not find the direction the animals had taken. The cross timbers to the west may have hidden them, but we could never chase them on foot. We lugged our saddles and gear back to the last cabin we had passed. We then further retreated to Gainesville in search of *trackers*."

"Trackers?" Lawrie asked.

"Trackers are a class of frontiersmen used to search for lost or stolen horses. We found no one to help us," Reverend Allen continued. "Failing trackers, Roger and I set out on foot for Alton, thirty-five miles due south. Having walked twenty-five miles, we were out of Cooke County and past Clear Creek, but still ten miles from Alton. Suddenly, riding up behind us came a 'somewhat remarkable specimen of humanity . . . a Delaware, united with a slight admixture of the African . . . his head . . . covered with a shawl à la Turk.'"

His name was Jim Ned, a chief of an Indian tribe camped not far from where they had last seen their horses. "He had a Delaware wife, and adopted the habits of that tribe, but at the same time he possessed all the social vivacity and garrulity of the Negro . . . he had the reputation of being one of the most expert, daring and successful horse-thieves among the southwestern tribes."

This day was a testament to the prowess of Jim Ned. Jim Ned had Reverend Allen's and Roger's horses. Allen, who always thought good of everyone, took a while to fathom the situation. "Although he [Jim Ned] was generous and hospitable in his disposition, he was eminently vindictive and revengeful toward those who interfered with his favorite pursuit, and it was said that several of his tribe had with their lives paid the penalty of incurring his displeasure."[18]

The European Roger understood at once that they were victims of extortion when Jim Ned's broken English thicket of "may be so" and "he," referring to plural horses, was penetrated to reveal a $35 return fee. Without a fight, they paid the asking price.

By then it was Sunday, January 7. After reporting their experiences, Cantagrel told Reverend Allen to get north to retrieve their gear and take Lawrie for protection. Near Gainesville, Allen discovered that his mare had the thumps, brought on by hard riding. They doctored the horse after finding shelter for the night at Mr. Brown's house, two miles from town.[19] Reverend Allen was now less interested in locations near the Red River or near the Delawares, having found their friendliness overrated.

Meanwhile, waiting in Alton, Bourgeois had heard of another potential surveyor-guide, a Mr. Jenkins. Cantagrel dispatched Roger to Fort Worth to ask Jenkins to pilot them while Bourgeois showed Cantagrel the land between Alton and Dallas. Bourgeois, having now met the Yankee minister, warned Cantagrel as they rode south that settlers hereabouts would have great prejudice against Allen's New England accent. Resigned to going much farther in search of land, in Dallas they procured a wagon and provisions for nights when no settler's cabin welcomed them. Reverend Allen and Lawrie, with effects retrieved, were to rendezvous with all of them in Fort Worth.

On Monday, riding again in their saddles on the trail south, Reverend Allen and Lawrie met rain. They took advantage of frontier hospitality to find shelter about dinner time at the house of a Mr. James Martin, chief justice of Precinct No. 2 in Cooke County. The host told them that they were following Considerant and Brisbane's trail, as the latter had stayed with Martin a year ago last June. It was still raining the next morning. Forced to stay over at Martin's, Lawrie used the time to write in his diary. Reverend Allen, sheepish over the loss of time and $35, fretted with his eye on the weather.

Midmorning they finally left. Wrapped in fog all day, distance beyond two hundred feet was annihilated but for faded, feathery black silhouettes of cedars or vague outlines of the fine-scaled branch structure, evolved to capture the most moisture possible for short prairie oaks. The ghostly silhouettes of post oaks, with their stiff trunks, angular branches, and thickets of fine branchlets at their outer perimeter, still holding their dead leaves, suggested the macabre in the eyes of visitors accustomed to the supple, tall silhouettes of water-filled tree forms in northern Europe.

On the ground, there was a hint of blue-green hidden in the straw-colored grass, encouraged by the rain the day before. While the men followed a vague trail through a creek-bottom forest, they saw through an occasional sudden hole in the wispy gray shroud a herd of antelope with their heads all turned in unison, peering out of the tall grass, as rigid as if they were a two-dimensional gray cut-out.

Pressing ahead into Denton County, the men stayed the night with a herder on Hickory Creek in the northwestern part of the county. The next night, still riding south toward Fort Worth, they encamped on the banks of what they supposed to be Elizabeth Creek, as they could see Blue Mound south-southwest in the distance. The weather was mild. They stopped for the night on the site of an old Indian camp, where its tent poles were still standing. They built a fire against a pair of hackberry trees, one of which was rotten. Fearing it might fall upon them in the night while they slept, they pushed it down with a pole. Unable to sleep with the sounds of coyotes barking and howling at the moon, they watched the clear moon in the West until the early morning hours.

Cantagrel, back in Dallas, faced another loop to the west. He now fully realized that finding free land on which to build shelters by the time colonists arrived was questionable. Based on his recent foray and Reverend Allen's Indian experience near the Red River, he had to consider cash purchase options. Gouhenant put the word out that there was a serious cash buyer in the village. It was in his and Bourgeois's interest, as well as that of the village, to have the colony near at hand. Others had begun to come forward with land offers in the ten days since Cantagrel's first arrival. There was a section of cleared land with river frontage in Long Bottom that Enoch Horton was willing to sell.

Cantagrel and Bourgeois rode over the offered section, inspected its cabin near the river, and then rode over an arid half section up the bluff to the south. After his last ten days in the saddle, seeing so many free-ranging cattle, Cantagrel listened more seriously to the argument that cattle could provide an immediate profit center on such arid land, though he knew that his Fourierist friends were not habituated as range cowboys. While the testament in *Au Texas* to the ease of growing cattle became clear, there was still the problem of a very distant market at railheads in Kansas.

The two Frenchmen continued from Dallas toward Fort-town with their wagon and provisions. They camped in the cross timbers, the ground still a bit damp from the rain two days before. The road through Long Bottom was "two parallel ruts with vegetation growing along the center line to the van pole. When the water in these ruts gains force, it washes out holes into which the wheels drop a foot or more on this side or that." Cantagrel was learning about the West. The ruts would overturn an ordinary vehicle, "so the Texas van is shallow with a narrow body set central on a wide axle." The driver knew that being flung from side to side was the lesser of two evils. Where the country is untimbered "and the road gets into too many holes, or a drove of bullocks puddle it into pudding, the next comers take their course to the right or left so that a much traveled road looks like the railway lines at Clapham Junction. Long Bottom . . . was a dreary stretch of mud."[20]

On Thursday, January 11, Reverend Allen and Lawrie left camp before sunrise. Again, fog occasionally revealed deer or antelope through the mist. Around Blue Mound they followed a trail edged in dew from the fog to reach Fort Worth about midday. There they found Roger, the "Doctor," who had been waiting two days. He had been to see surveyor Jenkins but had had no luck. Jenkins would not go with them. Cantagrel and Bourgeois had not yet arrived. Waiting for them in the afternoon, the two Yankees felt more comfortable on the prairie than in the fort amid settlers who were cool to their accents. Reverend Allen and Lawrie took a short hunt on the prairie to the west of the Clear Fork. The water was comfortably cool.

Cantagrel and Bourgeois had camped near Birdville Thursday night and driven the wagon to Fort-town midmorning of the following day. After six hours of a fruitless search for a surveyor-guide in the fort, Bourgeois and Reverend Allen identified yet another possibility. Cantagrel was ready to try anything. Speculating that Americans might do better at finding a guide out of the presence of foreigners, he sent Reverend Allen and Lawrie out of Fort Worth at midafternoon to find Silas P. Beebe, surveyor and member of the Denton Creek Settlement near Alton. Cantagrel and Roger would scout the West Fork while Luc Bourgeois brought the wagon to a rendezvous upstream.

Retracing their route back toward Alton, Reverend Allen and Lawrie traveled northeast until quite late, reaching Fossil Creek about nine. They camped on the creek, sleeping under the stars and trees until a "norther" came up about midnight.[21] The temperature dropped fifty degrees within two hours, introducing the suddenness of Texas winters to these Yankees. Sleep was impossible. Reverend Allen, the optimist, had his consolation. They had heard that the cold probably would go away in four days, the normal winter cycle.

They started for Beebe's before sunrise to reach there midmorning, but on arrival they found that the surveyor had left for Alton to procure a compass. The idea of sitting in a tiny, dark, smoky, and drafty log cabin in the cold was unacceptable. While waiting for Beebe's return, Reverend Allen and Lawrie took a hunt after deer and antelope. They came up to some but did not kill any. Both animals were very numerous.[22] Beebe returned late, and again the men were turned down.

Reverend Allen and Lawrie gave up on guides and started for the rendezvous with Cantagrel on the West Fork, reaching there midafternoon Sunday. Cantagrel and Roger arrived shortly, and Bourgeois drove up soon after. From there they rode to find a campsite farther up the river channel.[23]

The next morning the four left camp late after hunting. Allen's crack marksmanship supplied a "jackass" rabbit—so called for its nine-inch ears—which the travelers commented made a very savory breakfast dish. Bourgeois explained that for the best flavor they should roast it over mesquite, the wood of a short, spreading, thorny, and feathery legume tree with dark-purple bark.

After riding five miles from the previous night's campsite, their wheels broke down. The men devoted all day to repairing them. They camped that night only two miles on from the scene of the disaster. Because of their mishaps, Lawrie was made "chief of the teaming group" in charge of the vehicle. It would keep him to tamer roads than the others, who could negotiate trails on horseback.

By Tuesday, Cantagrel was feeling still more desperate until they came upon a Mr. Mann two miles after breaking camp. At last, someone agreed to act as a guide to lands on the West Fork. Under Mann's advice, Lawrie would continue with the wagon and meet them on the Belknap road, as it was impracticable to take the vehicle farther on the route along the Trinity. That night, Lawrie stopped at Old Man Woody's on Ash Creek and again had to mend the wagon.

Cantagrel, Reverend Allen, and Roger with Bourgeois and Mann began reconnoitering land farther up the West Fork of the Trinity. Each time they came up to the high divide between the rivers, the sky seemed bigger. They often stopped a minute to admire the long views, grading from beige, gold, and brown in the foreground to blue on the horizon. They understood they were on the surface of a vast ancient sea bed, grandly eroded by ancient glaciers to form two river systems. They turned back down the east side of the Brazos watershed south in the Keechi valley, encountering hills that reminded Cantagrel a little of the Vosges. At about the latitude of Fort Worth, they saw bits of island mesas left standing above the eroded plain, occasionally punctuating the horizon.[24]

On Wednesday, January 17, Lawrie returned a second time to Snyder's house on the Belknap Road. In the weather war overhead, the winds of which continually fluctuated between the Gulf of Mexico and the Arctic, the air again grew remarkably pleasant—positively warm—with wind in the south. The rule of four days of winter cold followed by warm air held for the men. Lawrie was bored. When was his brother James arriving? Sixty days would soon be up. How would he find them if he arrived early while they were wandering around the Brazos valley? It was ironic that part of his family was in this empty place with Frenchmen, and another part was going to France to be with Frenchmen. His brother Alexander was soon to go to Paris and listen to all that French while he studied painting. Brother John didn't approve of his and James coming to Texas, saying the whole thing was a land scam. It didn't look that way from here.

The next day, the weather continuing warm, Lawrie made for the house of a Mr. Sewell. On the second day, Lawrie wrote while he waited, "Here I am in the middle of northwest Texas, at the foot of the upper Cross Timbers on the ridge dividing the Trinity and Brazos on the road to Fort Belknap, and about forty-five miles above Fort Worth. Alone with two horses and a buggy and a dog." He was on unorganized public land fifty miles west of the last seats of government and forty-five miles east of the protecting Belknap army fort. Lawrie may have felt as James Beeman had nine years before: "When I was returning home one night on the other side of Richland Creek, I saw a herd of buffaloes. A storm came up that night and the buffaloes gathered in a great herd, which became wild with fright, and I could not tell the roar of the storm from the sound of the moving buffaloes. I sought protection in a skirt of timber close by."[25]

While Lawrie waited for the others, Cantagrel learned that vacant land was truly hard to uncover and that surveyors were as difficult to find as the land.[26] At the earliest, they might have returned to Fort Worth by January 22 or 23, but provisioned as they were, it is more likely that they got back on January 28. On that date, Cantagrel wrote the Paris management, reporting on his frustration. He wrote again from Fort Worth or Dallas on January 31.[27] Bourgeois took Cantagrel on a loop east to inspect the East Fork watershed and then back to Dallas, where he wrote a third time on February 4. The next *Bulletin* published in Paris for stockholders reported Cantagrel's recognition that "it is almost an impossibility to obtain sincere and true information from people who have, for themselves or for their associates, retained lands for resale and are interested consequently in not helping the new arrivals in their canvasses to discover free lands."[28]

To complicate matters further, somewhere along this route the group learned of the problems of verifying land claims. During the Hedgecoxe "War," which had been fought three years before, settlers' sentiment had run so high on the issue of verifying the land claims of the Peters Colony that the Texas legislature in 1853 rightly feared a voters' revolt. The legislature negotiated a compromise with irate free land holders, ordering titles verified by the General Land Office. Agents had come to interview and take affidavits from each settler of the colony. It was now nineteen months since most titles had been confirmed and located on the official maps filed with the Land Office in Austin. Cantagrel wondered, maybe that's what they should do—go to Austin and examine the maps. Cantagrel's letter of February 4 told of his decision. He had not found a landsman to help him. If he did not find better information in Austin on free lands, he would be forced to pay for a parent site for the colony. He took Reverend Allen with him as a translator.

To reach Austin, the two had a choice of continuing on horseback or taking the stagecoach, which had established Dallas's first travel service the previous July. After their strenuous six weeks on horseback, they took the stage. Four-horse coaches of the United States Small Line passed through Dallas Mondays, Wednesdays, and Fridays for Austin; they left from the Crutchfield House at the corner of the town square. "Through in three days," advertised the stagecoach line in the *Dallas Herald*.[29] Cantagrel and Reverend Allen left on Monday, February 5, arriving in Austin Wednesday evening. Based on the advice about abolitionists his French friends in Dallas had offered, Cantagrel cautioned Reverend Allen to refrain from offering opinions in the most westerly antebellum outpost in central Texas.

They ventured farther into settled country as their coach-and-four rolled south of the Brazos. They saw the land become dotted with more and larger motts of live oaks and a few buildings. At Salado they passed stone houses and log cabins joined by houses finished in milled lumber siding. They saw slaves building a building. Someone told them slaves built most of the buildings in this part of the state.

South of the hamlet of Brushy and ten miles north of Austin, they saw the flat rim of the horizon sprout low hills to the west. On the otherwise vacant skyline to the south, the late side light from the sun outlined a block surmounted by a small domed cupola. It was the year-old capitol of the state, Cantagrel's first reminder of Europe.

The building gradually sank from view behind hills as they approached the village and then emerged quite close on their left. They arrived in Austin on Wednesday evening. Their coach skirted the bottom of the capitol's hill and found a startling 120-foot-wide street sloping grandly from the capitol to the Colorado River a half mile away. Midway along this empty street to nowhere, lined with a sprinkling of one-story cabins and buildings, the village of two thousand huddled. Leaving the capitol in its splendid isolation, the coach descended the street to pull up at the village's center, Pecan Street, next to the two-story wooden veranda fronting Bullock's log hotel. With the legislature in session, the men were unable to find beds in this center of informal Texas politics. They stayed behind Bullock's in one of the small log buildings, where a slave lit a fire for them against the February damp.

The next morning the travelers walked up the grand street. Within a three-block radius, they saw four masonry churches in construction, perched on hills on either side. Governor Elisha Marshall Pease had inaugurated the capitol thirteen months before by leading a procession from the original log capitol, following the route Cantagrel and Reverend Allen were now taking up Congress Avenue to the new building on its dominating hill. The capitol, built of light-cream limestone, was plain but imposing, in contrast to the village below. Its silhouette showed two low and symmetrical hip roofs just visible behind the heavy cornice of a three-story masonry building. An undersized cupola sat in the middle of the building between the roof hips. The tiny cupola appeared to squash the roof. The building's center appeared sunken, exaggerated by the wide flight of stone steps leading to its piano nobile.

Austin's great axial street almost compelled a visit to the capitol. The ramped street ended in a flight of steps leading up to its portico. With an introduction to the governor from Brisbane's friend Merrill, Cantagrel and Reverend Allen climbed the flight of steps to see Texas government in session. Inside the building the cream limestone gave way to a harder white limestone, reflected in the marble tiles of the main floor. They watched the proceedings from the galleries overlooking the two chambers under their thirty-four-foot ceilings; the galleries' supporting beams were poorly fastened to columns, a fact not lost on Cantagrel. Gazing down over the Representatives' Hall, Reverend Allen was amused at the number of lawmakers who whittled while they listened to debates with fresh bundles of sticks supplied members each day.[30]

The two men attracted attention as they threaded their way through the hangers-on outside Governor Pease's office. The men were fish out of water, with one speaking with a French accent that no one could understand and the other with that odious New England sound acting as interpreter. With the introduction to the governor in hand, they entered the governor's office and stated their business. Other than confirm the fact that the lands in North Texas had been put on reserve for railroads, the governor could do little for Cantagrel but point the way to the Land Office. Their visit was enough to rouse the interest of the *Texas State Gazette*. On February 10, in the middle of their visit, the newspaper had other intelligence: according to a recent letter from Strasbourg published in the *National Gazette* of Switzerland, the Socialist Party in Alsace was about to immigrate en masse to Texas, where one of their chiefs, Victor Considerant, had purchased a large quantity of land. The first departure of immigrants was to take place during the ensuing spring.[31] Cantagrel and Allen walked around the ungainly capitol and headed northwest until they found the Land Office. It was a homely single-story stone building that had a corridor bisecting it, with three rooms on either side. Built three years before, it was crammed with people filing claims and seeking information.[32] The land boom had already attracted more people than the building could handle. Seeing the volume of people, Cantagrel and Allen surmised that the empresario grant Considerant had planned for was less and less likely. They spent Thursday and Friday in the Land Office, then waited for the next stage to return north on Tuesday.

Uncomfortable in this antiabolition, antiforeign environment, the men tried to be invisible. Walking the streets that night, they noticed "a very remarkable number of drinking and gambling shops" and the absence of a bookstore. Unfortunately for the European American Society of Colonization in Texas, Allen was indeed recognized in Austin. He was not only a Yankee but the New England Yankee who had been excoriated by a Mississippi newspaper as "a black leg of the blackest kind" for his antislavery militancy.

As newspapers in southern villages depended on journals passed down the Ohio, Mississippi, and Red River from the North, the editors of the *Texas State Gazette* had seen the article in the *Cincinnati Daily Commercial* the previous November:

Mr. John Allen, well known to the people of this and other Western States as a lecturer on "Association," and Victor Considerant,

a distinguished French Socialist, and a writer of considerable ability, have, we are informed, for some time been engaged in raising
funds, in this country and France, for the purpose of purchasing
a vast body of land in Texas, whereon to test the practicability
of Socialism on a grand scale. . . . We are told that half a million
dollars have absolutely been raised in behalf of this scheme, four
hundred thousand dollars in France, and one hundred thousand
in this country. . . . [A] number [*sic*, only Cantagrel] of Frenchmen
passed through this city . . . this week.[33]

A bit daunted by the cool reception they received from southerners
around them in Austin, Cantagrel and Reverend Allen left Austin on
Tuesday, February 13, and were back in Dallas the night of the 16th. They
had better information now, but finding free land was still problemat-
ical without a landsman to help. They rode to Fort Worth the next day
for another look. From map copies they had made in the Land Office
in Austin, they now knew who owned the land of the abandoned fort.
They had learned specifically where he had patented a headright at
the northwestern corner of the village. They checked prices with the
other owners. Cantagrel, Reverend Allen, and Lawrie debated what to
do next. "We either pay the prices thrust upon us by these speculators
or continue our search despite the fact that we are pressed for time,"
said Cantagrel. "I say we continue the search on the Clear Fork of the
Brazos." Reverend Allen agreed, but Lawrie insisted that they stop the
search, "the site of Réunion having been found, he insisted, in some way,
alleging particular instructions from Mr. Considerant, he insisted, shall
we say, that they stop there."[34]

Sometime in the later part of that week the men were all again in
Dallas, where the editor of the *Dallas Herald* quizzed them on their
findings. That Saturday he reported they were considering colonies
at three sites: one near Dallas, one in Tarrant County, and one on the
Keechi or Brazos.[35]

A large number of the settlers for these colonies are now *en route*,
having left Cincinnati in December last. They are probably detained
by the low stage of the rivers. We understand that industrial,

mechanical, and learned professions will be fully represented. It is their design to make everything they use within themselves, and they will engage largely in manufactures of different kinds. Such a settlement in our midst, of a nation celebrated for its intelligence, genius and skill in the mechanic arts cannot fail to add greatly to its prosperity—Some of the leading republican minds and most distinguished authors of France, who since the usurpation of the "man of the 2nd December" have been exiled from their country for opinion's sake, are engaged in this enterprise. A welcome and success to all say we—*Dallas Herald*.[36]

Cantagrel had seen lands in Denton and Tarrant Counties that had no potential for water transport to market. The farther west they looked, the less evidence of rainfall they saw. The colonization society was bringing French and Swiss farmers here, not cattle ranchers. The Trinity *might* be made navigable as far as the Dallas area; Major Ely and John Bryan, two of that town's leaders, had paddled down it in a spring flood a dozen years before. Everyone talked optimistically of its future for barge navigation. From Cantagrel's research in Washington, the U.S. Army Corps of Engineers had declared the Trinity "the deepest and least obstructed river in the State of Texas."[37]

Cantagrel also knew that a site higher up the West Fork of the Trinity most likely would not be navigable. Farther west, though this was a dry period, the upper reaches of the Brazos seemed too shallow even in the best of times to be accessible by boat. And Brazos waters were bitter from the mineral deposits through which they flowed.

On the upper areas of both rivers, the men had heard stories of Indian depredations and of the new reservations created the past summer on the Brazos where the red men *might* still be a threat. As they left Austin, the *Gazette* was announcing a company being formed to go west to fight the Comanches.

Cantagrel knew that for a year and a half, the Peters Company had been allowed to pick its own lands as payment for bringing settlers. As a result, much of the choice lands farther west on the Brazos had been claimed. The better river, the Trinity, was more settled. Around Dallas, land was harder to find and more expensive. Taller trees showed that the East Fork watershed had distinctly more rainfall.

It was not clear how long it would be before railroads were in place, though they were promised, and a twenty-mile line had been built west of Houston. Cantagrel balanced the need for a strategic transportation location with land cleared and ready for farm production. The first land acquired was to be for the colonization society's parent site. It had to quickly function as the center of operations. It had to produce food for the pioneers coming in the fall. He focused on sites in Dallas County.

Cantagrel could wait no longer. He had confirmation in letters waiting for him at the Dallas Post Office that people had left for Texas in December. He would be responsible if a reception place was not ready for them. After six weeks of looking, he had to act. In France they had talked of going to another state if the government of Texas was not favorable. But how could he scout land in another state after the École had sent all these people, now on the high seas?

He decided to buy the Horton section, the McCracken section, and land of L. G. Coombs, in all, 2,436 acres of land, situated three miles west of Dallas. They were higher in price than others offered, but they had more advantages: Cantagrel chose land that potentially would have access to water transport on the Trinity River itself. The east–west future railroad was projected to cross the land. And it straddled trails to several communities. The land had three characteristics: it offered a variety of soils—up to eight hundred acres of rich alluvial plain lowlands next to the river, with at least fifty of those acres cleared for farming, and on the north side of the river channel one reached a forty- to fifty-acre triangle by a rope-suspended footbridge.

In the middle of the one-by-three-mile tract—another seven hundred to eight hundred acres—a prairie highland of thin calcareous soil grew shorter-stemmed grasses. It would support a good town site, cattle grazing, and grape culture. Cantagrel could see that a good breeze in summer, important to avoid lowland fevers, would bathe the top of the bluff. On the chalky soil, cedar forests also grew. Springs flowed out of the oak-covered bluff overlooking the lowlands. Farther south, an area of hardwood forest shaded a flowing creek on the McCracken tract. On the southeast corner of that tract were two mounds, the site of a former Tonkawa village.[38]

In Cantagrel's mind, if he were too late to buy the fort site itself, he would buy land similar in prospect: a plateau with a bluff to the north, overlooking the same river hidden in a similar floodplain forest. He would locate a town site on a promontory similar to Fort Worth's. Cantagrel may have found a projected railroad route map in Austin, because Paris mapmakers, who drew from his information, recorded La Réunion landholdings and noted the latest route of the Atlantic to Pacific railroad passing west through their land, where ultimately it would be built seventeen years later.

Alexander Cockrell's major bridge of the region under construction—of cedar logs over the Trinity channel next to the village of Dallas—pointed toward their purchased lands. It appealed to Cantagrel's architect/engineer eye. It would direct travelers from the village to trails leading to his land chosen for La Réunion. The bridge, aligned with Bryan's Commerce Street, extended from the Dallas river bluff over the shoals of the river bed west-southwest for 525 feet. Its road surface was well above the floodplain bottoms, but its length did not reach a bluff at its western end. The bridge ramped back down to the floodplain, making it functional only in modest floods. Trails of a mile or more through the muck then reached for high ground.

The land Cantagrel purchased was at a crossroads of trails. Routes from Dallas to Birdville and Fort Worth, Johnson's Station, Mountain Creek, and Cedar Hill all crossed it going west and south. There was also a river-bottom trail that ran northeast to the town of Cedar Springs, where a mill had been built.

After six weeks searching and two negotiating, the men at last had a site. It indeed was similar to Fort Worth. The minute Cantagrel had a deed in hand, he, Reverend Allen, Roger, and Lawrie took up residence in the existing small cabin on the Horton section. Up the hill, Reverend Allen began making an enclosure and breaking ground for his five hundred vines, which were soon to arrive. He began working in the first days of March.

In announcing Cantagrel's purchases, the colonization society in Paris propounded its philosophy: in bargaining for land, the strength of union, and the solidarity, the superiority of a society over isolated individuals is clearly manifest.[39] In a society, the experience of one, which would be ruinous for each to acquire, profits everyone, and what it may have cost, if divided between the crowd, becomes an insignificant expense. Whereas the isolated individual, at the risk of seeing all his capital melt away even before he found a vacant tract of land, is obliged to buy, at second- or thirdhand, the first suitable place that is offered to him, the agent of a society can take all the time necessary to inquire, to discover the free lands, to take advantage of the bargains that, in all the fields where speculation is concerned, cannot fail to be presented to those who have the necessary capital for seizing them. Then what constitutes a very serious inconvenience, an obstacle almost invincible for the individual, becomes an obvious advantage for a group.

The settlers and speculators in Dallas might have a different view.

10

Sailing to America

Little by little as we approached, my eyes searched the sea with curiosity; at last we caught sight of the mouth of the Seine; on all sides we could see little ships, which sailed in different directions. As soon as we were into the city we saw a forest of masts because all the different dock basins of le Havre were crowded with ships. Every-where we see people chasing the slowing train and soliciting the travelers for their respective hotels.

JULIEN REVERCHON, 1855

When one is embarking on a sailing ship, the moment one is able to leave port is at the pleasure of the wind. Given the vagaries of the wind, the École Sociétaire had a balancing act: they had to choose a ship by reputation, negotiate passage rates, and organize groups of colonists from all over France and Belgium to reach the docks simultaneously without squandering resources on emigrants waiting in seaside hotels for indeterminate times. The École mothered steerage passengers by seeing that they bought adequate food and water for the trip and had sanitary spaces. In the winter of 1854–55, handling baggage, transshipping supplies, and negotiating last-minute exit visas for groups of colonists became full-time work for the École. Leaving Dr. Savardan to marshal his group, Considerant orchestrated the first group leaving from Antwerp. The rue de Beaune office handled all but one of the rest with the help of agents in Le Havre. The departure date was set.[1]

Twelve people bound for Texas left from Antwerp on Christmas Day. Their ship, the *Uriel*, a 156-by-33-foot packet of eight hundred tons with a 24-foot draft, was an eight-year-old American ship built in Boston.[2] Vincent Cousin, thirty-two, had been appointed leader of the *Uriel* pioneers, as Considerant called them. Cousin was the son of an industrialist and had practiced architecture in Brussels. He came from a wealthy liberal political family in Mons that had several involvements with New World communes. He carried gold to Texas for the needs of the colony. He was in charge of tools, supplies, and crates of plants being shipped for the colony's New World agriculture.

In Le Havre, on a crisp January afternoon, hawsers were loosened to the sound of ten more "pioneers" on the *Lexington* crying, "Vive Fourier!" to Ferdinand Guillon, Fourierist midwife for this sailing. A most favorable wind blew the ship out of the harbor. Guillon thought the magnificent weather was a good omen, and his twenty requests in three hours that morning for a passport for a settler named Topin worth the effort. He smiled as the ship disappeared into the purple of the setting sun. Alexander Raisant, a second-time traveler to the United States, led a group of nine in the *Lexington*. In February, Dr. Savardan and forty-five others would follow on the *Nuremberg*. Then Karl Burkli with twenty-five on the *Francisco*, the Reverchons on the *Wurtemberg*, and others would follow.

To be ready for the morning wind, passengers generally boarded at four. The ship would be crowded with unstowed baggage of every kind. A mass of emigrants, often Germans and Swiss, as well as French, would crowd the deck. Seamen would collide with passengers, or they would hoist onboard pigs, sheep, a cow for milk, and a mass of poultry. As one colonist put it, according to Julien Reverchon, "The confused cries of men and animals rendered a horrible mess." Curiosity pulled new arrivals immediately to their cabins and generally to disappointment at their cramped size. Julien Reverchon, the teenage son of Maximilien, felt lucky that one of four beds in his second-class cabin stayed empty, as it provided a place for the others' belongings, making the at first abominable place seem passable enough. As Reverchon wrote in his diary on October 31, 1855, "At last the ship cast off, we felt ourselves gently rock; we saw the buildings pass one by one before our eyes; at the window of a room in our hotel we saw a German lady whom we had met wave goodbye to us; opposite the jetty we also got a last farewell from Mr. Renaud, the phalansterian . . . who had helped us embark; the shores receded, and we said adieu to France." As the ship moved out of the harbor, the water lost its greenish, seeming transparency to turn an opaque, deep, threatening cobalt. They reached the open seas. The sea tosses, then the sea calms. Wrote young Reverchon,

> All is well; we go to bed; I lull myself with happy dreams of immense forests spread out in front of my eyes; a thousand birds swarm the solitudes. . . . Around midnight the wind comes up; we hear the voice of the captain, the sailors rush about; the waves beat against the flanks of the ship, which begins to roll in a much less agreeable manner; a moment later, all the passengers were sick; the noise of the masts, the creaking of the vessel, and cries of children formed an ensemble less harmonious, and which contributed to making the horror of this night more horrible still.

Reverchon recorded all the events that punctuated the progress of this small, 150-by-33-foot microcosm of human life bobbing on the top of the great ocean while seeking southern waters and western trade winds: the at-times suffocating heat, the odors of cooking and unwashed bodies, and all varieties of nature—polyps and jellyfish, schools of porpoises, squalls, petrels, a shark, sweltering heat. This rolling, distant capsule of human life, surviving at the grace of wind and wave, is both romantic and terrible in its implications. On January 15 Reverchon wrote, "Very violent northwest wind; all the high sails are furled; the ship lists in a frightening manner; the swell and the waves are enormous, and the ship is tossed violently; the rough sea has something of majesty; everywhere are black waves whose tops are covered with white foam hiding the horizon, and around the ship form deep valleys that seem to swallow it up; at other times it is carried on the crest of a foaming mountain." Then the speed slows down; the captain has a sail stretched at the stem to shield the first-class passengers from the extreme sun; they capture storm petrels; a dozen flying fish "lifted themselves out of the water and flew more than two hundred feet; the nights are splendid in the moonlight."

After a month on the water they begin to see an occasional tropical bird. Blown too far south to find the passage west through the Bahamas, the captain had to reach the Gulf of Mexico by sailing south of Cuba. They cross the Gulf Stream, where the sea appears divided into two distinct parts. In the intolerable heat and calm, they think they see

land in mirages. Julien spends the night on deck wrapped in his over-
coat and thinks of Chateaubriand, who said he changed dreams on
changing countries.

On the *Uriel*, Fritz Colas was famished and railed against the ration
given the passengers; he resolved to tell any followers back in France to
bring more of their own food.

On the thirty-fifth morning they, like Columbus, discovered Santo
Domingo and had their eyes riveted, questioning, to its jagged mountain
surfaces; there were circling boobies and a frigate, and a tropical sunset
with beautiful long rays extended over the vault of the sky.

The *Wurtemberg* rounded the end of Cuba into the Gulf of Mexico and
turned north into a last violent storm, where for two days waves washed
over the deck. Then, after forty-five days at sea, the ship crossed into
the Mississippi's yellow delta and finally into the river itself, surrounded
by low-lying swamps. Ocean crossings forged new bonds and new ani-
mosities. On the *Uriel*, Colas thought he had converted six Belgians to
his skepticism of Fourierism. He and Cousin were driven to opposite
poles and to a new animosity between well-off Belgians and Republican
French exiles. Colas bragged that his converted followers sent Cousin
to his cabin. Considerant had been wrong to mix other Europeanisms
along with his Fourierists.

11

Expectations

This time, he did not list himself on the ship manifest as "Prospero Considérante." Two years before, perhaps fearful of not being known in a milieu outside the pale of Europe, he had deliberately dissimulated his name so as not to be disappointed. Now he wanted—indeed, needed—attention.

VICTOR CONSIDERANT

Unlike those followers of Considerant who embarked for Texas via New Orleans on less expensive sailing packets and barques, the leader himself and his family were taking a steamship to New York. Considerant and his wife, Julie, and her mother, Clarisse Vigoureux, left Ostend on January 15, 1855. They had arrived at 4:00 p.m., and by 6:30 they were on the evening boat to Dover. A train took them to Southampton to embark. On the ss *Union*, a four-year-old ship built in New York, they put to sea on the 17th. In the middle of winter, the ship's manifest listed only twenty other passengers, most of whom had boarded the 1,200-ton ship at Le Havre.

Considerant, exhausted from the intensity of his departure, allowed himself to lie about in his cabin on the rolling and pitching ship. He thought of the past and was pleased. As he saw it, he was conquering all the barriers—the emperor, money, and doubters of Fourier's way to social progress. Like most emigrants, he gradually shed his orientation to his past as the ship plunged and rolled, creaked, groaned, and boomed. In a storm it was hard to concentrate on anything but the sea. One of the paddlewheels flapped when the ship's roll surfaced it on a sidewise plunge into a trough; the hull made great popping noises when unsupported at its two ends on the crest of a swell. He did not tell Clarisse and Julie that the ship he had boarded for his trip to the United States four months before, the *Arctichad*, had sunk when it ran too fast in a fog.[1]

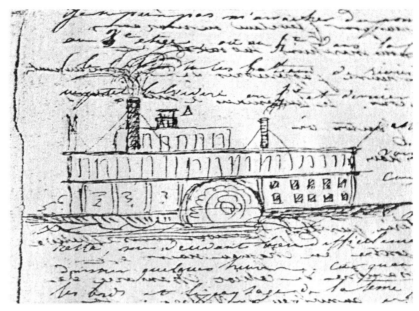

9. Paddle boat drawing by Victor Considerant. Courtesy of the author.

He busied himself mentally projecting his organization for the new social life. To maintain his new momentum, he laid out how to spend his coming time in New York, listing tasks for the social destiny of man:

See what American reactions were to Brisbane's English translation of *Au Texas*. Considerant liked the title, *The Great West: A New Social and Industrial Life in Its Fertile Regions*. With a preface written by Brisbane, coincidentally on the day Cantagrel had reached the United States, the book had been out a couple of months.

Set up banking relations between Paris, New Orleans, and Texas.

Go to Washington to solicit the Texas congressional delegation's support for a colony land grant. Tell them of the funds raised in Europe by the new corporation and the hundreds who were enthusiastic to come.

See how American investing is coming. Convince American investors, despite Cantagrel's warning that he did not see much enthusiasm for investing in their enterprise. And there was Reverend

Allen's inability to attract money in the Midwest—worrisome, but perhaps understandable, since Allen, in the past summer and fall, had been without proof of real European interest.

Make a tour to see potential investors. Look up acquaintances in New York. Go to the North American Phalanx and to Boston. Should he try Oneida? John Martin, Oneida's publicist, had been friendly in 1853.[2]

Had Brisbane succeeded in getting articles written in newspapers about the Texas enterprise? In Greeley's paper? In the French paper in New York?[3]

Find people to go to Texas to buy up headrights. He hoped for an empresario grant of free land, but if that failed, the corporation needed plenty of scrip to buy land cheap. In Texas he had seen a discounted, ready market in headright scrip.

Find a factotum or two to go with him to Texas. Traveling with women and children, they would need help going overland from the closest river port.

What had Cantagrel found at Fort Worth? Had he bought it? When would Cousin and Raisant get there to help him? Which way would they travel? Up the Red River through Shreveport?

What was the latest on railroad investment in Texas?

Set up commercial agents in New York, New Orleans, and Texas. The colony would need them, particularly when the industrial series got under way.

Start a friends group to stimulate American interest. D. H. Jacques?

Write Mama Vigoureux's nephew Jules Juif, an old friend and lawyer in New Orleans, to shepherd the colonists arriving there directly from Europe.[4]

Write his old classmate Weiss, the coeditor of the *New Orleans Bee*, that he would be passing through.[5]

Considerant thought again, The Mormons have established their own society in the Utah wilderness. Now we will.[6]

Unlike Cabet, he told himself, he was organized to succeed. Seven years ago, Cabet had not really thought through his colony coming to

Texas. Sixty people tried to live spread out on a checkerboard, everyone separated a mile or more from each other, while at the same time they tried to live as a share-and-share-alike commune. Another misfortune, that Champ d'Asile of the Bonapartists in 1818, farther down the Trinity at Liberty: just like the Cabetists, all land held in common; labor for the common good. Four hundred people. Military drills, social and literary activities, dreaming of life back in France. They only lasted from March to July; then the Spanish sent troops.

Instead of these failed idealists, Considerant identified with empresarios who had brought emigrants to Texas. Thirty years before, under Mexican emperor Agustín de Iturbide's Imperial Colonization Law of 1823 and then the following year under the Mexican Republic, the state of Coahuila y Tejas had passed another colonization law under which Moses and Stephen Austin had brought people to settle. A married man received up to 4,428 acres; an unmarried one got one-fourth of that. Some fifteen years ago, the Peters Company received an enormous land grant in North Texas from the Republic of Texas.[7] The company and each settler family who came and broke ground were rewarded with a section of land of 640 acres. The state of Texas was not giving that much recently, but a half section was still an opportunity for investors. If he could do the same thing, the European investors would love him.

With a lull in the ship's heavy roll, he pictured how life would be in Texas. That beautiful empty canvas, waiting to become their *champs d'asile*, their "place of asylum." Those ravishing wildflowers that had made the valley of the Red River an Eden on a Persian carpet.

For Julie Considerant and her mother, the North Atlantic was new and, as it was for most new emigrants, terrifying in the winter. The ocean had been simply majestic until they rounded Ireland. Then, for the first time, they looked out into that gray miasma of undefined sky or water and felt themselves rolling sideways down a trough as the wave beyond rose towering above the ship. With a blasting wind and great bangs in the hull, they wondered where Victor was leading them. Her mother's usual masked, anxious sensitiveness was shattered in the clutch of Julie's hand. The ocean detached them from the past or future; its intrusion

10. Julie Vigoureux Considerant self-portrait.
Photograph © Musée du Temps, Besançon.

on their minds made them neither emigrants nor immigrants but suspended in fascination for their lives.

Julie Josephine Vigoureux Considerant, now forty-three, did not have the haughty and fine beauty of her mother. Her cheekbones were a bit prominent, her features were strong, not very regular, "but she was tall

11. Clarisse Vigoureux. Archives nationales (France), 10AS35.

and slim with an elegant bearing and beautiful blonde hair that served to soften her features. In this long and tormented existence, far from hindering the work of her husband by an absorbing and jealous personality, she did not cease, at his side, to devote herself discretely as a faithful companion, valiant, and full of abnegation."[8]

Julie's mother, Clarisse Vigoureux, had been inspired by Fourier through Just Muiron in the early 1820s under the repression of the restored Bourbon monarchy. "Ties of old family linked Just Muiron and Mme Vigoureux. He had her read the galley-proofs of the 'Treatise of a Domestic Agricultural Association' and little by little introduced her to the theory [of Fourier]." That was thirty-five years ago.

Mme Vigoureux, no longer a vital young widow, had left one son and one daughter in Europe when she followed her Julie and Victor. After all, she had a stake in Victor too. She had introduced her now son-in-law to Fourier's ideas and nourished his interest as he listened to her salon conversations while a student in his teens at the Collège Royal de Besançon. She still

> had a very distinctive personality. Endowed with rare beauty, entirely of lines, of character, of expression that the era respected, refined even and lofty, far from seeking in the world of frivolous success, she was always withdrawn in a restricted circle, concerned with things of the mind. Her reserved attitude, in appearance perhaps a little haughty, kept admirers at a distance and, even in the intimacy of friendship, [she] always held some of herself back. She had a high mind, disdainful of banality and of the conventional, and at the same time, an odd imagination, an anxious sensitiveness that she made agonizing.

At age sixty-six, Mme Vigoureux was investing herself in the dream of her life. She was not that old, she reasoned. No, she had not stayed behind, as did Just Muiron, with the excuse that she was too old to travel.[9] She wanted to collect on her long investment. She wanted to be a part of the society in Texas. How would she fit in?[10]

Little by little the fearful ship's noises became commonplace and the passengers' stomachs ceased to complain. Shrouded in fog on the Grand Banks, comforted by the friendly blasts of the fog horn, the calmer waters making liquids again maintain their rightful places inside tumblers, the travelers felt they had survived the iceberg menace and might reach the unknown.

The nineteenth evening at sea, they passed the Nantucket lighthouse and spent most of the next morning reaching the narrows in the gray whiteness. Now the reality of America was upon them. They were becoming immigrants. Clarisse and Julie watched for clues about America. Inside the Narrows the gray sky was reflected in the almost smooth water of a windless morning; the world began to steady as they glided north. The Brooklyn hills gave off smoke, the low Jersey shore was a smudged line to the west. Finally, against a wall of four-story red-brick warehouses, they saw a forest of three-masted ships stuck into the soft cushion of the gray above. Most yardarms were etched in white from last night's snow. From the *Union*, Julie saw two thin spires but no imposing buildings. The reality of the New World hit her. This was not Paris. The wind gave a sudden snort and sent them a whiff of coal from the ship's stacks.

They arrived on February 5, their twentieth day at sea. A bitter winter day, with snow emphasizing Castle Clinton's brownness and roundness at the first tip of the city they encountered. The cannon ports of its tiered three-story walls were etched in white. Snow was piled up beside doorways and along streets. Slush. Snow dirty from coal smoke.

More than the weather was cold in New York. Considerant found that no fires had been lit toward gaining support for the Texas enterprise in America. Everything was still to be done for the financial organization of the colony. No one had taken a serious initiative. Were they waiting on what Europe did? Considerant carried the results from sales in Europe that the stock company had reached on December 31.[11] Now everywhere he went he told all he met the happy news.

These followers of Charles Fourier found something far worse than the lack of an American financial organization: they found the Know-Nothings. Antiforeignism in Texas was about to create one more barrier to Considerant's dream of free land. "During 1854 and 1855 the nation experienced outbreaks of two violent emotions. Two of the strongest prejudices which have been operative during the nation's history have been the antipathies which so many have held against foreigners and slave owners. The influx of foreign immigration, growing industrialization, and the western pressure to settlement caused a revival of anti-foreign, anti-Catholic, and anti-southern prejudices in the 1850s. The Kansas-Nebraska Act and the organization of Bleeding Kansas added fuel to these always smoldering embers."[12]

The Monday Considerant landed, the *New York Daily Times* already seemed weary of this new political phenomenon, the Know-Nothings, when it stuck its barb in an advertised book.[13] The word was that Know-Nothings were virulent in the South and in Texas. It was all confusing, as northern Know-Nothings had absorbed much antislavery sentiment that the Whigs were ignoring. Slavery and states' rights were becoming much more burning issues than Considerant had heard a year and a half before. Brisbane's friend Horace Greeley, who had coined the name Know-Nothings, also attacked them constantly in his *Tribune*.

Considerant had to get to work on his long list. He began by calling on all the friends of Fourierism he had met in 1853 in the United States and before in France. Brisbane must have carried him to Horace Greeley in his office overlooking the burned-out City Hall and green park. He might have shown him James Parton's biography of Greeley, which had been published a month before.

Considerant had a letter ready to send to Jules Juif in New Orleans, whom he could trust to smooth the way for the immigrants. He answered J. T. Fisher's welcome from Boston, offered felicitations for his recent marriage, and returned warm greetings to renew their friendship from their last visit in 1853—and to tell Fisher he would come to Boston to speak of their business affairs for La Réunion, which were going well.

A week after Considerant arrived, Arthur Young, a very old and munificent English friend of Fourierism, arrived unannounced in New York. He had undertaken an odyssey across the Pacific and North America from Australia to once again push a Fourierist experiment in the reorganization of society. More than twenty years before, he had funded Cîteaux in the Côte d'Or, one of the first Fourierist experiments in utopian living. He also had given the École 210,000 francs to begin publishing the *Démocratie pacifique* in 1843. Considerant was buoyed by this grandest of gestures of support by an old friend. He also began canvassing for American colonists to join his great experiment. Early on in New York,

Considerant met Paul Henri, a thirty-seven-year-old French lithographer with his wife and four children.[14] Henri had recently crossed the ocean and was convinced to join the colony later in the year.

A major objective of Considerant's itinerary on the East Coast was to take his good news to Washington to the Texas congressional delegation. In 1853 Brisbane had accompanied him, but this time Considerant was alone. He wanted César Daly with him to translate. Daly was supposed to arrive from England soon after Victor, but when he had not come by January 18, Considerant was pressed. He could wait no longer, as the Congress was about to adjourn. Without any specific news of American investment after two weeks in New York, he left the 19th. The free land question was paramount.

Considerant, a French Republican exiled under the tyranny of Napoleon III and bringing money and a group of European Republicans to partake of the American dream, hoped for a conspicuous welcome. But in going to Washington, he could not have chosen a worse time to seek influence. He arrived as members of Congress were trying to finish the session and depart Washington, which they did twelve days later.

12

Storm Clouds

Old parties, old names, old issues and old organizations are passing away. A day of new things is at hand.

ALEXANDER STEPHENS, in Congress, 1854

In Washington, Considerant called on President Franklin Pierce. At the White House, Considerant marveled with the other visitors at the presents just arrived from the Japanese government in response to relations recently demanded by Admiral Matthew C. Perry. Silks, swords, writing tables, vases, umbrellas, mats, jars, cabinets, agricultural implements, plants, sugar cane, two birds, and seven dogs represented the flower of Japanese art and civilization.[1]

In the United States barely a fortnight, Considerant expected an audience for his message of European support for a reconstituted society. Unfortunately, that audience was now otherwise occupied. The day he walked down the gangplank, the *New York Daily Times* had a full column reporting the lectures at Boston's Tremont Temple, where the governor and lieutenant governor sat on the platform to listen to abolitionist speeches, and Frederick Douglass was slated to substitute for a missing speaker the following week. The next day the newspaper reported antislavery demonstrations in Milwaukee.[2]

Just as Considerant appeared in the United States, the compromise forces that had put Franklin Pierce in power two years previously were breaking up. Southern and northern interests had been hovering in an uneasy balance. But that was not to last. New states were in favor of free labor. Every time a new state entered the Union, the influence of the South in Congress shrank. Southern politicians were used to dominating Washington, and now the Democratic Party was seen as the instrument of the South. This president and his cohorts were being dismissed as "doughfaces, abject servants of the lords of the lash." That they were men of high principle, upholding a time-honored constitutional interpretation created by the founding fathers to promote the stability of the republic, mattered not a whit.[3]

Near the end of this February, the president was consumed with holding his line of strict construction of the Constitution, wielding his veto in an avalanche of bills coming to his desk. Even more important to him, the signs portended that his Democratic Party might lose in the March elections in his own state. Pierce was bestirring himself to prevent his own mortification before the country if his party lost New Hampshire. He would be greatly embarrassed by the Know-Nothings and at the moment probably had little political enthusiasm for being in the company of any foreigner, particularly one attempting to establish a colony south of the Mason-Dixon Line.

In 1853 Considerant had heard nothing of any antiforeign movement in the United States. But at the beginning of 1855, Know-Nothingism constituted the most perplexing problem in American politics. Whigs, Democrats, Softs, Barnburners, Hards, Know-Nothings, South Americans (the southern faction of the Know-Nothings), North Americans (a free-state group and the northern faction of the Know-Nothings), Young Americans, abolitionists, Free Soilers, fusionists, coalitionists, Black Republicans, Republicans—this was different from the socialist clubs and Club of Clubs in Paris in the 1840s. The proliferation of parties was incomprehensible to Considerant, as it was to many in the United States that year.

It mattered not that England had outlawed slavery seventeen years before. Boatloads of immigrants appeared to be a threat, especially as Europeans were supposed to be opposed to slavery and were settling in the North. And Considerant with his followers were certainly immigrants.

The day after Considerant arrived in the capital, February 20, he wrote Julie in New York to send a message to César Daly the moment his ship arrived: "Get to Washington immediately!"[4] Faced with a confusing scene, he needed Daly, the dandy architect, to interpret.

The ss *Baltic* brought the forty-four-year-old Daly to New York on February 22, 1855, and he obeyed Victor's summons. He was a welcome help to Considerant. Considerant's poor English may not have let him penetrate the politeness of the Texians or the fact that the first great southern test of the Know-Nothings would be in Virginia in May, where the secret party was attempting to capture the governorship in order to control the legislature and elect a Know-Nothing senator.[5] With the Know-Nothings turning over everyone's dish, as the *New York Daily Times* put it, was there any time for anyone to take this Frenchman seriously?[6]

Nevertheless, Considerant pursued audiences with the Texas congressional delegates to the second session of the Thirty-Third Congress. It was set to adjourn March 3, two weeks away.

Texas's population gave the state two members in the House. Representative Peter Hansbrough Bell, a man three years younger than Considerant, was a Virginian by birth who had fought at San Jacinto, had been a captain in the Mexican War, and was the governor of Texas from 1849 to 1853. He was born in South Carolina. This self-taught lawyer was finishing his first term in the House and planning to stand for a second term.

The second representative, George Washington Smyth, was a North Carolinian who had come to Texas in 1828. He had been a signer of the Declaration of Independence and the Constitution of the republic. He was elected commissioner of the General Land Office in 1848. Both he and Representative Bell may have had their fill of empresarios, as they had felt the brunt of settlers' wrath over the management of the Peters Colony interests, until finally the legislature knew the heat of the volcano and passed legislation to give everyone the land they thought they were due. In Washington only two years, Smyth declined nomination to another term and was leaving Washington in the next two weeks. As southerners, he and Bell had to be polite to this Frenchman come calling.

One Texas senator was Thomas J. Rusk, who at fifty-two years of age was five years older than Considerant. He was born in South Carolina. Also self-taught, Rusk had practiced law in Georgia shortly before he went to Texas in 1835. In Nacogdoches he had quickly caught separation fever and was a delegate to the convention that declared Texas independent of Mexico the next year. As first secretary of war for the republic, he had fought under Houston at San Jacinto and took command of the forces after the battle. A member of the Second Congress of the republic, he next became chief justice of the Supreme Court for four years. In 1845 he became president of the convention that confirmed annexation to the United States. The following year he was sent to Washington along with Sam Houston as Texas's first senators. By the time of Considerant's visit, he had been a senator for nine years. A dyed-in-the-wool southerner, Rusk would have had little interest or help to offer the Frenchman who spoke of republican ideals and social experiments.

That left "picturesque Sam Houston[, who] sat in his seat in the Senate and whittled, occasionally sending a wooden heart of his own make to some fair observer in the gallery."[7] He was sixty-two, having been born the year the king's head was struck off in France. When Victor Considerant was five in Salins, Sam Houston had been fighting under Jackson at New Orleans. While the Frenchman lectured on Fourier to his barracks mates in the Metz Artillery School, Houston became a member of the Cherokee Nation. As the one sat in the Chamber of Deputies and was later exiled from his country, the other sat in the United States Senate, later to be deposed as governor by his state in 1861. When Considerant came to tell Senator Houston of the money raised in France to back an empresario grant, Houston was in his third Washington stint over a quarter century. Considerant wanted especially to see Sam Houston, since Houston had signed the empresario grant to the Peters Company for half of North Texas fourteen years before. Victor would certainly have been curious about this man, whose exploits had reached mythic proportions. It was known that Houston did not tolerate talk of the Union breaking up over slavery.

It may have been Houston who told Considerant that the Indians were being given land to settle west on the Brazos in North Texas and that Major Robert Neighbors, the patient Indian agent for the Republic of Texas, would help keep them peaceful. Captain Randolph Barnes Marcy had only recently returned from leading the Indians to the new reservations. Houston, towering over the Frenchman by a full head height, also may have been the first to explain to Considerant that Texas policy on land incentives had been shifted from settlers to railroads.

All four of these members of Congress had gone to Texas as Considerant now proposed to do, but all had gone twenty years previously. All were southerners.[8] Considerant was received politely but coolly by these men. After all, the Texas legislature, not they, had made this new policy to encourage railroads. They were preoccupied in a political fight with northern senators over routes for the transcontinental railroad. They had to be concerned about getting the southern route through Memphis established. "The Pacific railroad bill had failed by one vote in the House . . . and when [Jefferson] Davis reported, February 27, the results of the surveys and recommended a southern Pacific railroad, nobody paid any attention to him."[9]

Only Houston, who had negotiated the grant to the Peters Company, might have seen the value of continuing the precedent of the Peters grant. It had been such a headache as a process that Congressman Smyth would likely have laughed at another such endeavor. As land commissioner, he had had to contend with the arguments between settlers and the Peters Company, which had only been settled for two years—and there would be suits still, for years to come. All would have told Considerant that the Texas legislature was the place he had to appeal and that lands in North Texas had been put on reserve to pay for railroads. That would explain the tone of Considerant's letter to Julie commanding Daly's immediate appearance.[10] In that letter he told Julie that he planned to stay at least two more days. He wrote that "he had already seen several people and been presented to fifty, attaching himself naturally to the influential ones."[11] From talking with them, Considerant found out during his stay in Washington of the changed status of free Texas lands and the crumbling of his *Au Texas* argument.

Returning to New York, Considerant and Daly confronted the reality of a telegram from Vincent Cousin confirming his advance guard's arrival in New Orleans on February 24. They were on their way to the Three Forks on Considerant's instructions. The gray winter skies of New York were no worse than those in Brussels and Paris, but they did not help maintain his buoyancy.

Within a week of his return to New York, Considerant wrote the Paris office that southern immigrants into North Texas supported slavery. By then he had received news from Cantagrel. But he did not send all the bad news to Paris at once. It was not until March 13 that Considerant wrote Paris that things had changed. The best lands across North Texas were indeed now reserved for railroads. On March 15 he wrote again that the best lands west of Fort Worth had been put on reserve. He signaled a major change for the colony's location, saying they should look for land at twenty-seven degrees latitude on the Nueces or Rio Grande. With land already bought on the Trinity and seventy-odd people on their way from Europe to it, this Moses was suddenly improvising a new message to his people about the location of the promised land.

By now, Considerant had heard from Cantagrel about the unusualness of a Texas drought, though he did not realize its import. Still holding on to his grand scheme of transporting people, he wrote his old friend Gingembre in Ohio for information on buying a used steamboat on the Ohio, probably in Cincinnati. The latter's son advised him against such an idea, because a steamboat more than four years old was uninsurable. He warned Considerant that the specifications were different for boats operating above rafts in shallow rivers from those used in deeper waters.

But when Cantagrel sent him the *Texas State Gazette*'s February 17 article, provoked by Reverend John Allen's and his visit to Austin, Considerant faced a new dragon. The article proclaimed: "We had rather see Texas a howling desert than peopled with the likes of John Allen." Yankees, foreigners, and socialists were all abhorrent to Texas.

Texas newspapers now began to follow Considerant's movements. In LaGrange, Texas, the newspaper reported that Victor Considerant had arrived in New York, with the date set forward a month so as to seem current in Texas.

But money needed to be raised in the East. Boston friends who had helped Brook Farm would surely come forward with funds. Considerant remembered that heady summer of 1848 when France had restored the Second Republic and all socialisms were bright promises. The world had come to France to help and watch. Hugh Dougherty from London and Brisbane from New York were there. Charles Dana was spending eight months on a Paris news beat and had introduced Considerant to an idealistic young Bostonian, James Fisher, in the dappled, cool garden of the office of the *Démocratie pacifique.*[12] Those had been good days full of good portents.

So on March 21 Considerant sent James T. Fisher a manuscript souvenir—a two-page list of subjects, probably discarded draft pages, in Fourier's own handwriting. Considerant asked Fisher to prepare to help La Réunion. On March 22 he sent Benjamin Urner in Cincinnati the funds to cover a debt of James Lawrie and paid a Mr. Belmont a commission on a $1,030 purchase. Also, Considerant hired an American named Johnson, giving him $250 to leave for the colony.[13]

On March 26 Considerant deposited another $2,000 with Duncan Sherman. That day he mentioned a "memoir" to the American people.[14] He was writing again instead of acting. Since arriving and finding that Brisbane in New York had made no attempt to organize, Considerant's habitual reaction was to get Brisbane's translation of *Au Texas* updated with a translation of the statutes published so that it would, undoubtedly in his mind, have the same effect in America as it had had in Europe. Hearing Cantagrel's report of the people of Austin's reactions to the "socialist" colony, Considerant's method of overcoming this barrier was again to take up the pen.

Considerant's days in New York were consumed with details of land acquisition and money transactions. At the same time, he was trying to grasp the great events swirling around him. He could understand the reserve of land for railroads in North Texas for five years. But he did not understand that it was in this decade that the basic philosophical conflict of all American history, the battle between rational and mystical democracy, neared its climax.[15] It was a time for untrammeled expression. There was a drive for reform, change, and agitation, which boded ill for any arbitrament of intelligence.

After a month in America, Considerant's buoyancy was sinking. He turned to his wife, Julie, who saw days when his "daily burden exceeded his strength or he fell prostrate, helpless. . . . In his worst times . . . extended on a divan numb, immobile, to contemplate in silence the smoke from his cigarette curling in the air, or follow the various reflections and the languid movements of a certain chameleon, his host and his friend."[16]

His resilience was being constantly tested: after a month in the New World, a new worry for the Fourierists appeared. Newspapers shouted that the United States might soon be fighting Spain. The Fourierists would have to sail under a flag other than that of the United States to travel the hazardous Gulf waters around Cuba to reach New Orleans. César Daly, who earned at least part of his income and prestige as conservator of a major French cathedral, maintained his ties with the Roman Catholic Church. He had to be perplexed at what he found in the United States: antialcohol, antislavery, antiforeignism, and anti-Catholicism.

As Considerant in New York pondered the changes in Texas, in the March election New Hampshire went completely into the hands of the Know-Nothings, and Connecticut and Rhode Island followed suit.[17] The New Hampshire Democratic vote had decreased by only two thousand, but thirty-two thousand Know-Nothings had appeared as if by magic.[18] The president's state had indeed repudiated him. There was this mysticism engulfing foreigners that might have recalled for Considerant those aspects of Saint-Simonianism so odious to Fourierists.

Daly's English skill was employed for the Fourierist cause. Probably responding to an assertion in a letter from James Fisher to Considerant, Daly wrote to Fisher on March 29, 1855, from New York to refute the Boston socialist's thought, stating in part:

Many thanks for the list of names, and still more for your good advice about our land speculating. How such an idea of monopoly and all absorbing individual interest should have come to any man's mind with respect to us, appears to me miraculous. Now the most simple glance upon the statutes of the general Company or upon any of the five parts composing Considerant's volume, *Au Texas*, would suffice to overthrow completely so ridiculous a notion, which is in direct contradiction with all our written agreements. We cry out to all men of faith and good will to come with us to a land of liberty, of progress, of honest social competition. As socialists of every description may become proprietors, of any extent of land, even individuals are free to settle in the midst of these, for the principle, the basis of our Combination is to guarantee the most complete liberty of action to all settlers and to universalize as rapidly as possible the advantages of individual and associated property. Now as for us phalanstèriens, who have drank [sic] from the fountainhead since our boyhood, and who will shortly become or already [are] becoming gray headed men, we have such absolute faith in the superiority of our theory, that we are convinced that all other social experiments that may be carried on around us, will ultimately by sheer experience, be carried to take up our ideas.

2nd April—We, the phalanstèriens, only want to organize first a general company with powerful means in order to conquer the "land of general social experiment." This great company will have in its ranks numbers of individuals who will take active parts as settlers and be interested in different local establishments formed through the Company's Agency. These individuals may be socialists of other creeds than ours, for the General Company is a neutral body. . . . The lower the rate at which the general Company may obtain lands, etc., . . . the lower the scale price of their sale to the local establishments. It's also [in] the interest of social progress, that the members of the General Company be composed as much as possible of socialists and settlers, because the prices of the land ceded to local establishments would thus be determined by the instrumentality of a Company composed of representatives of social and settling interests.

We intend, Considerant and I, to join you at Boston on the 7th of April. Once more a thousand thanks for the frank expression of your feelings upon our subject. [W]e are always open to amicable and honest criticism. . . . So if you have still any difficulty whatever in your mind, then do continue your friendly communications to us. . . .

A good handshake, and my best compliments.

César Daly

Considerant and the ladies send you also friendly compliments.[19]

On March 30 Considerant gave Vesian $200 to leave New York on a real estate funding quest.[20] He deposited $3,000 in a Louisiana banking house for Vesian to draw from while accumulating headright scrip in Texas. This Frenchman from Marseilles living in New York was to depart immediately for Texas. The same day Considerant reimbursed Ben Umer in Cincinnati $1,100 and $600, probably for purchases that James Lawrie was transporting to La Réunion.

On April 4 Considerant prepared to leave for Boston, where he would spend twenty-four hours before starting for New Orleans.[21] He had left with Daly by April 6. Arthur Young was having recurring malaria and was unable to travel. Fourier's birthday was on April 7. This day had been feted for years past as a major annual event when followers reinforced their belief in Fourier at a formal banquet. But the numbers were small. Where were all the New Englander supporters of social causes? Considerant and Daly were mystified. No support from the heart of association leadership, Boston?

In Boston, Amelia Bloomer preached to her sex of the need for freedom from the thralldom of skirts, and Lucy Stone agitated the emancipation of women from the slavery of having to adopt their husbands' names. A few Americans like Reverend John Allen sought to recapture the heady times of ten years previous at Brook Farm, but they failed to recognize that the United States had moved on.

Did the Bostonians quiz Daly on his own role in the enterprise and learn his intent to visit Texas only as an observer? Did he admit that he had stated to the master of the *Baltic* that he was a "merchant" who would return to France?[22] Considerant and Daly did not circle back through Oneida. John Humphrey Noyes had attacked Fourierism in his newspaper after Considerant had visited there in 1853; John Martin, the chief disciple of Noyes who had written a friendly report of Considerant's fishing prowess on that visit, had since died.[23]

The two Frenchmen returned to New York on April 8, with little to show for their time. On April 9 Jerome Maguet and F. L. Willemet withdrew from the North American Phalanx, left Red Bank for New York, and considered a trip to Texas. In New York Considerant remitted $1,000 to Rupert Nussbaumer in Houston. Reaching Houston with the plant stock, Nussbaumer of the *Lexington* vanguard had seen that their stock would not make it another month in the chests rocked across the Texas plains.

These funds were probably for expenses in connection with their plant stock, now planted in Houston ground. Nussbaumer agreed to remain in Houston to superintend the new nursery and help others coming from Europe.[24]

By April 12 Considerant had hired Willemet, Maguet, Lanotte, and Haizé for $200 each to travel to Texas.[25] These men were in a sense refugees from the failed North American Phalanx. Two were to meet them in Houston, and two traveled with Considerant's party from New York. On hearing of these hires, Dr. Savardan roundly criticized Considerant for hiring these "commercial men," as he called them. Whether he knew it or not, Considerant was building factions.

On April 12 he advanced $400 to Arthur Young, who would follow when he was no longer ill with malaria. Daly received about $5,300 to carry to Texas. Madame Cantagrel was fortified with $120 for her and her two children's travel south with the Considerants. And Brisbane in New York? He came through with $7,000 of his pledge of $20,000 but was not going to Texas.

In France, to Considerant's news of Texas land changes, Godin in Guise had an instant reaction:

> Get to Texas; make a methodical exploration of lands to colonize; merge with the Peters Company; see if a railroad project is possible for us to promote. Worrying about American subscriptions is not the important thing now that conditions have changed. The theories of *Au Texas* I fear no longer apply. Don't leave us in the dark by your brief predictions; tell us all. It would have to be a very rich country to locate any distance from communication routes, the 27th degree latitude would be too hot, and we don't want to have to organize war against savages in a hostile climate, and it would be without connection to what we can do in the north.[26]

There was an acid ring to his further comment, "You asked what we are doing vis-à-vis the public. What can you conceive, nothing serious until

we can count hatched chicks; silence for now. I had a plan for a bro-
chure with a number of specific arguments, but all awaits your finding
a field of action."[27] By the time this advice reached New York, Considerant had gone south.

Considerant and Julie, Mme Vigoureux, Josephine Cantagrel with
Simon and the baby, and César Daly left on April 14. They took the cars
to Cincinnati. There, they ordered more things for the colony. Considerant bought a gig, a pretty wagonette, in which to travel in Texas.

New York had been an agony. Nothing was as Considerant had
planned. As the party plowed the Ohio and Mississippi Rivers toward
New Orleans, the frown on his forehead increasingly cast a dour look
about him. He really regretted that Brisbane would not go to Washington with him.[28] Why hadn't Brisbane helped more?

13

From Sails to Steam to Feet

Their first view of the United States at the mouth of the Mississippi did not charm the French bound for La Réunion. Its flat and swampy banks, its yellow waters choked with rotten or decaying tree trunks covered by hideous sleeping caimans—all that under a sweltering sun sullied somewhat the pleasant and poetic recollections from books of their childhood.[1] An electric telegraph at the mouth of the Mississippi signaled arrivals to New Orleans the instant ships entered the river, allowing newspapers to always announce their coming thirty-eight hours before they reached the docks a hundred miles up the delta. Thus Kalikst Wolski, the Polish engineer and Considerant's designated guide, knew to meet Vincent Cousin's and Alexandre Raisant's ships at the New Orleans dock. The *Uriel* from Antwerp and the *Lexington* from Le Havre, the first to carry colonists organized by the European American Society of Colonization in Texas, arrived within twenty-four hours of each other the last week of February 1855. Dr. Savardan and his group would not arrive until later that spring.

Wolski had been anticipating the arrival of the new pioneers, waiting in New Orleans for almost three months. Two years before, ten days after he had landed in New York, he had been taken to see the nine-year-old North American Phalanx. He was overjoyed at the communal living combined with personal freedom. Had he spoken English, he would have stayed. To cure his lack of English the Dutch consul advised him to go where only English was spoken. He chose Buffalo, New York. While there for six months, he met Albert Brisbane and likely renewed his acquaintance with Considerant when the latter passed through on his way to Texas in 1853. Two years later, when Considerant's request came to escort the colonists to Texas, Wolski had learned English and made himself at home in New York. Thus he understood Americans

enough to agree to meet the European vanguard in New Orleans. He
wanted to act on the Fourierist principles he had learned in Paris. He
would go with them to build a society in what Considerant called an
Eden, virgin, free, and uncorrupted.

That virginal image was in sharp contrast to Wolski's first hour in
the reality of New Orleans. When he entered the St. Louis Hotel, touted
as one of the city's greatest ornaments, he found men and women in
shackles being examined for purchase—a slave market proceeding in
the hotel lobby. He refused to register and fled to less heinous quarters.

While the people in Paris assumed Wolski would be joined by his
family on the caravan to Texas, Wolski separated entirely his private
from his social and public life.[2] No family member accompanied him to
Texas. He never spoke of his daughter or her mother. He did bring his
two-year-old daughter, Anna, with him to New Orleans and deposited
her with the Ursuline nuns. Anna, who was born in the middle of the
Atlantic during Wolski and his wife's trip to America in the fall of 1852,
would be cared for by the sisters in New Orleans until the age of sixteen.
Both Brisbane in New York and Considerant, at all events, knew Wolski
well enough socially in 1854 to give him letters of introduction to New
Orleans friends. Arriving on December 1, Wolski escaped the yellow
fever season. The deadly pestilence in the previous year, 1853, had visited
the worst scourge ever. Between 7,500 and 12,000 people had perished,
so many that no count could be accurate. It would be safest traveling in
winter to reach Considerant's future phalanstery.

Wolski also had an introduction from Considerant to a confirmed
brother Fourierist, G. F. Weiss, the co-owner and editor of a French-
language newspaper called the *Bee*. When Considerant returned through
New Orleans from Texas in July 1853, Weiss took Considerant's enthusiasm for Texas lightly and as being of the moment. But now he shared
with Wolski his concern for his old schoolmate. Weiss had been in class
with Considerant at the École Polytechnique in the 1820s and knew
Considerant's merits. But he remembered the Cabet followers who had
straggled back to New Orleans from Texas seven years before, their hopes
destroyed as they attempted to plow virgin land in the Texas heat. Weiss
told Wolski of his worries. Could Frenchmen accustomed to temperate

climes adjust to Texas summers? Would the emigrants be accepted in a Know-Nothing environment full of antiforeign sentiments? Texas had committed itself to a slave economy, though not as strongly in North Texas as farther south. How could a colony with a philosophy of free labor choice not threaten slave owners?

That Saturday Wolski climbed the levee and fixed his eye on the river until the *Uriel* glided into sight and finally into a slip. When the moorings were set and a gangplank dropped, he was at once on deck. A passenger hailed him by name, astounding the conscientious Pole. "Considerant described you to us so perfectly that when I saw you standing on the quay, I knew at once you were our man."[3]

Vincent Cousin greeted Wolski and immediately felt secure with the presence of a fluent French speaker and translator. The next day the process was repeated with the arrival of the *Lexington*, though Alexandre Raisant was not dependent on Wolski, since he knew English and had once been in America. Twenty-five Frenchmen and Belgians with a unique purpose landed from two ships.

That made news, but newspaperman Weiss was guarded in what he published in the *Bee*. The *Bee* was only impressed by the immigrants' descriptions of plants that Cousin's group brought from Antwerp on the *Uriel*. They included 450 Auxerre grapes, 100 white Chasselas, a grape of Ischia, 3,000 fruit trees, and 2,000 strawberry plants from a nursery at Vilvorde and another in Blêneau, Yonne, that belonged to a Republican refugee now fled to Brussels. The paper did not report that Raisant's group on the *Lexington* brought forty thousand assorted grapevines from different vineyards in France, as well as forty thousand fruit trees, several hundred grafted plants, an assortment of grains, pips of grapes and berries, fruit tree pits, and so on.[4]

The plants in this great number of chests were in danger of being lost had not Wolski soon found the hospitality of the Ursuline sisters. In their large convent courtyard, the chests were opened, and their cuttings and pips were refreshed.[5] Slaves unloaded ships, which took three days. Hands were hired from wharf masters to load and transport the stock to the convent. Utopian Republicans objected to the use of human chattel, and perhaps they managed to transport their own goods to their hostelry near the docks, but when overwhelmed by the strange New Orleans environment, where everything was new to them, pragmatism must have quelled their consciences.

Being released from the swell of the sea, walking freely, no longer cramped, using water as they wished, and satisfying their hunger was a relief. Gardeners Barbot, Michel, and young DeGuelle were refreshed by the sight of the big fig trees growing in the open, as Barbot had seen in North Africa—at home in France they were always grown under glass. The farmers walked about looking but were afraid of New Orleans as a money trap for their limited funds.

Once the plants were cared for, the chief question was what route these first colonists should take to reach North Texas from New Orleans. Should they choose to go up the Mississippi and Red River to Shreveport or Jefferson and then take a trail parallel to the Sulphur River to Considerant's Eden 150 miles west? Should they continue still farther up the Red River to Preston? Or proceed up the Arkansas River to Fort Smith, follow Considerant's route southwest across Indian Territory to the Red River, and enter Texas at Preston? Or should they travel via Galveston, take a boat up the Trinity as far as possible until they hit a drought, and then walk? How far up the Trinity River could a boat travel given the drought? If they went partway up the Trinity, could they find enough oxen to buy to haul their supplies? Or, failing water in the Trinity, would they have to go on paddle wheelers to Houston and there buy oxen to haul their heavy supplies overland north to the country of the Three Forks? They heard that the rivers north were low, too low to be depended upon for transport.

In the ten days while they questioned and debated, Wolski helped find canvas to buy and then have sewn into a dozen tents; he translated for them as they compared food costs and completed their provisions. Then the mood became agitated. After two weeks wandering about New Orleans as Cousin vacillated, hoping for better news upriver, Raisant, a man of action, took off for Shreveport to himself check on the water via that route. Meanwhile, after Cousin waited in New Orleans still more days, his conscience finally overcame his hesitation. He delayed no longer for Raisant to report from Shreveport. After three weeks in New Orleans, he made a decision on the next leg of a route to North Texas. Jules Juif, a French attorney living in New Orleans and a nephew of Clarisse Vigoureux, thought Cousin, as a leader of thirty-four persons, decided very tardily.[6] Cousin's message to Raisant stating his decision reached that lively gentleman in Shreveport, freeing Raisant to continue west alone, galloping a horse cross-country to La Réunion.

Meanwhile, Vincent Cousin and Kalikst Wolski bonded as confidants and shared decisions as leaders of the group. They led the colonists onto the large paddle wheeler *South American* on March 15.[7] The travelers from Europe were curious about this new experience, their first on a steam-powered ship. They expected it to be much nicer than their cramped ocean-going, sail-powered craft. And so it was for the twelve hours descending the river, accompanied by good food, wine, cigars, and promenades on deck. But once on the open sea they discovered seasickness to be much worse on a steam-powered craft, for the motion of the engine was never synchronized with the rise and fall of the waves. The advertised forty-eight hours for this voyage stretched to fifty-eight after a burst pipe. This delay caused them to wait for high tide to enter Galveston Bay. Cousin and Wolski may have regretted their decision to be egalitarian and refuse cabins for themselves. Instead, they slept on deck with the rest of the party.

Deposited on the Galveston wharf, they had to make their next decision on the route to follow. Considerant defined in a letter where they were to go, three miles west of a little village called Dallas on the Trinity River, but he did not say how they were to get there. Earlier he had pointed out that the Houston and Texas Central Railroad had its franchise ratified by the state legislature on February 7, 1853, but they had not heard that construction had begun. It was springtime, and the Trinity River usually could float shallow draft paddle wheelers up to Buffalo for at least two months in the spring flood. Farther was questionable, even in good years, because of a channel filled with rafts, which were accumulations of floating tree debris that clogged Texas rivers when river currents were slow. But this year the news of rainfall was dismal. The travelers would certainly find it more comfortable on the river, but they might wait sixty days for it to fill, even if the drought ended.

They knew for certain it would take thirty days to walk from Houston. These chests of plants had to get into the ground. After several days of questioning, they transshipped to another vessel of shallower draught that could carry them across Galveston Bay into Buffalo and Houston.

Bivouacked outside the town to save money, they set up their tents in a circle to protect their goods and began camp life. Rupert Nussbaumer, forty-eight years old, was one of those concerned about the plants they carried. In his early life he had farmed in the Swiss canton of Soleure as animal husbander, driver of teams, operator of a cheese dairy, and manager of a pigsty. But for the past eight years he had found work and participated in the Fourierist cause in Paris. With him on the trip was his twenty-six-year-old son, Jacques, also a farmer.[8] He knew the value of the nursery stock, much of it species unknown in Texas, these pioneers told themselves.

After again inspecting their plants in Houston, Rupert and the others tending them saw that the persistent heat of an advancing Texas spring would kill them. When they opened the chests, they were certain their stock could not be packed for another month of travel. But Vincent Cousin, the keeper of the purse and not a nurseryman or farmer, hated to spend company money, for which he was responsible, not to mention the fact that he was a major investor in the colony who expected a good return. Rupert Nussbaumer saw Cousin as pound foolish and told him so in one of several run-ins that the two men had. Cousin's gold weighed nothing with Rupert, an opinion shared by the anarchists and the young idealists in the caravan.

When finally persuaded to seek land to buy, Cousin began to see the advantages of acreage as a way-station for colonists on the very bayou they had passed through, but he wanted to bargain a price. When they returned to view the prospective purchase a final time, the Texian owner sat in his cabin in the middle of the land, reading his newspaper while his wife rocked in her chair, not acknowledging the Belgians and French. The cabin was typical: one room, a fireplace, no windows, but an unglazed opening above the single low door to let in light and air. A large bed draped in mosquito netting was set opposite the fireplace.

All the gardeners and farmers in the group climbed over the property fence, walked its length, and fingered and smelled the soil. Wolski explained to the Europeans that it was the custom to omit gates in
property fences in remote locations, forcing everyone to climb over
them. The owner had used two acres to grow sweet potatoes, carrots,
and cabbages; he used the other four acres for corn. Neither occupant
came forward nor acted in the least interested in whether the colonists
bought their land or not.

When the gardeners and farmers finished walking slowly about the
entire expanse of the property, a favorable report led Cousin and Wolski to return to the owner with an offer to buy. The owner still sat in the
same position in which he had been left, "his feet on the table, chewing primka (the best tobacco) and still reading that paper. His wife, as
before, was rocking back and forth in a rocking chair. Neither of the pair
got up or made any sign of stopping what they were doing in order to
greet [them]. The couple did not ask whether they wanted to purchase
the property. They did not even nod a head." The colonists' visit was of
no matter to the farmer and his wife.[9]

The price was $400, and Cousin's offer of $300, which Wolski
was required to haggle, might as well have been spoken in the next
county. Nor did they compromise on $350. Wolski knew that bar-
gaining was not a thing Americans did, but under Cousin's urging,
he pressed both the owner and the Houston broker. Neither blinked.
No true Texian did. About March 27, Cousin released $400 of society
gold to buy the six acres of land, three miles from Houston, fronting
on the bayou. The seller gave buyer Cousin no quarter; the Belgian
even had to pay all the closing costs. Three days later, the transac-
tion concluded, the colonists moved their tents and gear to take
possession. Everyone in the group took up an implement to clear
last year's corn stubble, turn the ground, and, under the gardeners'
supervision, plant their treasures and water them. It was decided
that the single-room cabin would hold Nussbaumer, another gardener, and a helper to continue tending the plants.[10] Fortunately for
Cousin's conscience, the plants immediately sprouted in their new
home on the bayou.

With the plants stored in the land, the colonists began a search for oxen and wagons. A land broker told them that

it was necessary to go looking around on the outskirts of the city, for in Houston, or in fact in all Texas, there were no horse and cattle markets. On one of the city squares was a huge building where trading went on every day, but the commodities dealt in were only wheat flour . . . and corn meal milled in the city. Also whiskey, salt pork, sometimes fresh meat, either veal, mutton or beef, and Negroes of both sexes. For everything else it was necessary to go . . . a few miles or more outside the city.[11]

Next they were referred to a man everyone called Captain, a Hungarian. He would know what persons were likely to have the items needed for the next leg of the odyssey. They found him. He knew the region because he made a living finding and breaking in its wild horses. He spoke fluent English and would take them to various persons who would have what they needed.

First, they needed to purchase horses to manage their future oxen. Horses were used to find and drive the oxen back to the wagons in the morning after being let loose at night to feed. Cousin, Wolski, and the Hungarian purchased three horses for $25 to $30 each so that they could more easily find four large wagons and twenty pairs of oxen. Transport was purchased here and there over the countryside, so the men searched for two weeks every day but Sunday. They eventually settled for fifteen pair of oxen.[12]

The Europeans saw more elements of the strange new culture they were invading. New Orleans had shown them an exotic mixture of French, Spanish, Creole, Negro, and Anglo cultures. In Houston they saw primarily southerners of English Protestant antecedents. Here, they were told, it was strictly taboo to work, shop, or even play cards on the Lord's Day.

When they departed from the camp in the mornings on that day's equipment quest, they carried in their saddle bags ham, rolls, and whiskey, but usually they were offered other fare. "The universal hospitality prevailing among the Texians," commented Wolski, "almost never permitted us to use our food when we sat with them at their tables. The Hungarian told us before hand of this hospitality, and now we saw it with our own eyes, and were convinced he had spoken the truth, that it was, as he had said, simple and sincere. The custom was to invite each and everyone arriving at a settler's to sit at the table without ceremony and to eat whatever was set before him." Wolski thought the diet "not much to boast of, consisting in fried salt pork and cornmeal pancakes; settlers served with it weak black coffee or strong black tea. But the fact that everything [was] offered with a good heart makes it the more tastier. The most serious offense would be to question the food in any way, or make comparisons with any other."[13]

They searched for men to handle the oxen. Texian teamsters were essential to communicate with the animals, as they would answer to no other tongue than that of the born Texian they were trained in, or so Wolski and Cousin were told. To go even two kilometers with their heavy equipment, the foreigners needed four teamsters. The teamsters they found agreed to work for a dollar a day plus food and whiskey. Some colonists provisioned themselves with guns, powder, and small shot. All hung small horns around their necks so that if they were lost in this unknown wilderness, they might announce their whereabouts.

Cousin and Wolski thought hard about the large amount of gold entrusted to Cousin. How should they secure it in the wilderness ahead of them? Eventually, rather than try to secrete it in the wagons, they divided it into parts for several colonists to carry. Certainly, everyone carrying gold was also armed.

On April 1, 1855, Wolski crossed himself as he departed Houston.[14] He and Vincent Cousin and thirty-two colonists pressed on into the unknown wild land toward the country of the Three Forks. There they were, marching down the big street of Houston, with a caravan of four wagons, three yoked to eight oxen and one to six, the men marching on each side. The inhabitants stared from their windows, and those with whom they had become acquainted came out to wave. As everywhere, they left behind only good memories.[15]

Later that spring the third group of colonists, led by Dr. Savardan, approached the United States from the Gulf. They saw the spring floodwaters of the Mississippi made even more yellow in the wet heat. At the mouth of the river, "a pilot steam boat placed itself between the Nuremberg and another ship just arriving from Central America, grappled itself to them and towed them at a very satisfactory speed for bored navigators, tired from the long crossing." Otherwise, traveling only under sail, the trip upriver would have taken anywhere from three days with the best of winds to three weeks with the worst to ascend the 105 miles to New Orleans against a two-to-six-mile-an-hour current.[16]

Dr. Savardan had mixed feelings about this ship from Central America.

Permission was given us to visit, and it had a full load of pineapples and bananas from which we could draw abundant refreshment. While savoring the excellent fruits . . . I was gripped with a queasiness. . . . Would it be thus, I told myself in looking with anxiety at that merchant fruit ship, that the figs, oranges, lemons, dates, pineapples, olives and other tropical fruits . . . abound in the southern parts of North America? Who would bother in carrying them from the tenth to thirtieth degree, if they abounded? And what would it be in Texas, five degrees further north?[17]

In the river on their fifty-second and last night on the *Nuremberg*, they passed their first big river steamboat. She looked magnificent in the dark, her lights shining like many sparklers, and the cinders flying out of her pipes forming huge and tortuous columns of fire that cast a luminous light far around.

Dr. Savardan's question about tropical fruits growing in North Texas was put aside when New Orleans came into view on April 20 after two months at sea: his earlier impression at the mouth of the river softened when he saw pretty white houses. Their galleries or airy verandas, framed by thick groves of trees, exuded a freshness really worthy of envy as he stood on the scorching bridge of the *Nuremberg*.

Dr. Savardan and his followers who landed in the New World were not met, as Cousin had been, by Wolski and as promised by Bureau and Guillon back in Paris. Feeling the forgotten unyielding firmness of the earth, Dr. Savardan walked the dockside levee in vain.[18] At once he was overlooking a city unlike any he had ever seen. Four-fifths of the people he saw were of mixed race or black. Streets all led away from the levee parallel to each other. There was a formal square with obviously new buildings on three sides. Long three-story brick buildings faced with lacy balconies flanked a cathedral with three high Norman towers.[19] Its architecture was unmistakably French, but not practiced in the florid fashion the doctor had just left in Paris. There were still-green palm fronds hung over doorways, as Easter had passed two weeks before.

The seafarers at last felt freed from the confines of the voyage. The farmers went to see what was offered in the market and to judge the quality of the produce. They compared prices with French ones. The architects and builders looked for differences in construction practices. They had heard of the wooden houses with balloon framing but were surprised at seeing brick columns and high steps to raise the buildings above the damp of a high water table.

Though Savardan spoke no English, there were many along the wharf speaking a corrupted French called Cajun, and he was armed with a list of contacts. He soon found Jules Juif, lawyer and nephew of Mme Vigoureux, Considerant's mother-in-law.[20] Juif found Savardan help with customs. The colony equipment was released for transshipping. Yet, with Dr. Savardan's penchant for order, this failure to meet the *Nuremberg* appeared to be a fissure, though small, in the leader Victor Considerant's armor.

Two days later Considerant arrived on a river boat from Cincinnati. He no longer seemed the same man who had come from Europe to New York less than three months before. Even to himself, he seemed filled with guilt, which at times took the form of depression. The news he found in New York of slavery politics in the South, the news in Washington concerning the suspension of North Texas land grants, the news from Texas of a serious drought—all threatened his dream. He had written Paris more than a month ago that they had to move the theater of operations from North Texas farther southwest.[21] That idea too was a gamble, since he himself had not seen the land he now advocated.

He would not be able to fulfill his *Au Texas* promise of free land in North Texas if the legislature did not make an exception for the society to its settlement suspension policy. That land five degrees farther south was more arid, less defended from Indians, but less populated; therefore, it could be bought cheaper, although the waterway might be less navigable and railroads might not come as soon. Godin had reacted by return mail: "Do not buy land where we would have to fight the Indians."[22]

As he traveled down the Mississippi from Cincinnati and now here in New Orleans, Considerant had the definite feeling that they would need to go overland from Houston because of the drought. His old university classmate Weiss confirmed it.

Considerant heard even more about slavery now that he was in the South. Britain was trying to end the slave trade on the high seas. Would Britain persuade Spain to free the slaves already in Cuba? "This was a terrible bogey to the South, for it could produce the rise of a Negro republic comparable to that in Haiti, which would offer a perilous contagious example to the slaves in the American cotton belt. But some argued that further Cuban imports of Negroes, of which there continued to be many . . . or the arming of the blacks there in case of a war with the United States, might precipitate the same result anyway. Such anxiety over 'Africanization' was no light matter to the 'slavocracy.'"[23] Considerant tried to dismiss such talk as having nothing to do with the colony in North Texas.

It was too late for Considerant to stop Cantagrel. That sturdy builder had not been able to buy Fort Worth but had already bought a substitute. It appeared a bad choice to try to seek land north of Indian Territory with all the fighting in Kansas going on between free-state men and slave holders. Considerant's communication with his followers was strained. He had to go through with what he had started, but he seemed to regret everything that was happening.

Considerant couldn't go back. There was no place in France for him. Louis-Napoléon called himself emperor now, and all of France was submissive. His Sûreté Nationale had almost eliminated all Republican plots against him; the very idea of the republic seemed lost. The socialist and Fourierist presses had been smashed. The emperor was the "restorer of the overthrown altars," which gave him the men in black. He had even let them get the university in their hands. He gave away sausages and used certain Orléanists and Saint-Simonians to make himself palatable to the industrial classes. He extended credit and developed the means of communication; he strongly backed business. Through foundations, charitable gifts, and subsidies, he posed as one seeking always to remember those who suffered. He assured the people cheap bread, jobs in big public works, and fetes emphasized by a brilliant imperial court. Republican France was decimated politically by this man. No, Considerant could not go back.

Considerant's wife, Julie, and her mother, Mme Vigoureux, could do little to change Considerant's view of his plight, though they insisted on drives about the city—this exotic place, showing its mixtures of Creole life. Mlle Gaudel joined them on walks viewing the white blooms of giant catalpa trees against their heart-shaped leaves, fuchsia hibiscus, yellow jasmine vines, pink queen's wreath, and white gardenias flourishing against dark green broadleafs in the thick humidity. Spring in full flower—what was known as summer to those northern Europeans—certainly attracted Julie's painterly eye. Mme Vigoureux shook off her tiredness and was cheered by Aimée Beucque's letter that Dr. Savardan had carried for two months.

When Dr. Savardan met up with Considerant, he found him "prostrated in a most wretched despondency" and from that time on never saw him without more or less marked symptoms of that depression. Dr. Savardan watched his leader gradually become a different man. He heard Considerant expound, like all sick people, at great length to everybody concerning his malady. To hide his guilt, Considerant feigned disdain, even repugnance, for the majority of emigrants who had followed him five thousand miles across the ocean—those who saw in him the embodiment of their hope and confidence in the life he had espoused, in the land and place that he had chosen. There were five from Considerant's own Jura who stayed in New Orleans because of their leader's frozen attitude.

While the leader hid from contact in New Orleans, New Orleans was, in one sense, a balm to Considerant. Clarisse Vigoureux's nephew Jules Juif welcomed the three family members and housed them after their trip down the Mississippi.[24] Being welcomed in the bosom of his wife's family by a host who was a respected lawyer representing the interests of the Baron de Pontalba in New Orleans was a haven. Of course, Considerant could depend on Juif to help with transshipment and, most importantly, ease the arrival of future colonists.

But Weiss's reserve when the subject of the colony arose did not help Considerant's depression. Weiss, like Considerant in Paris, was a newspaperman and a Fourierist. He should be able to help inspire Americans to participate, but as far as Considerant could see, the *Bee* had done little for the cause. Only Wolski had given him a little hope. He had written Considerant five weeks earlier that in New Orleans he was trying to discourage many from joining the caravan to North Texas until buildings were ready to receive them.

Perhaps Considerant convinced himself that free land wasn't everything. As a fail-safe, if they could not get it free, as he had counted on, he still had Vesian, the young former lieutenant of the French African Army, who had been sent with $3,000 to buy headright scrip in Texas at the end of March.[25] After all, the stock company Considerant had caused to be created the year before *had* to succeed, or there could never be a phalanx trial of Fourier's principles for reorganizing society.

By late April 1855, as Dr. Savardan continued planning the trip north, the newly arrived colonists suffered in the New Orleans humidity. They already had baked under the spring sun on their ship crossing the Gulf of Mexico. It was particularly oppressive to the colonists from the Hautes-Alpes.[26] One of those was Jean Nicolas, the doctor from a valley in the western flanks of the Cottian Alps, in the Dauphiné, who had practiced medicine in the village of St. Bonnet for almost thirty years. Nicolas felt ill in the stifling heat.

Dr. Nicolas immediately started organizing escape from this exotic, languid home of humidity and pestilence so that he would not have to spend his fifty-seventh birthday, one week away, in New Orleans. Encountering in New Orleans a twenty-year-old French mountain stockherd named Marius Mouren, Nicolas swept him along too.

Dr. Nicolas had been a widower for a quarter century but left a married daughter and grandchildren back in the Alps. When he was a student, his thesis at Montpellier medical school, "Essai sur la topographie physique et médicale du Champsaur," showed the effects of climate and manmade environments on health. The extremes and changeability of

North Texas were going to be a surprise to this doctor. Within four days, as quickly as he could, Dr. Jean Nicolas found passage to Galveston and sailed with ten "of the most impatient" of the new colonists on April 25.[27]

A few days later, the bulk of Dr. Savardan's group left New Orleans with Charles François Bernard Bussy, a former Republican government functionary from the Paris suburb of La Villeté. They carried the equipment brought from Le Havre as soon as they could get it transshipped to a paddle wheeler bound for Galveston on April 29. Bussy, fifty-three, listed himself as an accountant and in agriculture and industry. His ventures made numerous dupes; he was accused of being a swindler who twice had declared fraudulent bankruptcy. As a proclaimed Republican who had gotten jobs under the government of the 1848 Revolution, he was very likely now out of a job. He probably felt uncomfortable enough in France after the emperor's coup in 1852 to need to join the Fourierist pilgrimage to the New World.

Bussy was the same age as Savardan and Nicolas, though he traveled in a better class than steerage. He was the only person crossing to La Réunion with a servant. Certainly, he appeared to possess more than average funds. Perhaps age, money, and a habit of commanding made him a logical leader to take the colonists on to Houston.

Dr. Savardan stayed behind to conduct business and buy provisions for their overland trip through Texas. His primary goal was "to provide for the existence of the group during the long trip on land that we would have to make. This trip, all information considered, should last a month at least, without allowance for unexpected circumstances," so his mission was to procure provisions for two months. He purchased twenty barrels, weighing around a thousand pounds, of biscuit of two different types. One biscuit was sweetened and the other unsweetened. The first was a little smaller but was the same price as the second and could be used to sweeten coffee. He then bought ten half barrels of beer, weighing two thousand pounds. Buying beer was at least partly for health purposes, in the doctor's mind. He had observed during the ocean crossing that "beer like almost all the light bitters, was a valuable relief for impairments of digestive functions." If it were good for seasickness, the good doctor reasoned, it would be salutary for overland travel where water might be bad.[28] It also might be hard to purchase in the part of Texas where they were headed. The French had been hearing that there were Protestant sects that militantly disapproved of any form of alcohol.

Savardan bought 30 pounds of candles, 100 pounds of coffee, 50 pounds of chocolate, 6 liters of d'esprit-de-vin, 130 pounds of Gruyère cheese, 200 pounds of beans, 180 pounds of cooking oil, 200 pounds of smoked pork tongues, 150 pounds of lentils, 370 pounds of plum marmalade, 20 pounds of mustard, 25 pounds of onions, 20 pounds of pepper, 110 pounds of dried apples, 650 pounds of rice, 100 pounds of lard, 20 pounds of sardines in small bottles, 100 pounds of sausage, 100 pounds of salt, 68 pounds of white and 137 of brown sugar, 120 pounds of vermicelli and macaroni, 1,000 pounds of wine in two barrels, 360 pounds of vinegar, and 300 pounds of whiskey. Finally, he bought 25 pounds of powder and 100 of lead for hunting. All that totaled about 7,000 pounds and cost, including transport, $1,000.[29]

As for Considerant, he saw a need to set up banking relations as close as possible to La Réunion, given the fact that they were about to go into an environment in which there were no banks.[30] He also would need to carry gold. The bank in New Orleans did not honor Considerant's letter of credit. A check had also bounced in New York because Brisbane failed in his responsibility. Amédée Simonin, the society's newly appointed representative to handle affairs in New York, received a letter from Juif on which Considerant had scribbled, "It won't happen again, tell August Belmont. Juif paved his way."

Dr. Savardan left New Orleans for Texas with five ladies who had preferred to wait for him (or spend more time in New Orleans recovering from the ocean before going out on the water again) and a Monsieur Christophe from Hautes-Alpes, who had just joined them from another ship. Mademoiselle Gaudel was in this group, as this lady of a certain age had traveled second class with Savardan on the *Nuremberg* and probably spent time with Clarisse Vigoureux. When Mademoiselle Gaudel had gone to Paris from her home in Rouen the past winter, she and Aimée Beucque had planned to communicate through the spirits back to the rue de Beaune office in Paris. Aimée Beucque had even identified a particular spirit who could be summoned in a séance at the tables to carry their secret news.[31] Catherine Bossereau, Dr. Savardan's late wife's woman in service at their home in La Sarthe, also traveled with him.

Still concerned by the change in Considerant, Dr. Savardan noted, "We have seen little of M. Considerant. He was, though better, still suffering from his illness from New York. He seemed preoccupied, anxious, sad; consequently, we had understood that we were not to worry him with any of our affairs. We would join each other in a few days in Galveston, then Houston, . . . and continue our trip together."[32]

Bound for Galveston from New Orleans on the *Louisiana*, a large paddle wheeler, they all went back down "the great river gaily to the sound of military music of an American regiment, which was going to take up a garrison" on the Texas-Mexican frontier. The travelers soon sought shelter and breeze from the Gulf sun and heat until twilight, when the rails became festooned with people.[33]

One of the passengers, hearing the group speaking French, came over to greet them. He was a Monsieur Castagne, a merchant from Bordeaux who was established in Galveston. He shared with the group helpful information on Galveston, Houston, and Texas in general. But it was not all good news. He confirmed the news they had heard in New Orleans, that it had not rained for a year in Texas and that the harvest had been almost nothing.[34]

On the *Louisiana*, a few moments after meeting Castagne, they were approached by another man with a French "good day" and a friendly inquiry on the purpose of their trip. The man's accent was a curious mix of Anglo and French inflections. His intelligent and pleasant physiognomy, expressing as his speech only good will, and showing some respectable signs of the beginning of old age had invited us from the first into his confidence. Their conversation, steered by the stranger's questioning on what ideas the immigrants' enterprise was based, which the preceding groups had made an object of almost general curiosity en route, soon became a discussion, remaining always on the best terms." Savardan sensed he had discovered a Catholic priest. Then a moment later he noticed the ring, a large emerald, a sign of the episcopate. Dr. Savardan remarked on the ring to the questioner, who then admitted that he was the Catholic bishop of Galveston and Texas. "His face, as his speech, entirely evangelical, reminded [Dr. Savardan] of the former archbishop of Bordeaux, M. de Cheverus, who had begun his apostolate in America, and of a former grand vicar of Verdun, the abbé de Gaulme, and [his] uncle, whom emigration had kept in Poland for nearly twenty years."[35]

Several times on this passage, Monsignor Odin sought out Dr. Savardan to return to their conversations on the goal and the future of humanity in this world and the next. While their minds were not completely in accord, their hearts were in sympathy.

Finding the gap between two coastal sand reefs marked by a low lighthouse on May 5, the *Louisiana* passed Point Bolivar and fed fuel to its engines to overcome the current flowing out of Galveston Bay. To the left, as they passed between the sand barriers, Galveston revealed itself first by the rigging of a half dozen three-masters puncturing the sky in the distance. Galveston perched on the leeward north side of a mile-wide sand bar that separates the ocean from the great bay to its north. The true gateway to Texas and the largest town in Texas, Galveston had doubled its population to nine thousand since the last census. The colonists saw a two-story, wood-and-brick Galveston, protecting itself from the sun behind verandas and porches, its buildings disposed along neat, wide, clean streets. The streets were lighted throughout with gas. Though the yellow fever season had not yet begun, and Galveston's sea breezes supposedly reduced the pestilence, everyone was mindful of the terrible epidemic the past fall, and those with means moved north as soon as possible after winter had passed.

On the Galveston wharf, Dr. Savardan did not seek in vain the provident solicitude of a friend, unlike the lack of a greeter in New Orleans. From the bridge of the ship, he heard his name called by an unknown voice. He had no trouble in recognizing the face of Mr. Vesian, a decommissioned officer of the African Army who had come to America to make his fortune. A friend of Considerant, he had put himself at the leader's disposal for the work in Texas. Vesian had been dispatched by Considerant from New York to purchase cheap headright script, in which there was a market in Texas, and then to meet the colonists' ships, as they would know no English and need help.[36]

They found in Vesian a helpful contact for all the difficulties of landing, the rules of the dock, and the transshipping of their numerous goods. A ship left a few hours later for Houston with the small group. Dr. Savardan waited behind for Considerant to arrive and to settle business with Monsieur de Saint Cyr, consul of France and designated broker, and with his partner, Monsieur Saltzmann, concerning their interests in this place. "M. de Saint Cyr seemed to [him], as all business men in America, to have two different faces."[37] In his office, he was all business, looking after his interests but solicitous also for his employees. He had come when very young to Galveston by way of Brazil and a few years with the Indians. He prospered and contributed a great deal to the life of this little island, but at home he shed his "grand and cool manner" of managing his commercial affairs and became a French gentleman educated by travel, in the midst of his family. Savardan contrasted him and the monsignor, both well-traveled patricians, as understanding the genuine Christian values of individuals much better than those of similar station in "countries where the nobility and church dominate" and "conventional" values predominate.[38]

Bishop Odin, before disembarking, offered Dr. Savardan the hospitality of his modest episcopal palace. The latter could not accept, having also, as he told the bishop, "charge of souls." The two did visit several times in Galveston. Raising eyebrows among anticlerical republican colonists, Savardan's friendship and dining with Odin were gossip to the ears of Fritz Colas, who reported it to his friends in Paris, and thus it reached an old columnist antagonist and the press. To Republicans in France, the Catholic Church had never been on the right side of change but always associated with reactionary monarchists. It had been a chief target to topple in the first revolution and continued to be for socialists throughout the nineteenth century. Though they had no power, they canted. In the political soup of La Réunion, here was another factional element dragged from Europe to help spoil the broth.

Dr. Savardan's meeting with Saint-Cyr, Odin, and Vesian in Galveston gave him a good opinion of the long, narrow, and low island, a sand barrier protecting Galveston Bay. The town was commodiously laid out in rectangles, contrasting the plans of medieval and constricted French towns. Its sand foundation may have worried Savardan, but he was charmed by the blankets of blooming oleander and the refreshing moist Gulf breeze. Watching the glistening foam of the surf's edge break against his horses' hooves as they pulled his carriage for long miles down the beautiful sand beach at high tide, he felt better about Texas. Here, following the beach toward a seemingly endless infinity, inches into the land he had dreamed of when reading *Au Texas*, and with the great waters he had crossed still at his side, he thought better of Considerant's opinion of the place. But as Dr. Savardan and Vesian rode down the beach, they commented that they saw no evidence of the bananas, coconuts, oranges, and olives that Considerant had promised. There were a few planted date palms and gardenias in the town, but no rank tropical vegetation. Still, both men regretted having to take themselves away from their long ride on this beautiful beach.[39]

In Galveston, Vesian recommended to Considerant that he open accounts with Saltzmann and St. Cyr to act as customs brokers and forwarding agents. Their business completed, Dr. Savardan with his young friend, without waiting longer for Considerant, took passage in another steamboat and followed his shipmates to Houston. Across the bay, they did not have to wait—as did their predecessors—for the tide to rise so that they could enter Buffalo Bayou.

In the evening with the wind calmed, the great, expansive bay mirrored the black smoke from their funnel in the twilight. The smoke wafted in front of them while they churned north. Dead ahead was San Jacinto, where Sam Houston and his troops had surprised Santa Anna to win Texas freedom from Mexico nineteen years before. Suddenly the paddle wheeler steered to port as the seamen hoisted large, flat, iron baskets at the prow. Soon they approached a seemingly solid wall of vegetation. Pine-wood fires were being lighted in the iron baskets as the boat slowed, seeking the mouth of Buffalo Bayou.

The narrowness of the bayou channel reinforced their sense of retreat from civilization, especially in contrast to the bay they had left. Wolski commented that no one in Europe would venture on such a stream, even in a small skiff, much less in a large paddle wheeler.[40] Branches scraped the sides of the ship. For almost the entire length of the bayou, the ship fitted in the channel as if it had donned a glove. There was certainly no passage for a second ship running in the opposite direction; this paddle wheeler had to stay the course to Houston so that it could turn around. To disembark, only a gangplank was necessary; travelers all along the bayou were met at their landings by slaves with lanterns. Meeting sharp turns in the channel, several men with heavy poles pushed the boat around each bend.

Almost everywhere the great trees of the waterside, many gray bearded with "Spanish" moss, came together to form a thick vault over the ship. The ship moved forward throughout the night, following its own beacons, hung from the prow and sides. Numerous tall magnolias waved their great white flowers and red seed pods above the ship. "Enormous clusters of these flowers were placed in large vases here and there, on the sideboards and the pier tables of the long, splendid interior gallery, partly two stories high."[41]

"Those fires, that dark night, those thick vaults, that interior gallery, that rapid and silent movement of the ship, all the passengers wandering or sitting along the exterior galleries and on the poop deck, everything lighted and perfumed in a manner so unusual for us, all that was indeed, whatever else it may have lacked, the Texas of the book and the Texas of our dreams," wrote Savardan. "We spent the entire night without going to bed in contemplation of it."[42]

At the break of day, the morning of May 9, the ship's deep whistle announced their arrival in Houston. They found themselves in a tiny turning basin with dock space for barely two ships. Having arranged for wharf space while they sought their next conveyances, Dr. Savardan went off to seek their companions already in Houston and to inspect their new plant nursery. He began asking about sources for oxen, horses, and drovers with wagons.[43]

Considerant just missed Dr. Savardan. Considerant arrived with his group in Galveston the evening Savardan left. While Savardan was plying the bayou to Houston, Considerant slept to the comforting sound of a torrential rain on the coast. He judged news of this rain as important enough to be included in his letter to the Paris office.[44] Perhaps the drought in Texas was not real—or was providence changing Texas for the arrival of the Fourierist leader?

A week earlier Dr. Jean Nicolas awoke to his birthday, looking out of one of the two paddle wheelers oscillating between Galveston and Houston as it was being moored to the Houston landing. He opened his eyes at the blast of a neighboring ship, the only other one that could fit in the tiny basin, and the one that had to immediately leave or risk getting stuck at the mouth of the bayou in the waning tide. The ten-hour tide and width of the bayou regulated Houston commerce that reached it from the sea; these two ships filled the port's capacity and were its total complement.

He saw a thirty-foot-high wall of dirt, which he climbed to find his first view of flat Houston, a perfectly rectangular grid of streets laid at right angles to one another rigidly with a compass. Houston had doubled its inhabitants in the past five years. Still, only five thousand inhabitants resided on this grid, interrupted on the west by the meandering tidal shallows of Buffalo Bayou. This was the place all the products of their phalanstery would come for sale. Except for Jefferson and Shreveport in rainy years, or if the Trinity could be cleared, this was the closest port they had to get their products to market. It was a long way. They were really in Texas now, at the frontier. Wild Indians were only two hundred miles west. They could feel the shrinking of civilization.[45]

Beyond the dock and the two- and three-story plastered buildings lining the side of the basin, the streets in Dr. Nicolas's view ran straight to a converging infinity in the southwest, their perspective only interrupted by enormous, low, spreading trees offering a dense shade under small, convex, and pointed glossy leaves. In the foreground the streets were lined with offices and a street or two of "handsome dwelling houses, of wood, to be sure, but very elegant, with gardens surrounding them and very comfortably arranged, all lighted by gas, as are all the streets."[46] The small town, serving a quarter of this frontier state, awaited the coming of the railroad to overtake the center of trade in Galveston. It would serve North Texas in the future. Now there was a rail line projected, even with a franchise from the legislature, but no tracks had been laid toward La Réunion.[47] United again in Houston, it took Dr. Savardan's group eight days to find oxen and horses and hire six additional wagons to transport the mills, forges, and tools of all kinds. After loading the wagons to travel to the colonists' final destination, they were well on their way.[48]

14

From Houston to the Three Forks

The teamsters would keep going from one pair of oxen to another, talking to the animals in very tender words, trying to persuade them to keep together, and flattering them by stroking them on their muzzles for ten minutes or so, after which they would begin to drive them forward. But the oxen never heard the first word, and each would go in a different direction.

> Then there would ensue a pitiless beating of the beasts with long poles, and cries from those who but a moment before had chatted with them in such a friendly manner. Refractory and accustomed to freedom on the Texas wastes, the oxen still remained obdurate, each pair going where it wished, as if it were determined to show by this means the impossibility of coming to terms with them. At times like this the teamsters would fling their straw caps on the ground, tear their hair, and confer with each other, usually in a highly tempestuous manner, for each put the blame on the other three.[1]

"It was a blessing for all to think that for 300 miles we were going to travel in the early mornings with the leader of our school over this magnificent Texas so brilliantly described by him, and to enjoy, from this moment, at each stop, the benefit of hearing his eloquent words."[2] But Dr. Savardan, who based that thought on the previous examples of Cabet and Brigham Young leading their Icarians and Mormons by sharing their labors, was to be disappointed. Those leaders understood how to gain their followers' confidence and to sustain that confidence and enthusiasm for long periods, however unreasonable and insubstantial might be the basis on which it rested.

Considerant did not see himself in that role. When he caught up with Dr. Savardan in Houston it became clear that he did not intend

to travel with the colonists. Though he gave no such excuse, he perhaps felt responsibility to hurry ahead to La Réunion to better decide
whether they should try to move the colony to a new location at once.
Dr. Savardan had made his own excuses for Considerant in New Orleans, but now the leader's actions did not conform to his dream of how
a leader should act toward his own brainchild, the communal society.
Dr. Savardan had questions. The hands-on doctor did not understand
the actions of the social theoretician. Did traveling apart mean that
Victor Considerant did not see himself as part of the group? Savardan
remembered his friend Fugère's warning in France. Was Considerant
in fact a leader?

The divergent perspectives of the leaders on this trip colored the views
of all. Colas, a self-proclaimed anarchist, had walked to La Réunion
with the earliest group to escape his exile in Belgium. In a letter to Jean
Journet in Paris, Colas accused Dr. Savardan of leaving Mademoiselle
Gaudel in Houston "on the pretext of loose talk on the crossing; she
was 52 years old! It is true that she was destined to nurse the sick, and
they had decided her services would be of no value at Réunion."[3] Savardan's benign comments about Mademoiselle Gaudel suggest Colas was
spreading unfounded gossip. She probably stayed in Houston so that
she could come to the colony when it was better organized. Later she
did come north.

In Houston, the word was widespread about the drought and the poverty of water in rivers. There was no possibility of navigating the Trinity. At last, with a chance to talk with Considerant, Savardan raised his
concerns. Considerant's response? "There is no rule without an exception, and there only remained for us, after this disappointing news, the
difficulty of beginning during such a serious exception." Considerant
could certainly not be blamed for the drought and, given his intellectual
rationalism, could have had no more reassuring answer to Savardan's
fears. Considerant probably also pointed out to Savardan, as he did to
the Paris office, the torrential rain he had just experienced two nights
before in Galveston.

With Vesian to interpret, Dr. Savardan soon bought a horse for himself
and found his way to the colony's land on the bayou and to his *Nurem-*

berg charges, whom Charles Bussy had led from New Orleans. Those of the thirty-three bivouacked there who spoke English helped in the search for wagons, oxen, and drovers. Rupert Nussbaumer and the two left tending the colonists' plants and trees brought by Cousin's group took charge of the Bordelaise grape root-stock carried on the *Nuremberg*. Those from the ship smiled to see them immediately start to sprout.[4]

Leaving the colonists to travel under Dr. Savardan's care, Executive Director Considerant launched his own overland trip to La Réunion on May 16. He harnessed his pretty little gig, which cost him $100 in Cincinnati, with two beautiful gray mares bought for $400. Such an extravagance raised eyebrows among colonists who had paid $35 for theirs and thought that they as Fourierists were in Texas to end the bad habits of class distinctions. Did their leader need those fancy horses and that gig, unsuited for rough roads, for his appearance, or were the Texas roads better than they had heard?

Considerant rode mounted with César Daly and Louis Willemet, who cooked for the group. Considerant commandeered Dr. Savardan's saddle horse, to which he had taken a liking, and persuaded its owner to let him buy it the day before they left. With Jules Haizé flicking the reins of the gig, Julie Considerant, Madame Clarisse, Josephine Cantagrel, her son, Simon, and her infant daughter-in-arms started for La Réunion.

Two days after Considerant left on the morning of May 18, teamster Black, a settler who lived in a neighboring county to that of Dallas, followed, leading Dr. Savardan's long convoy. Black was returning to his farm after selling his two wagon-loads of cotton in Houston. Four teamsters cracked the whips over the oxen transporting the colony's heavy machinery. Their wagons were in bad condition and often broke down, delaying the caravan. Mr. Black himself, in spite of his sixteen good oxen, did not have wheels strong enough to hope for a trip without damage.

For the most part, the six teamsters with their six substitutes, whom Dr. Savardan had selected from the colonists, had considerable trouble coming to terms with their role as part of the caravan; the beginning days were disorderly and, as Savardan described them, of "perplexity." At the end of the first one, Savardan was presented with one of Considerant's horses, a horse Considerant had recognized as useless.[5] He abandoned it at the first farm he encountered, along with a part of his heaviest baggage. Savardan's group then had six horses, two owned by those who rode them and four belonging to the society. One of the society's horses was adopted by Vesian, another by Charles Bussy. A third was reserved for tired walkers. Dr. Savardan drove a four-wheeled cabriolet buggy drawn by a "good old" horse. The convoy of nine wagons and forty head of cattle sometimes stretched out for a mile. Savardan's group, six on horse, a few riding in the ox-drawn carts, and the rest walking, comprised thirty-three people and drovers.

Considerant dispatched Vesian to continue to travel with Savardan as interpreter.[6] Since there were few among the colonists who spoke English, Savardan was delighted with this decision, though Vesian was disappointed, even vexed. He had counted on traveling with the great leader.

Colonists began their trek north traveling for a mile across a swamp on a road paved with tree trunks laid in the mud perpendicular to travel. The first three days of the journey took them across what they referred to as the "so-called meadows," "that is, uncultivated plains."[7] After four days along a well-rutted road across this flat coastal plain, they passed into a great forest and began to encounter occasional cleared farm patches skirting small swampy lakes surrounded by trees festooned in Spanish moss.

Impatient with their rate of six or seven miles a day, Sauzeau, the anarchist Considerant had invited to join the Réunion "field of social experiment," persuaded Topin to ride ahead with him. Soon after, they encountered Alexandre Raisant coming south toward them from La Réunion.

Engineer Raisant was dedicated. Having left New Orleans in early March to scout the routes from there via the Red River, he was greatly astonished to get a letter in Shreveport saying that Cousin, an architect and Considerant's confidant, was taking the pioneers by way of Galveston instead. Realizing they were no longer behind him, he at once beat it to the colony. In seven days he covered seventy leagues, reaching La Réunion at the end of March. Scarcely two hours after he arrived, a letter came from the coast from Cousin's group saying they would have to haul with slow oxen. Meanwhile, Cantagrel, Reverend Allen, and some twenty hired Americans were busy cultivating and building, but they were not ready to receive colonists. Seeing how much had to be done, Raisant got back on a horse and rode south to commandeer more hands from the slow caravan. Galloping south for five days and another 270 miles, he found Cousin's group only 20 miles north of Houston. Inviting seven "capable of working wood" to ride a forced march back to La Réunion with him, he was indefatigable.[8] Less than three weeks later, he made a *second* twelve-day forced march to Houston for supplies, arriving about May 22.[9]

It took the trail leaders some time to organize novice caravans. Dr. Savardan exerted leadership in the form of reasoned appeals. With patience he established order in both travel and camping. No longer did all the horsemen rush off ahead to seek shade or refreshment at a farmhouse, leaving the walkers and drovers to overcome all the difficulties with the carts. No longer did the drovers constantly pass each other in competition to be the first at the next creek. No longer did everyone abandon a disabled vehicle to its own devices. Savardan taught the "sentiments of fraternity and the principles of association in the name of which [they] had embarked on this long pilgrimage." And in the evening the drovers at last learned to circle their carts around the two food wagons to simplify service.

Of course, they constantly compared this place with home and, wanting to stay in communication with their old world, wrote letters while waiting for the drovers to master the next feat. One night Dr. Savardan wrote to his adopted children while on this trail:

> Perhaps you would be interested to know how our days are spent.
>
> Every day, I get out of my bed chamber at 2:30 in the morning. I get up our teamster, who on his horn, sounds reveille. While everyone is rousing himself and waking up, I rekindle the fire from the old one. Our cooks come successively to heat up the chocolate and the soups. The délité devoured, the wagoniers collect their oxen, the horsemen curry, saddle their horses and give them their ration of corn; the ladies wash the tableware and pack it in baskets; the men fold the hammocks, roll the mattresses. When the whole caboodle

is put away in the wagons, the call to mount sounds and the column sets out on a march of 4 to 5 hours, preceded and followed by
a part of the horsemen, so that they can forestall alternatively what
happens at the two extremities. The hunters stretch out along the
flanks of the column, and thanks to them and to small resources
that the American farmers place at our disposal, until now we have
lacked neither calves, fowl, nor good game.[10]

Creeks were a new problem for Europeans used to bridges. Imagine these cultured Europeans arriving at "ravines sixty to ninety feet
deep . . . across which the Americans have traced with their wagons, in
the middle of tree trunks, brushwood, vines, and brambles, the most
impracticable roads that one can imagine." The steep sides of the narrow waterways often made skids impractical and forced the unloading
of wagons, requiring numerous trips to portage all gear. On reaching
the edge overlooking one, teamster Black went first, shouting great
epithets at his oxen while delivering two-handed blows and cracks of
his whip. Savardan may have exaggerated when he recalled Black's skill
with his whip, which reached from one end of his yoked team to the
other, some sixty-five feet. His skill was most manifest on the climb
up the other side, when he repeated *Cows!* at each crack of his whip,
continually for as long as the climb lasted, and interspersed them with
Goddamn! Savardan observed that these sobriquets "appeared to prick
in a singular manner the self-esteem of the oxen. Vexed at being treated
as mere cows, they redoubled their efforts in order to prove that they
are useful." When they again reached the rim of the defile, they got an
All right! for their reward. Being a good lead ox also rewarded that animal with being unyoked and led back across the river to help another
team—for several trips.

The group faced hazards at creeks of every condition. If it had rained
recently, the descent and ascent in the mud required at least twice the
time as in dry weather. If it were dry and the oxen caught the smell of
water, they immediately hurled themselves toward the creek, regardless
of what they pulled or of the shouts of the drovers. Carts and goods,
as well as men, were at hazard. To overcome these perils, experienced

drovers unyoked their animals in advance in order to water them before they attempted any crossing.

If it were storming, and waters became torrential, there was nothing to do but make a camp in the damp and wait, a soggy, dispiriting affair. This required patience. François Santerre and his family had to wait three weeks to cross the Navasota River while on their trip from Houston to La Réunion.[11]

The morning brought another time problem. Finding and assembling the oxen could take hours, half the day, and occasionally even whole days. If the campsite did not have both good water and ample forage, the animals might have wandered several creeks away and be hidden in thick woods, satiated and no longer jingling their bells. To cure this problem, Savardan instituted a two-hour watch of the herd, the men on duty counting animals through the night. This worked for those nights the sentries did not fall asleep in the middle of a prairie.

In architect Cousin's group, Wolski suddenly saw fire on the floor of the forest ahead of them on their tenth day. After horsemen explored in three directions, they determined to reach safety by crossing what they thought was a few hundred steps through the fire. All grabbed spades and axes to make a path for the oxen in the burning grass. It was neither thick nor high, but it turned out to extend for a mile and a half of long, anxious labor. The sweat poured from them in streams as they worked first in terror and then to exhaustion. Crossing a little stream, their anxiety was finally relieved.[12]

Out of the forest, all the colonist groups saw the first small hill, on top of which grew a hamlet called Anderson. The town was unique in Texas, a medieval village in format, without surrounding walls. At its north end stood a courthouse. From it a spine ran along the hilltop between houses and a Baptist church. At the spine terminus, on the south brow, stood the Fanthrop Inn, an eighteen-year-old stagecoach stop established the year after the Texas revolution. On both east and west slopes down from the spine, a couple of streets were sprinkled with houses, draped down the hillside. The inn was the last public hostelry the colonists would encounter on their route north.

The reality of their travel on the frontier bore in when "two wild Indians with arms on their breasts, almost completely naked, with long hair in long braids, and faces painted a brick color" appeared. Wolski's imagination immediately pictured a hidden horde with whom the colonists would have to do battle to save their scalps. The teamsters, recognizing them for being only horse thieves and not dangerous to an armed party, calmed the Europeans as the Indians disappeared in the underbrush.[13]

As they moved farther upland away from the coast, they saw more and more signs of the ambiguity of the Texas climate. Thankfully, they had brought kegs of water.[14] Parched farms on the prairie offered no water for either their animals or themselves. Then a green bottomland encountered would revive their enthusiasm, but it mired their slowing oxen. They had to make more and more frequent stops and were depressed by finding a dead oxen belonging to Jean Nicolas's group, which preceded them. Then they had to abandon one of their own.

On making camp in the evening, wood was gathered and big fires built immediately. The teamsters told Wolski the fires would keep away the snakes. A wide and deep trench was built around each tent site or wagon for the same reason. Oxen were unharnessed but left yoked two by two, and they had their forefeet hobbled before being turned out to graze. Horses, more subject to thievery, were staked and tethered on a circle of grassland near the camp.

Dr. Savardan organized the handling of meals. He encouraged the colonists to combine friendships and tastes. The thirty-five travelers self-divided into four groups for meals. An officer for each recorded the supplies used, as the Society of Colonization in Texas charged back to the individuals everything they used, including the transportation. Generally, this was an orderly procedure. From eleven to noon, they unhitched in the midst of some beautiful prairie and near a bayou or river. They kindled four fires to start cooking. As described by Dr. Savardan, dinner was a "good soup, whether of meat or onion or of beans. Bouillon in which appear, with the beef or the mutton, prairie chicken or poultry-yard hens; lastly all that is old, except me. Lacking boiled beef, sometimes an omelet, or beans, or lentils. Roast meat, made up of all that the hunt or the farmyards can supply us of young ones. Lastly, for dessert, apple sauce or cheese and the cup of coffee."[15]

At two in the afternoon, they departed again to walk until six in the evening. After the wagons were put in a half circle, the horses were picketed, and the oxen were hobbled with each other, the four fires were again built so that the women could prepare the evening meal. The canteen was opened and supplies were distributed as needed to supplement the hunting bag of the day. They nearly always shot game birds—prairie hens, dove, quail, or wild turkey—and rabbit. Occasionally, a farm sold the group eggs, milk, or fowl to share. On bad days they might encounter no game and be offered only a cow by settlers. That was refused by Dr. Savardan as being prodigal, wasteful of at least half the animal, since they could not eat it all and were not able to carry it. Rice, beans, sardines, baked apples, good coffee, and excellent biscuits were the easy example he set for his charges. Once, the former lieutenant of the African Army decided he would requisition a pig from a nearby farm. After shooting it, he had to be persuaded that the colonists could not accept it in their stew. At least within his sight, the doctor's moral authority held sway.

At twilight, a colonist was detailed to fetch water for cooking. He descended in the creek bed and immediately noticed the cooler air that had settled there. While at the creek, he bathed the red bug bites on his ankles but was soon encouraged to retreat by mosquitoes breeding in the seepage waters and waiting for rain. Coming back up to the level of the prairie, he regretted leaving that air settled over the creek, which was perceptibly cooler than that on the open prairie. In the still dusk, the campers yet waited for the evening breeze.

Around the campfires, women and children made their beds in the wagons. The men strung hammocks or laid their rolls under wagons. "Almost all the men of the convoy dressed in red flannel, according to the custom of American sailors, and wore a long beard."[16] This red, bobbing in the firelight among the wagons, horses, and cattle, together with myriad fireflies and the barking of coyotes, made a fairy-tale tableau of all who traveled.

Abel Bossereau, from Dr. Savardan's estate in La Sarthe, became especially proficient at hunting, even of snakes. One day Abel killed a fine rattlesnake more than a meter in length; the next day he killed a six-foot-long python. Abel, with his nineteen-year-old eyes, surprised and discomforted Dr. Savardan by diving in front of his white beard to dispatch a viper in a twinkling. A fisherman as well as a hunter, and despite Savardan's prohibition, Abel stuck his leg in every hole to fish. One day he pulled out a big black snake that had bitten the upper part of his left hand. After the wound was washed, squeezed, and sucked twice, Abel showed no effects from the bite.[17] Wolski was told by settlers that a rattlesnake bite was incurably deadly. Settlers advised him, for snakebites, colonists must have ready at all times a small tinderbox, a piece of meat, some gunpowder, ammonia, and a flask of whiskey. After sucking the wound, spread gunpowder over the spot and burn it, then cover the bite with a handkerchief soaked in ammonia. Finally, the person should drink as much whiskey as he could hold, a whole bottle of it if possible.

Sickness also came to dog them. Ex-lieutenant Vesian repeatedly became inexplicably irritable, with his disagreements gradually growing into threats. He succored his fatigue with liquor, making his health visibly worse. Dr. Savardan finally invoked his authority to limit Vesian's outbursts, while Vesian countered that he had authority from Considerant. At last the despondent man asked to be allowed to take a society horse and leave in advance so that he could announce the group's arrival and sooner rest at La Réunion. Since they were at Chambers Creek, impatience overflowed after twenty days on the road. Bussy, since he had his own horse, asked Savardan to let him go ahead and to allow his servant, Robert Martin, to take a society horse and accompany Vesian. Henri Montreuil, a young Paris notary who had his own horse, jumped to follow the two older men and Vesian. This left no more saddle horses with the group, now twenty-nine.

The landscape changed and changed again as they traveled toward their destination. Little prairies with small forests became larger prairies separated by large forests and then an immense forest. Some of the French were entirely unprepared for the wilderness of Texas. Hipolithe Barret, a well-known riding master and gymnast from Saumur, became lost in a forest crossing the Navasota.[18] Barret had achieved great discipline over his own body and over that of a horse, but having spent the night lost in a forest, his mental discipline failed him, and he became terrified through his imaginings of fearsome Mexicans and Indians in the patterns of trees. Badly crazed by his experience, he stayed within a hundred feet of the convoy at all times thereafter. Barret rode a horse of his own, and after the departure of the four other horsemen, he was the only mounted person left by the time the convoy reached Lancaster, fifteen miles from their goal.

Needing two or three pairs of oxen to reinforce the flagging teams, Savardan could not persuade Barret to ride those last few miles alone to La Réunion. He had to set out himself to seek help. Savardan spent the day getting his buggy and horse across Ten and Five Mile, Cedar and Coombs Creeks, which he termed abominable, and came at last to the edge of the chalky mesa and La Réunion. Translator Edmund Roger endeared himself to Dr. Savardan by volunteering to ride back to the caravan with the news that there were no oxen that could help them to reach La Réunion. They would have to make their own way as best they could for two more nights on the prairie. Even with the drought, May brought storms on the prairie, as Dr. Savardan wrote home:

> Yesterday one of those storms as the newspapers tell you about sometimes, and of which we only have very rare examples in France. It was at the end of the day, at about a mile from our camp; we were going toward an electrical storm cloud that only showed us its existence by some rather infrequent flashes of lightning. All at once with a deafening clap of thunder, a torrential and very cold rain pounced on us without letup. . . . [M]y horse that, following my old habit, I chose among the wise and benevolent types, and who (as God wanted to infuse all inferior creatures) is a model of submission, all at once turned about, in spite of my efforts and in spite of the bridle, and at the risk of breaking and upsetting everything, in which he would have succeeded, if I had not quickly yielded to him. He only wanted . . . to show his rear end to the storm, and that done, he remained as calm and immobile as if the wind was only a puff. But it was altogether different for all the others: several

of our riders and teams passed successively by me, swept away as madmen by a truly awful terror.

The bulk of this scene of confusion lasted more than half an hour, and happily without accident other than our wagon tents carried away and us all soaked to the bone.[19]

As they neared La Réunion, they left the forest and entered an immense flat prairie. Day by day the scrub plants were replaced by more lush vegetation: wild wheat, rye and barley, verbenas, sunflowers of all sizes, and larkspur.

In the afternoon, they rode into a colony situated near the road where they stopped to refresh themselves with sour milk. Wolski asked the host, "Do you know of a Frenchman who bought land nearby?" "Ah, yes," the host responded. "Some five kilometers away a large new building has been put up by this man. It is a big attraction! The neighbors living closest to him are constantly going to look at the building. We only build small houses around here." When Wolski repeated this to his traveling companions, they were overjoyed. They decided to make the remainder of the trip that day and ordered the teamsters to hurry the oxen. Unfortunately, they did not anticipate the riverbed that appeared. "Once again the usual comedy with the oxen would have to be played, and so [they] spent one more night in camp."[20]

15

First Days Building and the Bloom of June

We have everything to create in Texas; thus, we will have to create more than we consume; consequently, we must be true workers there; it is the price of success.

JEAN-BAPTISTE ANDRÉ GODIN

In early March 1855, as soon as agreement on the land was reached, Cantagrel, Reverend Allen, and the two young men accompanying them set up headquarters in the cabin on the Horton section in the lowlands near the Trinity River, the first land for which Cantagrel had contracted. Cantagrel then hired workmen around Dallas County, directed the clearing and plowing of riverside land, bought several pairs of oxen to move trees, stockpiled a good reservoir of logs for future construction, and, on the mesa top, selected a townsite around a small creek. It was there that he began construction of the first sizable building.

To the west, outside the building area, a cedar forest limited the view from the townsite. To the east, beyond the spring and still on the high land, some areas of chalky soil had been cleared of their cedars and left to grow grass among the stumps. Through this snaggy area ran a trail toward Dallas. A mile south, the prairie gave way to mixed hardwoods surrounding a larger creek that was called by the name of its land patentee, Coombs. Trails led off to Pleasant Run and toward Houston and Austin. To the southwest a trail followed the upper edge of an eroded escarpment to a village called Cedar Hill. To the north, the prairie mesa on which the townsite stood fell away precipitously into the forested Trinity River valley. At the bottom of this bluff, a trail north through the rich, alluvial lowland led to the Trinity River, to a rope suspension bridge over its waters, and thence to trails northeast to the village of Cedar Springs and northwest to a tiny hamlet called Buck-and-Breck.

In addition to the first nine or twelve local hands hired by Cantagrel from around the county, another six had come from Cincinnati. In all, twenty-four persons, including one woman, two youths, and two children, were erecting the future colony when Alexandre Raisant, the first of the many colonists who were on their way, rode into this scene the first day of April.[1]

Raisant had ridden west from Shreveport with the news that architect Cousin was leading his charges from New Orleans to Galveston, hoping for better waters to transport colonists up the Trinity River. On reaching the colony site, Raisant found people busy cultivating and constructing. There were the beginnings of a building in a clearing, but not enough hands to ready it and other housing for the Europeans soon to arrive. Two hours after Raisant arrived, a letter came from Cousin on the coast stating that the first pioneers would come overland. And so the same day, Raisant got back on a new horse and rushed south to meet Cousin's caravan. His mission was to detach from the caravan needed builders and double-time them back to the colony site. On the way south, he met Sauzeau and Topin, Frenchmen of their group who had anticipated Raisant and who beat him back to the colony by a week.[2] Seven Belgians followed Raisant back to the colony site to give Cantagrel needed assistance with construction.

Cantagrel's big buildings were unlike anything around. Most days at least a few locals within gossip distance paid a visit to gawk at them. Verandas ran around the four outside walls of the first house. Through the entire depth of that house a wide hall bisected the building. On either side were two large rooms yet without doors or windows, "according to the Texas custom to be found in all the villages."[3] The eating hall held the colony's only furniture, a long table with surrounding benches.[4]

Arriving at last on May 3, Cousin, guide Wolski, and their group saw the large building they had heard about when they stopped to refresh themselves at a nearby settler's home. The report was true. Even more, construction on a second large building had been started, and an isolated kitchen had been set up near the first structure. Wolski admired the remarkable speed with which Cantagrel had managed the construction

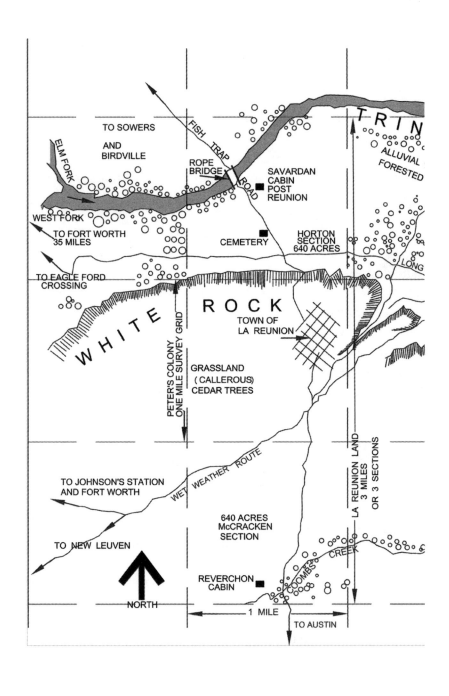

TO SOWERS
AND
BIRDVILLE

ELM FORK

FISH TRAP ROAD

ROPE
BRIDGE

SAVARDAN
CABIN
POST
REUNION

TRIN

ALLUVIAL
FORESTED

WEST FORK

TO FORT WORTH
35 MILES

CEMETERY

HORTON
SECTION
640 ACRES

LONG

TO EAGLE FORD
CROSSING

WHITE   ROCK

TOWN OF
LA REUNION

PETER'S COLONY
ONE MILE SURVEY GRID

GRASSLAND
(CALLEROUS)
CEDAR TREES

LA REUNION LAND
3 MILES
OR 3 SECTIONS

TO JOHNSON'S STATION
AND FORT WORTH

WET WEATHER ROUTE

TO NEW LEUVEN

640 ACRES
McCRACKEN
SECTION

COMBS CREEK

NORTH

REVERCHON
CABIN

1 MILE

TO AUSTIN

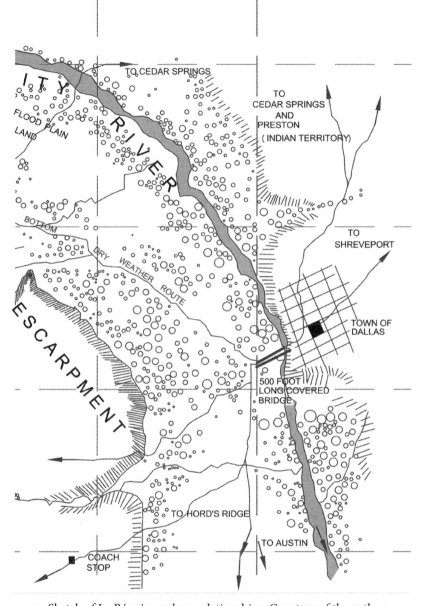

TO CEDAR SPRINGS

TY RIVER

FLOOD PLAIN LAND

BOTTOM

DRY WEATHER ROUTE

ESCARPMENT

TO
CEDAR SPRINGS
AND
PRESTON
(INDIAN TERRITORY)

TO
SHREVEPORT

TOWN OF
DALLAS

500 FOOT
LONG COVERED
BRIDGE

TO HORD'S RIDGE

TO AUSTIN

COACH
STOP

12. Sketch of La Réunion colony relationships. Courtesy of the author.

and credited the American laborers, who, "it is true, they demand to be paid lavishly, [but they] work at the same time with tireless energy."[5]

When Cousin and Wolski's caravan finally stood in front of the big building, they realized their camping life was not over. Cantagrel had as yet only provided them with a wooden roof instead of the canvas one they had become used to on the trail. It began to dawn on them that they might be camping for many more months.

They removed their goods from the carts. Each found a spot in one of the four rooms where he could stake out a space with his mattress and trunk. For the month they had been on the trail, everyone had endured discomforts because they were temporary. But here at La Réunion it was clear they faced a continuing lack of privacy and war with insects. Wasps and flies joined them under the roof. "It would have been better if Cantagrel had put up say a dozen or more small houses. Here such houses can be built with extraordinary speed. Then each family could have had separate quarters. One or two of the bachelors who got along well with each other could have gone together, and so escaped the communism, which, even if only temporary, was so distressing to all." Wolski was apprehensive that there would be a certain amount of discontented "murmuring."[6]

Wolski was not one to overlook housing options for himself. Hearing from Roger that a two-celled cabin existed down the bluff a mile or more to the north, Wolski petitioned Cantagrel to let him, Cousin, and Roger occupy it. Cantagrel had to stay on top of the bluff to manage the enterprise, and Reverend Allen had moved to the top of the bluff with his son. The twelve other adults and nine youth and children, including two families, would stay in Cantagrel's new building.

As the light faded that early May evening, Wolski and Cousin stood for the first time on the bluff overlooking the darkening forest. The medium-green cottonwoods formed a sinuous line in the distance, rising forty feet above the other trees, still bathed in horizontal sunlight against the black below. Edmund Roger explained to Vincent and Wolski that the trees marked the river course, otherwise invisible under the leaf canopy. On a trail down the bluff flanked with delicate, deeply serrated leaves of dwarf oaks, Roger led the newcomers toward the forest. They saw in the dark-green distance a small cleared patch of light green in the alluvial plain framing a cabin. This was the settler's lonely cabin near the river that had sheltered Cantagrel, Reverend Allen, Roger, and Lawrie two months before.

Near the bottom of the bluff, the small shin oaks with a unique dappled bark, growing on their white rock ledges, gave way to grasses that sloped down to a line of trees. Passing into the trees, the men walked north to the clearing they had seen from above and reached their cabin. That first soft May night at La Réunion the three men, full of hope, congratulated themselves on their arrival: "Despite the hardships of the day's journey and the unpacking of the carts, almost the whole of that first night the three of [us] spent in front of our little house, exchanging impressions, discussing the things that had happened on . . . [the] journey, and marveling at the starry majesty of that ravishing night."[7] While the men sat on stumps at the Horton cabin under the velvet dome, the breeze blew softly and fireflies flew in a stately manner, occasionally broadcasting their languid green light signal. A chorus of frogs sang from the river. Considerant's Eden cast its spell over them.

After inspecting the area in daylight, guide Wolski began his war with nature by attacking the snakes that feasted near the river and preferred to nest under the cabin floor. Back on the bluff at breakfast the next morning, the men heard the ten of their companions on the *Uriel* and *Lexington* who had been wielding axes and froes now for two weeks tell of their experiences. Snakes were part of those experiences.

While the rest settled in, Raisant took pen and paper from his bag, sat under a tree, and dashed a letter to Paris:

We dream still of expanding towards the northwest. Considerant, who should arrive from New York in a few days, will decide for us in this regard. In a country where, so to speak, only corn is grown, the inhabitants have been simple enough to let their whiskey come from New Orleans at an insane price. It is the same with shoes and a thousand things for which we have the raw material. It goes without saying that we will not follow this example. The railroad that must cross Texas is already started, with activity at different points in the country; it will pass twenty miles from Dallas and the most peopled country of the world.[8] Now, in a state that is as large as France, one counts no more than 300,000 inhabitants. Up to now there is scarcely any interest in mining. I myself have seen iron in profusion and on the surface of the ground coming from Shreveport to Dallas, 70 miles from Dallas. Near Preston, and in Indian Territory, coal, iron and slate are in profusion and do not present any difficulty for extraction.[9] The Indians are the most charming men in the world; I believe that their women would be more beautiful than ours if they had lighter complexions. Today there are many who are quite rich; they work, they have their machines, their young ladies are dressed in the French manner. I believe that they have been much maligned. The pillagers were none other than white skins disguised in red skins. These Indians like the French very much. They will gladly make them perpetual concessions without cost. Their country is magnificent.

Until we have the railroad, communications will be somewhat difficult to get to us, all the same. Meanwhile, we will have our wagons moving back and forth to the north and south. . . . The plan is magnificent and I am very sure will attract the curious. The water gushes out of five springs from these hills, and goes spreading over the valley. It is excellent and always abundant in every season. We have made an immense basin in one of them in order to be able to bathe.

He added a cryptic sentence at the end: "I would have yet much to say, if I did not want to keep myself in the positive."[10]

Wolski saw the other new arrivals in his group, like all good Frenchmen, first attack their food problem: "On the second day after our arrival here, that is on the fourth of May, our gardeners selected quite a piece of ground for a kitchen garden. They fenced it in and began to dig it up. Then they planted various kinds of seeds brought from Europe. They laid it out attractively and neatly, and made little paths where one could walk of an evening."[11]

But they were too late in the spring. The followers discovered what Considerant had not: the sun, so beneficent in other countries, burns mercilessly in Texas. Watering night and morning does no good and is besides too much of an effort. Their water source for filling kegs was a spring some distance away. On an errand in Dallas, Wolski asked a settler if the harsh sun was normal. They answered, yes, in fact, few vegetables are found. The only way to grow them is to plant them in the midst of rows of corn, the stalks providing shade. And watering the vegetable plants actually harms them if they are not shaded. Helpful advice for next year, Wolski thought, but too late for this year. Wolski now knew that the months of April to October, which are so delightful in France, change this place "into a sorrowing waste."[12]

Cantagrel was pressed for time. But for that, he might have waited for architect Daly, who was traveling with Considerant, to help give an aesthetic form to the physical layout of the townsite, for they had all worried over and discussed the proper image for their cause during the past twenty years. But Cantagrel made physical decisions immediately, as he had to prepare shelter for the hundred people about to arrive. After all, he was an architect and engineer himself. He did not follow Major Arnold's plan for Fort Worth, a place turned inward and focused on a public space—the parade ground—and where a palisade surrounded all buildings as defense from Indians. Nor did he lay his town out as John Neeley Bryan and Coho Smith had done for Dallas, with square blocks extending out from a central one containing the seat of justice, an important symbol of civilization on the lawless frontier. And in Dallas the streets were open-ended, ready to grow into the wilderness.

Cantagrel lived up to his French heritage by laying out an orthography like Baron Haussmann's latest model for civic design then under way in Paris. Ironically, the emperor was commanding Haussmann to cut grand, straight boulevards diagonally from one point to another so that the populace could no longer barricade the narrow, crooked streets and disrupt this self-proclaimed emperor's control.

On the North Texas frontier, Cantagrel, a Republican who was no friend of the emperor, imitated the emperor's plan for Paris. Cantagrel began with a street parallel to a small draw, or streamlet, and being from northern Europe, where sun was prized, he anticipated a need for his future platted properties to receive sun on all four faces during the day, a tradition of Latin surveyors established in Texas before its revolution. Cantagrel was bringing culture to the wilderness and did not want to lay out just any old pragmatic frontier settlement like those of the Americans he had seen everywhere. His had to be distinguished.

Cantagrel also had to hurry, with his compatriots from Europe soon to descend on him. The choice for the townsite location within the sections he purchased had been in part, he reminded himself, dictated by the speed of the state of Texas in issuing land patents. In the nascent county of Dallas, so far from state government, most people did not bother with legal formalities until they had a reason to prove their possession. Leven G. Coombes and his wife, Jane, had rushed to Austin once they saw the prospect of gold on the horizon for their land.[13] Coombes had received a patent on March 16, giving him the ability to legally transfer ownership to Cantagrel, who could then be secure in committing work to a particular spot for construction.[14]

Hearing town gossip that Cantagrel had actually bought two tracts of land and was contracting for more in the first week of April, J. Wellington Latimer, representing the *Dallas Herald,* interviewed Cantagrel. Latimer had been in the village publishing a newspaper for some six years.[15] It had grown enough to become a weekly and for Latimer to hazard adding Swindells to the staff a year before.[16] The *Dallas Herald* reported the interview, in which Cantagrel acquitted himself and his enterprise well. The *Northern Standard* echoed the *Herald* a few days later, wishing the Colonization Society success.[17] The attack by the *Gazette* in Austin the previous February seemed distant. As soon as news of the endorsement reached Paris, the *Bulletin* of the Colonization Society used the warm Texas welcome to point others toward investment.[18]

On May 16 Cantagrel reported to Paris that fifty-one people were now present at the site. A "Furyite," as the census-taker called Reverend John Allen and his son from Massachusetts, along with one of Allen's brothers-in-law from New York, had been the first on the land with Cantagrel and his Belgian medical student translator. A half dozen American workers recruited in Cincinnati arrived with a sawmill and other equipment to begin building. A French miner family of four adrift in Texas thought they saw an opportunity to settle; a Cabetist who had already become a settler in Dallas, as well as the son of another Cabetist newly immigrated to find his father, joined them. A former North American Phalanx member probably came overland from New Jersey. Four exiled French anarchists, bored with being marooned in

Belgium, arrived with Cousin. Five young Belgian architects just out of school and an older one from Louvain rushed to help with what they thought would be their first chance to practice their profession. A teen-age son of an exiled French deputy, another scion of a major Belgian investor, a Belgian poet, exiled news writers, Republicans out of place under the emperor's new government, a Polish and a French engineer, two doctors, and a Belgian accountant all followed Considerant's words as first "pioneers." Also attracted to this migration in New Orleans was a French tailor and a Parisian family of seven led by a seasoned construc-tion superintendent, Pierre Frichot. He and Raisant, of all these people, understood American scale, as they had traveled in the country before. They came a second time sensing opportunity and waited expectantly with the others for their leader to arrive.

16

Confronting the Vision

Considerant's group—four men, three women, and two infants—rode light and relatively fast, not burdened with oxen or heavy baggage. Most nights their sleeping accommodations were the hammocks they brought from Paris hung between the trees. However, when they passed through Anderson, they slept at the Fanthrop Inn. There a rocking chair for Josephine Cantagrel to nurse the baby was a welcome luxury. César Daly rode beside them to translate. With two former members of the North American Phalanx, Louis Willemet to cook, and Jules Haizé to drive the horses hitched to the gig, Considerant, the ladies, and Daly maintained some semblance of their own views of their station in life. They reserved their energies to tend to their own toilets and rest after their day's twenty miles of jostling, jarring bumps. The exception was Josephine's caring for her baby and small son. There were no maids to handle diapers and linen, duties none of these three women would have handled at home. The baby had to be held, as the gig was too small for a bassinet next to all the luggage.

Already at the colony site since March 9 and dribbling in since April were over twelve American men and women, as well as over forty émigrés and Fourierists, French and Belgian immigrants, working furiously while acclimating to their stunning new surroundings. As Josse Vrydagh, a young Belgian architect, described, "Toward the South, the ground is elevated in hills. From these hills, when you turn your eyes toward the North, you see a magnificent spectacle. At the foot of the hill is a prairie bordered by woods resembling—I don't know what to compare it to because I have never seen nature such as this. The English gardens compared to this prairie view from the heights are as faded artificial roses to the natural ones in gardens."[1]

All these first arrivals assembled at La Réunion could be proud of what they had accomplished in under three months. While Cantagrel crisscrossed the county checking on surveys, looking for sellers, and buying sections of land, Reverend Allen and the hired Americans plowed. They planted Reverend Allen's grape root cuttings on the chalky mesa.[2] They tended the inherited wheat acreage, planted crops in the rich lowland, and built fences. They bought oxen. They felled trees, cut and froed them to become construction logs, and coached the oxen to drag them to the future village site. A Dallas saw mill supplied cut lumber. Belgians arriving helped the Americans finish erecting the walls and roofs of two large buildings, the wonder of local settlers because of their size. They raised other smaller buildings. They built a second corral and a saddlery and added a smokehouse. Three streamlets seemed to produce adequate water; one had been dammed. A wellhead was under construction.

On May 30 first one member of the colony and then another saw the dust kicked up along the road by men on horses and a small gig. "He is here! Considerant has arrived!" An echo rang through the site. Considerant and his party had covered the distance from Houston to Considerant's promised land in just fourteen days. The men at the site gathered around the newcomers, shaking hands and helping the women and children from the gig. Cantagrel came running from the building site to greet his wife, Josephine, his son, and his infant daughter.

Stepping out of the gig and turning his head from side to side, Considerant at once absorbed the reality of the quickly built shelters. He stood with Cantagrel and a few other workers, staring at the new structures. Then, making no allowance for time, place, tools, or the pioneers' ingenuity, energy, and goodwill, he dismissed Cantagrel's two big buildings, large and unique in local settlers' eyes, calling them "mastodons."[3]

There may have been a laugh in his voice, but underneath, his listeners felt criticism. In contrast to translator Wolski, who saw at La Réunion an Eden with a few problems, Considerant felt scorn. Could not the leader of their new utopia see the enormous work they had done for him?

The twenty who had come on the first two ships began to remember that Considerant had promised to meet them at the dock in New Orleans but did not. He had not traveled with them to Galveston. Nor had he cheered them on as they prepared to leave Houston for a painful month's walk; instead, he had left them in the dust of his pretty surrey.

As Considerant silently walked the land and observed the new construction, everything was becoming more and more indeterminate. Cantagrel had bought all this land, all of these colonists had descended on him, and more were coming. Dr. Jean Nicolas would arrive with eight more colonists ten days later, and in less than another week some thirty-five under Dr. Savardan would appear—and there were these crude buildings. Considerant stood with hands on hips and stared at the enormous structures. He shook his head. His imagination had projected whitewashed building walls set amid gardens in rows around a quadrangle, a kind of civility in the army-imposed order that he had seen two years ago at Major Merrill's Fort Worth, not the rough unfinished structures he faced. And, from the evidence of his mood in New Orleans, what Considerant had learned upon landing in America had already instilled in him a prejudice against his colony by the time he reached it. After Considerant had heard in February from Texan congressmen in Washington that lands in North Texas were now reserved for railroad building incentives, a young New England farmer, recently back in New York from San Antonio, had contacted him. Frederick Law Olmsted had become impressed with the character of the Germans there and advocated Free-Soil for western Texas. In his campaign to keep slavery out of the western half of the state, he sought to send Considerant's colony west of the Nueces. From New York, Considerant, after this encounter, had written Jean Godin in Guise that perhaps they should seek land in the west or on the Nueces or the Rio Grande.[4] Godin's rebuttal now reached Considerant upon his arrival at La Réunion: "A climate too hot? The Comanches? We want to work for the pacification of humanity under the auspices of a friendly nature, and not to organize war against savages in a hostile climate! Is the state of things such that you should think of going elsewhere?" Godin's reaction put Considerant in another kind of bind, restricting his choices from another direction. Bleeding Kansas was out.

Indian Territory was closed to Europeans. Seeking a home on the western plains would be "straying from the natural means of communication."[5]

As Considerant looked down at the prairie below he wondered. Now there might not be the double advantage of this "theater of operations" of which he had written in *Au Texas*—accruing wealth in land speculation and creating homes for Fourierists in great phalanxes. These crude buildings only reinforced Godin's chiding that Considerant should stop writing and seize the moment. He had written a book about, had theorized about, a communal Versailles. He dreamed of a planned, rationally ordered, rectilinear home set in bucolic nature. These buildings before him did little more than provide shade under their verandas from the increasingly hot sun and only served as campsites free of dew. Considerant went mute, failing completely to report to the Paris management.

And Considerant hid from himself as well. He of all people was not at fault, he thought to himself. Others had blundered and created a mess of his vision. Cantagrel, his dedicated friend, had this March been responsible. As Cantagrel now felt cold water, not praise, he stood next to their leader and ran through the events of the last few months. He had been under enormous pressure to find land and get shelters built for 130 people, dutifully following Considerant's orders. He had been an effective engineer for Fourierists and for Considerant. He had had no time to reflect on carefully conceived building plans while he was riding boundaries over the county as he looked for more land. Trying to lay out a future town on the diagonal principles of Paris, a plan partly generated by small streamlets, might work when built and filled out, but it was not at all evident with only these few scattered and rude buildings extant. Cantagrel knew that to Considerant, all this appeared thoughtless and without order. And for Considerant, these shelters were not contributing to a phalanstery; they were only making it harder for him to find a new site. That depressed him further.

Within moments of Considerant's arrival, it was evident to Cantagrel that their leader presumed special treatment for himself. He already had illustrated that by traveling separately and arriving in an expensive gig. Matched horses and a gig were a waste of resources! Matched grays, at four times the cost of ordinary horses, were not necessary to pull a conveyance. Considerant, on the other hand, assumed that he had to project the image of a powerful empresario. Rather than seeing his purchases as a double standard, he saw the gig and horses as needed comforts for the ladies in his life and for Josephine Cantagrel with a baby and a young child.

On this next to the last day of May, Cantagrel could only offer Considerant the promise in three more weeks of a small cabin for Considerant's family when he, Cantagrel, would ready one for his own. Cantagrel planned for Considerant, as well as for his own family, the construction of separate quarters apart from these communal shelters.[6]

Now standing on the land with Cantagrel, the executive agent, Considerant again had confirmation from his faithful follower that great empty domains were unattainable and that Cantagrel had spent seven times the going rate, in precious dollars, for a single section of land next to this townsite. Considerant did not want to face the reality but likely only thought of another empty, remote domain for social experiments while temporizing about all that concerned La Réunion. Could he become a railroad promoter to get land, as Godin in Guise suggested was an option? Should he follow Olmsted's advice, even though he might become entangled with slavery issues or Indians? Should he try to merge with the Peters group in Texas as Godin asked? With all the bad odor of lawsuits between settlers and the Peters Company, it would seem a bad idea. Was his vision at La Réunion to become nothing but a failed second edition of Cabet's Icarie? He did not confide his thoughts to those around him, but Considerant's actions soon showed his rejection of La Réunion.

Within weeks of his arrival, all the paid American help that Cantagrel hired had left or been dismissed—but for one, Johnson, the man Considerant had hired and paid to come from New York. The Americans faded away, many leaving because the executive agent did not want to pay American wages.[7]

To the European Fourierist "pioneers," as Considerant called them, he offered far less in ready cash than to the Americans, in fact, cash only for a third of their wages. The other two-thirds were to be invested in stock paying 6 percent a year. This saved the stockholders initial capital, which then could be invested in more land, and allowed much cheaper company operating costs. The enterprise depended on each pulling his or her own weight and on all agreeing to the wage rate system, under which five different levels of pay were assigned to different jobs based on their difficulty.

When Dr. Savardan arrived two weeks after Considerant, he saw in La Réunion a different glass—one that was half full. As he walked the land with Cantagrel, rather than mastodons of ugly buildings, he saw the beautiful view over the Trinity Valley. All could not be done at once, but someday artists among them would paint that view. He hung the portrait of his wife and began.

New arrival Pierre Topin wrote his father, "So we have at last arrived. Cantagrel has found a magnificent domain to buy. Construction has begun on a cliff that has a view! You have to see it—flanked on each side half way up by three beautiful springs. When all this has been cleared, irrigated, landscaped, and cared for as we propose to do, and as we have the means, it will be difficult to find a more beautiful and more agreeable place to be."[8]

Competing visions for what they were about and how they were to proceed in America soon took hold among the immigrant pioneers. Considerant had written in *Au Texas* that there would be space and time for various experiments in living. One could live alone and perform all drudgeries separately, as those now did "in civilization," and buy goods and tools from a company store; or one could share labor and drudgeries in a communal system with cultural assets not normally found on the frontier. Well-financed colonists such as Vincent Cousin wanted to move gradually toward the reconstitution of society.[9]

Others, led conspicuously by Dr. Savardan and Reverend Allen, wanted to immediately organize to live communally in a phalanx. After all, prior to agreeing to join the pioneers, Dr. Savardan had traveled to Brussels and specifically queried Considerant on his view of all sharing food preparation, a laundry, a library, a carriage. Considerant had assured the doctor that their visions were aligned.

One of the first tests was Dr. Savardan's request to open a school now that the Bar family of highly trained teachers had arrived. There were twelve children at the colony, and locals were anxious for their children to join the school. The fee charged to the locals would cover most of the expenses. Yet when Dr. Savardan sat down with Considerant and requested the commencement of the school as promised in Brussels, Considerant ruled that a dozen children were too few. Considerant assigned Mr. Bar to a low-paying position and Mrs. Bar to the laundry.

Then there was the matter of the much-needed irrigation system of farmland from the canal. Dr. Savardan had constructed one at his home in La Chapelle-Gaugain to reach the local spring. He could do the same at La Réunion. But Considerant answered Dr. Savardan's suggestion for irrigation with a paternal smile and "Doctor, your ideas are truly ideas of a giant!"[10]

The organization of farming trades on Fourier's model as proposed by Dr. Savardan would be too difficult, according to Considerant. And it was apparent that Considerant had approved too many artists and not enough people who actually knew how to farm. Dr. Savardan remembered what Henri Fugère, a man of practical disposition, had warned him the past summer. "You are wrong to enlist under the direction of Considerant; that man, whom I have seen at work, is completely incapable of managing men and business."

Besides competing internal debates, by the time the last of Dr. Savardan's forty-three colonists arrived on Cantagrel's site, the Austin papers had been at them again: that summer newspapers were peppered with comments about the French colony come to North Texas. Considerant's "Address to the American People," written in March but only published in April, had now reached Austin. It mistakenly gave fodder to the southern antiabolitionist press and to the Texas Know-Nothings. Said the *Texas State Gazette* in an article titled "The Socialist in Texas" three days after Considerant reached the colony, "We have had enough discussion of the principles of Socialism from Greeley, Brisbane, other fanatics and abolitionists. . . . Whatever may be their *new views*, they are at least not the class of men to do a state any good. We believe them to be a mischievous element of population, did we not believe their wild theories would not long stand the test of experiment, and would soon be abandoned, we might urge our objections more seriously than we have done."[11]

In the same issue a letter from "J.L." in Washington dated May 2, 1855, appealed to the "Southerners of Texas" not to permit that "band of lawless and unprincipled foreigners to settle in our midst." The letter listed six reasons: the purpose of the socialists was to overthrow existing government; they were opposed to Christian morals because that would check their liberties; they were infidels; they condemned marriage and "avow[ed] promiscuous intercourse of the sexes"; they were abolitionists; and "they would divert individual property to their own peculiar organization."

When Considerant read this, he cringed. He had worked very hard to suppress the public knowledge of Fourier's opinions on sex and, indeed, left them out of his three-volume explanation of Fourier's thoughts, *Destinée sociale*, twenty years previous. By and large, he had succeeded in transforming the master's thoughts to conform to bourgeois mores. However, these words struck very close to home in all their points. And the *Texas State Times* offered still more against foreigners.

John Salmon Ford, physician, ranger, and lawyer, had made this paper the foremost spokesman for Know-Nothingism in this its year of ascendancy. The principles that Considerant was advocating were such, said the editor, as the "vilest Red Republicans of France have repudiated, in the most licentious and stormy days of that wavering government." Even though the whole scheme was to be experimental, it would be very much better, so the editor thought, that such experiments should be done by "our own people rather than by a deputation of French philosophers" whose attempts to "half-sole and heel-tap society in days gone by" ended in "miserable failure."[12]

It took three days for such information to reach the colony from the Austin press, and of course few of the European colonists were fluent in English, but the American workers at La Réunion could read. Though for the most part they were committed Associationists, they sensed a hard southern battle threatening. This was another frustration for Considerant. In all his forty-five years, he had never been where he could not use his pen as a device to establish his position via the press. As it turned out, and as Godin had told him a year previous, this was not the time to write, and certainly not the place.

Architect César Daly, a rational Republican but an emotional aristocrat from Paris, had an equivocal role for the stock company and as Considerant's long-time friend. Daly, more than many, was shaken by the reality of the crude frontier now manifest in colony buildings, in the extreme raw nature before them. Yet he intermittently participated in the practical needs of the colony while he was forced much of the time to stay in bed, the results of serious bouts of pneumonia in 1851 and 1854 and now bronchial ailments brought on by the effects of extreme allergic reactions in Texas's worst month of spring.

Still, he responded to a call for help from Dr. Savardan in his first month at La Réunion to assist in the building of a cave to keep perishables cool. For several weeks after his arrival, Dr. Savardan had walked the land in the evening in search of a place that would be convenient and cost little to build. He found the place and called upon his friends to assist. All who participated donated their time to the community, not requesting remuneration for their work. Daly took over the management of digging the cave. The stone cutter laid out the height of the door in the solid rock. Daly designed an entrance door that Savardan described as delineated with "the greatest simplicity, yet with a very satisfying monumental character."[13] It was at that point that Considerant, with his Belgian aides-de-camp Roger and Cousin, confronted the workers, demanding, "You started to make a cave there?" "Yes," they responded, wondering why this would be a problem. The second-guessing began: "But could you not have chosen a better place nearer the kitchen?" The questioning continued. The placement of the cave was moved. Undaunted by this episode, Daly also was helpful in creating a check-out system to control the whereabouts of equipment.[14] Strangely, Daly antagonized his friend Considerant, likely over Considerant's failure to lead. With seasoned architects Cantagrel and Daly present, Considerant in his prideful pique appointed Vincent Cousin as architect of the colony, with disastrous results.

Architects often become consumed by the manipulation of form to the exclusion of other needs in building. At La Réunion Daly had no form, in his terms, with which to be engrossed. From his London childhood and French mother, he could contrast Anglo-Saxon and French ideas.[15] But his émigrée mother had given him French values. There was no bishop with an Albi or a Chartres cathedral to challenge him at La Réunion. The nineteenth-century view of progress that he had expressed in drawings in his *Review* was nowhere yet present in the country of the Three Forks. He was therefore a writer, a publicist, and a fastidious dresser who would mainly hold himself apart as an observer in Texas.[16] The colony, indeed Texas, made him a fish out of water.

In his writings, Daly entirely hid the colony's existence under a year of "travel in America" with those three words. True, he was indisposed a good bit, but when he finally did communicate, he sent to Paris only one sentence on the entire subject of La Réunion: "Considerant will always be as he has been, and will never change." Daly left the colony after three months but fell ill crossing Indian Territory and had to return to La Réunion to recover. He never mentioned La Réunion to Paris again.

In the spring of 1855 Considerant was holding fast to the architectural vision he had conjured in accord with Fourier's precepts back in the 1830s, those images on the walls of the Paris bookstore of the École Sociétaire that showed a major tree-lined way leading from a river to a great square surrounded by buildings on three sides and with wing extensions. This image implied efficient living in enormous ranks of private apartments. Towers, domes, and portals symmetrically added to the facades in good Louvres or Versailles fashion. Interior covered streets allowed people to function in inclement weather. The smaller courtyards provided space for communal sharing of responsibilities, for child care, education, cooking, and cleaning. And there was beauty. The followers of Fourier aspired to prerogatives that the Bourbon kings had enjoyed with formal gardens, fountains, pavilions, and promenades.

Also in this image, opposite the principal facade of the square, the buildings housing workshops and manufacturing "series" echoed the quadrennial order. Smokestacks and less imposing facades demarcated these functions. In the near foreground, overlooking all from atop a hill, five uniformly dressed maidens, one of whom led with a banner and four of whom carried scythes, marched forward. Three men, also sporting scythes, and ten children gaily accompanied them, presumably to reap the harvest. Considerant held these images for his phalanx at Réunion.

All during the spring of 1855, François Cantagrel labored to put land reflecting those grand images under the control of the Colonization Society. He had tried to acquire land adjacent to the south of his town-site almost as soon as he had first invested in the area. The land that he wanted included a running creek and mature tree cover, but his offer had never been enough to dislodge the owners. They sensed his want, smelling blood, until he finally advanced the price to an unheard-of $7.50 an acre! His offer—in gold—for the McCracken section was accepted on May 15.[17] Anson and Mahala Ann McCracken must have rushed to Austin to have their headright recorded so that they could do business with Cantagrel: they received $4,800 from him, agent and trustee of the European American Society of Colonization in Texas, for 640 acres. Dallas speculators and settlers were smug at this new confirmation of their land's worth. Previously, land had commanded fifty cents to a dollar per acre. And McCracken's land wasn't even among that of Dallas County then considered prime.

While the colonists' illusions were confounded by reality, they began to adapt to their new home. By June 1855, some 105 persons needed to be housed and fed. By the end of June, four small buildings had been completed. Considerant and his family were moved to one of the buildings, in another Cantagrel lived with his wife and small children, and the other two housed what they called the staff of the commander-in-chief, the ex-deputies and ex-editors. Architect César Daly was one of those, and accountant Charles Bussy was another.

When Considerant's cabin was finished, the small structure did not suit him. He rejected it, asking Vincent Cousin to build at Considerant's own expense a larger, two-story house with a painting studio for Julie above and separate quarters for his mother-in-law.

The third week of June the colony was faced with its first death. Young Vesian died of typhoid fever on June 21, twelve days after he reached La Réunion. Considerant walked the land with Dr. Savardan, Cantagrel and others, looking for the place to situate the colony's cemetery. Considerant made one of his first decisions, choosing for a cemetery a low-land plot in a handsome grove of trees. Pragmatist Cantagrel argued that they should not waste their best land for that purpose, but

Considerant thought it a nice spot, by a pond, along the trail north to the river.[18] Dr. Savardan was upset at Considerant's choosing a site in low, flood-prone land instead of a hilltop for such a purpose—it was an insult to the dead to not protect them better. But it was Considerant's choice to make. In preparation for the funeral, one of the carpenters made a coffin. Someone gathered flowers after the body was washed and dressed. The colonists followed the coffin down the escarpment trail behind Considerant, who as leader gave this man, whom he had chosen in New York to come gather headrights for his own future and for the other Fourierists in Texas, a graveside eulogy. They cleared the understory near the grave and built a wooden fence around the plot. For the moment, for a marker they settled for the soft, white limestone they found on the escarpment bluff farther west.[19]

Once Considerant arrived on site, it became unclear where leadership really lay. Cantagrel continued his direction of activities necessary to the colony's survival, while Considerant lay on his bed smoking his pipe. Sometimes Considerant gave conflicting directions, undercutting pragmatist Cantagrel. This ambiguity would endure. Considerant often refused to implement ideas that would bring income to the colony and ease the life of the colonists.

A mill carpenter named Pascal offered to make use of the saws and the mills that Godin in Guise had selected and transported to La Réunion at great expense. The equipment had been sitting gathering dust and rust. Pascal knew well how to install the equipment, having owned and constructed his own machine saws and mill, but Considerant deemed him incapable and opened negotiations with Americans to sell the equipment. Pascal recoiled at the idea and asked Considerant if he might demonstrate at his own expense "the usefulness of the mill and saws, and to work them at his own risk and peril in the capacity of contractor." Pascal also offered to "build a distillery for maize, sorghum grass, and wild fruits and to attempt the manufacture of beer."[20] Considerant rejected all of Pascal's suggestions. Discouraged, Pascal left La Réunion.

Dr. Savardan argued for organizing workers in groups, with each group assigned a leader. After much discussion, each individual was assigned work to perform.[21] The "ordre du jour" for one day at the end of June showed that Considerant had appointed five others along with himself "chefs d'ordre." Cantagrel and Savardan were understandable as surrogate chiefs. Architects Cousin and Daly were theoretically needed for construction. But what made Considerant choose translator Edmund Roger as a chief? Roger was no leader. Why not Reverend John Allen? Considerant acknowledged that Reverend Allen had been responsible for much of the early success in organizing. Perhaps Considerant responded to either his own or other colonists' French prejudice. The French should be in charge; it was their money.

Considerant's vision for a self-sustaining utopian community included agriculture and a garden, but not just any garden. He had hired on salary Alexis Barbot, a vigorous journeyman and market gardener from the suburbs of Paris, to be the general director of horticulture, although Dr. Savardan said Barbot knew nothing about farming. Barbot planted a large garden with nursery stock from France that had first rested from its ocean crossing at Buffalo Bayou and then was trundled north by Alexandre Raisant and planted in uniform geometric patterns.

The order of work this day in June showed Reverend Allen as busy at a variety of essential jobs: planting potatoes with three others, repairing a road, fabricating pipe for a pump, and hunting wild grapes. The grapes were not yet ripe, but Reverend Allen, because of his recent background in growing them as a vintner in Indiana, was out spotting them in the bottomlands for harvest later in the summer, perhaps while he shot game with the new gun Considerant brought him from Belgium. He certainly was checking on the five hundred cuttings he had had carried from Patriot, now in good chalky ground on a Texas mesa top.

Three men were caring for the horses, pulling burrs from their withers, brushing and saddling them for the day. Two mountain men from Hautes-Alpes were scouring the brambles of creek draws, seeking to find contented hidden cattle so as to round them up and ride herd with a young buck teenager and an American from the North American Phalanx in New Jersey. Not far from the kitchen, one was butchering as summer smoke fanned out from the improvised chimney over some curing meat. Three men in the twelve-acre field now turned golden with mature grain bound, hauled, and threshed the wheat. On this second day of summer, with water already drying up in the three springs that had seemed so copious a month before, two were hauling water from the river, two others were digging a well, and two more were making barrels.

Two youths were at their early morning ritual, sitting under cows milking before sending them out to pasture and bringing their product to the kitchen. Two men were covering the live yeast, punching down a great trough of dough, and pulling hot loaves out of the portable metal oven, of which they complained. Nearby, three women were cleaning utensils left from early morning use, stirring pots for the dinner meal in the kitchen building, and trying to keep order among ten children and youths assigned to help them. Five other women were doing small washes in pails and feeding wood to a fire under a cast-iron pot of water. On one of the verandas in the morning shade six women sat mending and sewing.

The cobbler was busy, along with two tailors cutting out fabric to keep workers in pants and shirts. One of them, Jean Priot, who had joined in New Orleans, was becoming concerned about pay. He had not agreed to the proposal of one-third cash salary, with two-thirds being invested in the colony. He was preparing for a demand for payment with a long list of all his work to date. (A few weeks later Priot had had enough of La Réunion and his lack of pay. He left for Dallas, hired a lawyer, and sued Considerant for his money. When Considerant was served a summons, he hired a lawyer. At the first hearing, Considerant's lawyer asked the judge to require Priot to post bond in the amount for which Priot was suing. The judge agreed. Since Priot had no money, given the fact that he was not paid at La Réunion, the case was dismissed.)

Two men turned dirt to begin the big garden under the direction of Barbot, who considered himself above manual labor and only watched. Considerant and Barbot had already decided this was to be a formal French garden, organized as André Le Nôtre, principal gardener of Louis XIV, would have designed it. Vegetable plants were organized in designs inside borders of other plants. Large glass houses were to hold exotics and tender plants.

Doctors Nicolas and Savardan, alumni of their own long garden experience in La Sarthe and Hautes-Alpes, had an immediate visceral rejection of the expenditure of energy in this formal garden fashion at such an early stage in harnessing the wilderness. The doctors watched Barbot in his big garden squander over $3,000 in funds on walls, irregular canals, long sandy paths, the planting of pepper trees in geometric patterns, and those great glass hothouses.

They almost immediately went off to clear a few acres in a valley off the side of the mesa toward the village of Dallas for a more pragmatic result in vegetable produce. They also saw their own work leading to a pleasant, organized-out-of-nature idle in which to walk for recreation after hours. It would be a place of order, free of the endless chaos of out-of-place plants around them. Considerant and Cantagrel came to observe. Considerant sat on a dead tree trunk and said, "Well, so you want to destroy this thicket?" In response, the gardeners reminded him, "We have cultivated gardens all our lives." Without deigning to respond, Considerant rose and walked away.

Four Americans were off felling trees in cedar brakes to the southwest while two were hauling logs back to building sites near the edge of the bluff. Two others were improving a road east toward Dallas. On the building site, eight of the Europeans were putting their axes and froes to the logs brought them to produce lumber for more needed buildings and enclosures, while two were making bricks, filling wooden molds from piles of clay, sand, and straw, and turning them out into improvised racks to dry. Six finish carpenters were trimming out buildings, fitting shutters, doors, latch strings, and shelving, and making elemental furniture.

Until a few acres of corn ripened from the first harvest and their gardens began producing, the colonists were dependent on food they had hauled from Houston, what meats and birds they could catch in the forest or slaughter from their beginning herd, their small wheat harvest, and what they could buy in Dallas. That day in June two colonists were hauling supplies from Dallas with translator Wolski. When they returned, the goods were placed in the care of a former member of the North American Phalanx who oversaw the supply shed, chinking it to keep out field mice. Eleven persons were indisposed that day, principally from boils caused by microscopic insects and a few cases of diarrhea.

Doctors Savardan and Nicholas and medical student Roger administered to them. Only a fourteen-year-old was actually sick; he had jumped in the river when he was overheated. There was very little fever. Raisant, who had twice taken the responsibility to gallop to Houston and back to hurry needed trades to the building sites, all after he had raced across the prairies from Shreveport, was not on the complement list of June 22. Sick in Houston in early June, he was recovering or directed the Swiss in improving a road from the bayou landing to the colony way station and had already assumed management of the Houston farm along with Rupert Nussbaumer.

Finally, besides the women accounted for in the kitchen and laundry, the complement listed seven other women, most wives of *gros-bonnets*, as critics among the workers called the leaders. Class dictated these women to be above duties. Though Fourier had spoken of it and Considerant had introduced a motion in the Chamber of Deputies to liberate women, the men of the colony all forgot that point in Fourier's teachings. And the wives of *gros-bonnets* found it in their personal interests to easily forget to pick up the laundry soap or scrub brush. As a footnote to Fourier's notion of equality, women earned four cents an hour, while the men were paid up to ten cents an hour.

As for the rest, one colonist stated:

Here each of us works where he is needed. A professor of music (Mr. Steere) cuts stone with his friends. . . . A former Anglican pastor, Universalist, Mr. Allen, goes at four in the morning to round up the oxen, and plant sweet potatoes, peas, beans, with me. The same Allen kills the beef to eat, strips off the hide, etc. Roger, the doctor, carries shingles over a rope bridge on his back to the West Fork; goes to buy provisions at farmers' houses in the neighborhood, and brings back on horseback up to 6 or 10 dozen unwrapped eggs, without any cushion at all, not even hay, except the basket, at a great trot for three miles without breaking one. Cousin, architect, cooks the bread, serves the potage twice to each, etc., (the job of the grocer).

Everyone, or at least almost everyone, did a bit of everything.

Then there was the serious business of coping with Texas nature. Women had to guard constantly not only themselves but also children from innumerable insects and poisonous plants: gnats, chiggers, sand ticks, wood lice, bed bugs, mosquitoes, flies, poison ivy, smilax sticker vines, stinging nettle, tarantulas, scorpions, centipedes, mason wasps, snakes, wolves, coyotes, wild cats, skunks, and alligators greeted the Europeans, who were accustomed to poppies in the fields of Europe—a nature tamed and benign under temperate skies. Mme Despars, a cook in the early days of the colony, was bitten by a copperhead, the most poisonous of snakes. She was given a Texas folk cure: the wound sucked to remove the venom, the spot spread with gunpowder and burned, a handkerchief soaked in ammonia laid over it, and as much whiskey as she could hold poured down her throat under protest.

But life at the colony was not all work. On Sundays there were expeditions into the creek and river bottoms to find what the settlers called "hog plums." When their fruits turned a gorgeous salmon-rose color, they made marvelous jelly and preserves. There was also the grape to be found: "The last Sunday in July, we went to pick a wild early grape, very common in the woods. This harvest was conducted with much pomp. A wagon pulled by two pairs of oxen carried the food, two empty barrels and the lady harvesters. We gathered, without much difficulty, about two loads of grapes and returned as true winemakers, crowned with vine branches and flowers. Our convoy gravely made the tour of our buildings and with much spirit we sang 'Friends, among us, happiness will be reborn.'"

This small wild grape, with very dark blue-purple thick skin, red on its inner side, contrasting its light green pulp, festooned the forests near watercourses. The lady harvesters likely continued the ritual of gathering by lifting their skirts to dance in the tubs piled with grapes as the fruit gave up its juice. Then those with wine-making experience added sugar to cut the extreme astringency and hoped for something drinkable out of the effort. Later in the season, in the bottomlands came a pecan harvest, considered a rare cash crop by the settlers but unknown to the Europeans. They soon learned to flail the trees, or "shell them," as the settlers described the process of reaching distant branches with poles to knock the small, thick-shelled nuts loose from their carapaces.

Victor Considerant's wife, Julie, held an evening cedar salon for select colonists. Near the dwellings at La Réunion was a small woods overgrown with cedars. Mme Considerant transformed this cool retreat into a salon. After the work of the day, colonists were invited to enter the vault of green branches. They sat on the rug she placed on the floor of the woods or rocked in one of the hammocks hung from tree to tree above the snakes and the insects below. By the bright light of the moon, they enjoyed their conversations, often until one or two in the morning.[22]

And there were other social events this first summer at La Réunion. The colonists held dances on Sundays, to which they invited the locals. The locals were at first scandalized that dances would be held on the day held sacred to most Americans. Americans did their dancing on Saturdays. Reverend Allen used his oratory skill and succeeded, after several speeches to the locals who attended the balls out of curiosity, in making them understand that in France they did not have two days of rest, one devoted to religion and the other, Saturday, devoted to pleasure. In France these two things, both essential in different degrees, shared the same day.

As Josse Vrydagh, a twenty-three-year-old architect, wrote home to Belgium:

> Already we see that the beautiful sex is here. Last Sunday everyone was dressed up and decked out like the Sunday race to church. Today, Sunday, June 24, I hear songs in the other house, a violin. We're practicing a chorus to go to Dallas the 4th of July. . . . This evening after dinner there is a dance on the lawn. The program promises refreshments. In fact, we are hearing the violin and flute. Some couples venture out, a little shy, a little embarrassed, and then it livens up. Each person gets a mug of beer. We haven't drunk any for three months, and even as bad as it is, it seems delicious to us. Waltzes and quadrilles follow each other, and at 10 we retire.[23]

One of the Brochier brothers, a man from the Hautes-Alpes, added, "The women and girls make garlands and bouquets to decorate the site. The Americans and their ladies come from rather far."

Life at La Réunion had begun.

17

―――

Trying Out Life

At the latitude of the Three Forks, before September 20 the heat always breaks. In the hard hot summer sky on the horizon in the northwest at sunset, a low line of clouds full of lightning may promise rain; during the evening they will push away the last hot air with a fresh moist and cooling breeze, ending summer. To be sure, there are hot days well into October, but never with hot nights after mid-September.

At La Réunion, as the weather cooled, dining was moved within the big hangar space, with four large tables set up around the room. "Each of these was served with a large bowl of soup and a great platter of meat, which was passed around the table; but it was unfortunate for . . . those who received the platter last. Very often the plate was empty and it was not always easy to obtain additional food, especially if one was not in the good graces of the maître d'hôtel." For food costs, "the consumers were divided into four categories. The men paid 22 sous per day; the women 18 sous; the children from six to twelve years of age, 12 sous; and the children under six, 6 sous. A communistic table is then evidently an aristocratic institution in which, and for each of the categories, the nobility is represented by the big eaters. That nobility has, for its claims, powerful stomachs, jaw strength, quick movements, which establish in fact its right to extra portions over the people represented there with less energetic physical constitutions and more timid characters."[1]

In the fall of 1855, the colony of La Réunion was showing a few hints of success. More than a hundred La Réunion colonists had been settled on the land for five months. Eight days of rain had recently washed away the extreme dryness. Some 12,900 acres of land in western Dallas County had been optioned or purchased. The Belgian parent corporation in August had turned over to the settlers the management of the lands purchased, called the Company of Réunion. It then became these settlers' responsibility to earn a profit for the European investors, as well as for themselves. One of these properties included a sawmill, so sawn lumber became much cheaper. Myriad plant cuttings, seeds, and pips shipped overseas had been safely stowed and were now growing outside Houston on land bought along Buffalo Bayou. By midfall several buildings had been erected on the site. The company store was beginning to do business outside the colony, as it offered products such as brandied peaches not otherwise available in frontier villages; the keeper of the labor books, Auguste Savardan, reported with satisfaction its $200 to $300 a month in sales. The colonists had harvested wild grapes and put up the first vintage of wine.

But fall also brought the further deterioration of Rupert Nussbaumer's health, which had been in decline since the summer. At the Houston farm, around the end of July, Nussbaumer, forty-eight, who had spent his adult life in Paris and whose wife and family were still there, developed intermittent fever.[2] As a representative of the colony, he managed the Houston nursery station until the end of July. Then he came north to escape the yellow fever season. At Réunion on August 22, Rupert came down with another attack of intermittent fever and sought care from Dr. Savardan, his phalansterian friend for eight years. There had been only two other such cases, and those were among the Swiss when they arrived six weeks previously.

The doctor prescribed quinine, sending the fever away within two days. However, Nussbaumer soon developed violent pains in his bladder and intestines, pains to which he had been subject over several years. On September 10 Doctors Savardan and Nicolas, having no leeches available, decided to administer the wet cupping glass to relieve the pain.[3] Two days later, Nussbaumer's pains returned. Considerant, on the insistence of his wife, Julie, intervened and directed Roger, the medical student, to take over from the two skilled doctors and nurse Nussbaumer night and day, despite the fact that Roger did not even know how to lance a boil. Evidently, medical student Edmund Roger had the ear of Julie Considerant on advanced medical practices. On the 15th, Nussbaumer was up and taking his habitual walks. Considerant, on the insistence of his wife, discouraged the sick man from allowing use of additional cupping-glass treatments.

When Nussbaumer again became ill, he refused the use of the cupping glass, though Savardan and Nicolas thought cupping should be continued. Dr. Savardan, already acquainted with his fellow local practitioner, Virginian Samuel Pryor, felt confirmed in his practice of cupping after seeking out Pryor in Dallas on the subject. Dr. Pryor vouchsafed the use and efficacy of the procedure. Savardan, Nicolas, and Pryor wondered at the effrontery of a student like Roger and argued that proper medical attention was not being paid the poor patient. It was a rejection of age and experience in medicine.

Since Considerant had rejected Dr. Savardan's plea for an infirmary, Nussbaumer was sleeping in an attic. Unfortunately, the attic ceiling leaked rain onto his bed, thanks to Belgian architect Cousin. During the spring and summer Cousin had directed the building of shelters hurriedly roofed with boards "for two large workshops, the kitchen, the bakery, a laundry, and the grocery store."[4] These board roofs were quite common among Anglo settlers, who improvised quickly on their first arrival at a wilderness site, thinking of them as never more than temporary shelters. However, approaching the equinox, rains came. Reacting to the leaky roofs, the colonists conferred an honorary degree upon Vincent Cousin for the invention of pock-pitted roofs. Cousin was angry at the jest at his expense. No one gave him credit for helping get quick shelters built for the approaching numbers of colonists. The administrative council passed resolutions on September 5 and again on September 11 that a substitution of shingles for weather boards should be made for all the roofs that did not protect the inhabitants from the rain. These resolutions were an attempt to overcome what Dr. Savardan called Cousin's stubbornness but what may have been only hurried pragmatism when he had been early on the site with Cantagrel.[5]

And so with cool nights and rain, poor Rupert Nussbaumer felt the chill of his disease even more. Nussbaumer's protests about the change in doctors went unheard, and he gradually declined over the next two weeks. In the attic of the carpentry workshop, where a tent cloth had been nailed above Nussbaumer's bed to prevent rain from reaching him through Cousin's board roof, Nussbaumer died on September 26 of typhoid fever.[6]

While the body was washed and dressed, Jean Louckx's carpenters hurriedly made a coffin. A ceremony was improvised, the coffin carried the mile down the escarpment hillside, followed by a procession of his friends, to lie in a grave dug next to that of Vesian.[7] After Vesian's death, they had been able to soon smile again. He was, after all, a young single man out of the army from Marseilles, an agent of Considerant barely known to them, not a fellow Fourierist. His typhoid fever was an unlucky accident. It was different with their comrade Rupert Nussbaumer, who had hosted their Paris meetings in his family bar. He had two children and a wife who didn't yet know and wouldn't for six weeks. He was buried in that lowland muck that Considerant had chosen for a cemetery site. It rained at least all of eight days.

Nicolas and Savardan retreated to their gardening daily in the late afternoons. They took advantage of a little seep working its way east down the side of the plateau, sculpturing its own ravine, which protected plants from the wind, sun, and dryness. Their fruit trees and vines from France flourished with the special care, the watering they lovingly provided them. Dr. Nicolas, a clever bee-master, began raising a hive. François Cantagrel called the garden an excellent idea.[8] Colonists ventured into the garden to watch plants growing.

The doctors extended their gardening idea by means of a "serial constitution," and amateur gardeners began to join them. Eventually, there were about twenty volunteers, so that the administration council assigned to that gardening society the landscaping of the entire valley in order to make it a colonial park.[9] That garden under those beautiful oaks gave consolation to the colonists for their numerous disappointments and for the growing nostalgia for their old homeland. The afternoon shade offered recreation for the people of the nearby village, as well as the ladies of La Réunion.

October brought a sudden freeze, which formed a thin layer of ice on the water. The dryness ceased, followed by magnificent days. The daytime temperature soared, but the air remained cool. The Sunday night ball resumed. Anglo settler Sam Jones and Frenchwoman Louise Dusseau were becoming attracted to each other.

Victor Considerant had announced in the summer that he was going to have a two-story cottage built at his own expense. Cousin began plans. Dr. Savardan suspected that the ideas built were only those of Considerant. The cottage had shingles on the roof, but one was required to go outside to get from one room to the other, climbing up a stair without banisters.[10] Stonemason Renier objected to Cousin's idea of the chimney design for the home and built one of stone that he knew would draw, provoking Considerant's criticism of "monumental." It was common to build kitchens as separate structures, but this house did not need a kitchen because of the communal one.[11] A veranda lined the front. It was the only house at La Réunion with two stories. And it was white-washed inside and out.

From La Réunion, Cantagrel wrote Godin in Guise on October 7, "Only well-off Phalanstèriens, without children, should come to Réunion." Godin replied, "Have no illusions; they [well-off persons] won't budge. It's poverty that makes them willing to change their lives, move, etc."[12]

Dr. Savardan commented, "There are in our [phalansterian] school some intelligent people who believe that a community of men should and ought to live without rules, without legislation. Reproach for our opinion [against this] . . . came to us first from Paris, from even the management; then . . . those of the emigrants who seemed to believe much more in democratic radicalism than in the judicious theory of Fourier protested against the whole formula determining the duties and the reciprocal rights of the Fourierists."[13] Cantagrel resisted this protest and lost his popularity, as did the doctor.

Considerant, the ambivalent leader, stood by, either out of failure to understand his own duties or because he considered La Réunion tentative until the Texas legislature had given the society his dreamed-of empresario grant, now of indeterminate location because of railroad reserves. Regardless of Considerant's state of mind, the administration council of La Réunion met with some regularity. A typical meeting went like this.[14]

Considerant, president of the council, lay in one of his two hammocks, around which the councilors seated themselves either on the ground or on logs, as in an Indian pow-wow. "Cousin lay in the other hammock and from time to time passed to his master the flame destined to preserve the eternal fire of the nicotiana. One would have said that the two, thus nonchalantly stretched out, amply justified more and more the name faineansteriens (sluggards) that someone had concocted for them."[15]

Director Cantagrel presented all the questions that were of interest to the colony. He asked for solutions. "Roger rarely failed to raise on each question, with crafty forms of insinuation . . . personal criticism and interminable difficulties." Having been attacked by Roger, Cantagrel then defended himself "like a brave bull harassed by the darts and the feints of the picador; but . . . M. Cousin never let go his hold."[16] These arguments often lasted several hours.

Meanwhile, Considerant created elaborate smoke rings and solemnly whittled small pieces of wood in the American manner. He "appeared to enjoy himself either by rocking to the rhythm of these endless and useless discussions, or better still by letting his imagination wander everywhere except in this little world which ought to have so seriously occupied it."[17]

At one meeting Dr. Savardan dared to smile and raise an eyebrow at Considerant for the smoke rings. Considerant answered gravely, "Don't you know that is all that is necessary to frighten the Indians into a veritable stupor and to save my life, if I were ever their prisoner?"[18]

These meetings lasted for hours, in part because of the constant acrimony between what Dr. Savardan referred to as the aides-de-camp Cousin and Roger and the director, Cantagrel. Cantagrel would speak with Considerant privately to emphasize to the leader that "his spirit of favoritism and his meddling in the smallest details of the administration by continuously caviling with the responsible administrator [Cantagrel] led to a duality of action contrary to all [their] theories, but always in vain." As a result, to the detriment of La Réunion, "they divided the immigrants into two centers, two factions perpetually hostile, paralyzing themselves mutually in their best intentions and in their best efforts."[19]

Considerant was beginning to mystify his followers. His actions were at odds with what most of those who had come to the site wanted and what *Au Texas* proclaimed.

Even as Victor Considerant blundered at La Réunion, newspaper editors proclaimed that he had blundered into the southern frontier, not at all understanding it. His naive, misinformed, really ignorant view of people and how to communicate with Texians "where they were" in understanding and his attempts at betterment (in European eyes) were entirely ineffective. Yet other papers did not fear socialism and were anxious to see the colony tried in Texas. The *Galveston News* even thought that the experiment might discover or explain certain social regulations that would bring to humanity "greater happiness and a higher degree of civilization." However, in that statement the mind of the writer communicated a certain pessimism, for he also wrote, "Discord, which creeps into all human organization, may cause it to riot in infamy."[20]

In Clarksville, DeMorse, editor of the *Northern Standard*, described the postscript to the pamphlet Considerant had written, "Who We Are." DeMorse opined, "For ourselves only, we say that we think. The immigration of such a class of persons as he describes would be eminently beneficial to the State, and tend to its enrichment, by the introduction of Manufactories, without which no state is truly independent, and free from tribute in an eminent degree to other States. The agriculture, manufacturing and commercial elements all confined in a body politic, give it great power as the result of great resources—Texas has the elements for the successful development of all three, to which may be added mining in coal and iron."[21]

In Austin, John Marshall, editor of the *Texas State Gazette*, stated on October 13, 1855: "It is a matter of deep solicitude to all Southern men, that these Socialists should know in advance the opinions and views of our people. We are far from being fit subjects for the transcendental theorists of the North and of France. The thousand isms of the day find no congenial soil in the South, and besides this, the hatred of the Slave Institution, cherished by these Socialists and avowed openly by them in our State, must only the more remind us of our duty and awake our action."[22] Marshall was likely remembering Reverend John Allen's visit to Austin back in February and Allen's notoriety as a lecturer on abolition for more than fifteen years, as well as Brisbane's investment in Considerant's enterprise.

The writer of the editorial received numerous letters praising the paper's stand against socialists. In support, the *Sentinel* made a statement:

> Yet when an effort is made to plant among us, and that, in a Slave State, a colony of French Socialists and abolitionists (They are endorsed by the *New York Tribune*) then we demur, most positively and absolutely. We want no abolitionist plantations or colonies here, whether they be foreign or native. We want no European ideas of liberty. We carved out, by our own strong arms, the independence

VICTOR CONSIDÉRANT.

Dessiné d'après nature à la tribune le jour mémorable où orné de tous les attributs d'un disciple de Fourrier, et prenant la pose de l'anti-lion, il cherche à phalanstériser tous les membres de l'assemblée nationale.

13. Victor Considerant attracted mockery. Bibliothèque nationale de France.

of this country, and we want nothing of foreign origin infused into our system. But socialists are system-makers, government-builders, and communists—they are political incendiaries and propagandists, and would not only plant themselves and their social institutions upon our soil, but would endeavor insidiously and furtively to erect the system of government which they espouse, on the same soil. Their system is altogether different from our system. . . . Besides, it is an abolition system. It is useless for Mr. Considerant or Mister Anybody else to attempt to disguise it. They want to get a foothold here, and they will adopt any means to do so. It is vain for Mr. Considerant to attempt to hide his purposes under the rubbish of pedantic and scholastic phrases. Those purposes are plain and palpable.

Even as new colonists arrived, others left La Réunion to find work elsewhere. Said Fritz Colas to his friend in Bonneville, Savoy: "Now all those who have been able to find work in the neighborhood have left the colony; there are at this time about thirty of the best workers who have all left, and no one would remain were it not for the difficulty with the English language." For those who left La Réunion, there were complications: "When you leave, the society refuses to sell you seed or implements; they refuse . . . to pay them as one pays rural workers. Consequently at this moment they have at least twenty lawsuits in Dallas."

Architect César Daly had seen enough. On September 22, 1855, he wrote accountant Simonin that he would return north across Indian Territory to Fort Smith, then take paddle wheelers downriver and east to New York. He had had a rough time on the prairie. For three months he was so afflicted with insect bites that he had to remain in bed nearly the entire time. During that time Considerant never visited Daly until he was about to leave, when, according to Dr. Savardan, Considerant begged Daly's forgiveness. As Daly prepared to leave, Dr. Nicolas wrote home: "Our wine, about which we refrained from speaking, was almost forgotten when the departure of Mr. Daly gave us the occasion to present it at table. It was acclaimed and celebrated, found delicious though a little murky. (It had just fifteen days in the barrel.)"[23] However, Daly may have had another occasion to drink it. In early October he returned to La Réunion, having fallen sick at Fort Wichita.

News of the closing of the North American Phalanx (NAP) after twelve years of operation near Red Bank, New Jersey, was received as a blow to faith in the hopes for La Réunion. Those who thought some would use the NAP as a way station for La Réunion were now without common fellows on the East Coast. Englishman Arthur Young, that munificent donor who paid to found their Paris daily, the *Démocratie pacifique*, in the early 1840s, was ill at the NAP and now without funds. Considerant had sent him $400 before he left for Texas. They could only rationalize that Considerant was right, that the NAP had not been a true follower of Fourier's precepts. The NAP had survived a splinter group's leaving but not a fire. Yet La Réunion had gotten young Renshaw, son of a dedicated Associationist and member of the NAP for several years, because of the NAP closing. The Texas colonists hoped that his father and others would join La Réunion. The NAP stockholders had voted the prior July 4 to sell their property, then had set September 25 for the release of all obligations and the following February 1, 1856, as the date to vacate the land.

At La Réunion, about September 26, Reverend Allen's conscience overcame his zeal in establishing La Réunion. He had told his wife that he would return to Indiana in March or August, and now it was late September. Recognizing the need to superintend his vineyard harvest in Patriot, Indiana, he left La Réunion to return up the Mississippi. Perhaps, clinging to his dream and thinking he would come again to La Réunion after the harvest, he placed his son Fred, now nearly fifteen, in the care of Dr. Savardan and his friends at La Réunion.

Belgian poet Adolphe Leray, forty, and his foreman, Désiré Desutter, twenty-five, who had come with him the winter before, left La Réunion, as he wittily but trenchantly wrote in a poem, "without even a carrot." The two men found work first in New Orleans and then in New York in their trades as dyers to accrue funds for the passage home to Tournai.

About September 28, Chavennes, the young French clockmaker who had come with Nussbaumer to the colony the month before, returned to Houston following Nussbaumer's death.

Yet at La Réunion, optimism continued among the leaders. On October 7 Cantagrel wrote announcing the addition of 640 acres south of and contiguous to 2 acres on which were established the central buildings, the mill, and the sawmill of Green-Coombes. Cantagrel summarized land then bought as 12,926 acres total, of which 5,194 had been rented to a single tenant, 2,240 with some plowed land and some construction. The remaining 5,000 were obtained by "localization" of headrights.

The workers continued in their demands for permanence, while Considerant seemed to think that every shelter, machine, and process should be kept impermanent. In October Dr. Savardan and Abel Dailly asked Considerant for permission for Alexis Renier, thirty-one, a skilled mason who had grown up on Savardan's estate in La Sarthe, to build a stone chimney for the forge, the current mud-and-sticks chimney having disintegrated. On being refused, the three determined to pay for it themselves. After it was built, Considerant dismissed it as "monumental," and Roger said, "The company's funds will all be eaten up soon." Dr. Savardan made a cost comparison to the administration council of the two ways of building and found they both cost $30, even though Renier's preferred one contained three cubic meters of masonry. The latter had two furnaces and two bellows, whereas the former had only one. "It was the same with the pavement of the kitchen and the bakery and with the chimneys of the house built for Considerant. Everywhere and always there were groans, complaints, choleric and bitter criticisms from Considerant's two Belgians over every idea and every construction having the character of solidity, perpetuity, and desire, in brief, of a serious Fourierist settlement on this plateau."[24]

The bakery oven was the focus of another division in values. Dr. Savardan sarcastically called the argument over its size and portability another striking example of the Belgians' practical sense. Cousin insisted on building a larger portable oven than the bakers wanted, anticipating future population growth. The bakers wanted a brick oven, which would cost $100, but the larger iron oven sanctioned by Considerant when built cost $200, and because of the terrible winter of 1855, it was not finished until the following spring. The bakers pointed to the iron oven as producing the softer crust, even with the right winter wheat flour, while missing the masonry that yielded the hard crunch quality in crust that all Frenchmen insisted upon.

Considerant wanted land to be cleared, saying, "If I could at least this year announce in Europe that we have a thousand acres of land cleared."[25] But according to Dr. Savardan, the least harvest that a thousand acres would produce would be 4,000 bushels, and if the population doubled to three hundred, and each person annually consumed 8 bushels, the wheat harvest would produce a surplus of 1,400 to 1,600 bushels. The planting and tilling work would require seventy oxen driven by seven laborers working every day for six months. For the harvest, it would require fifteen days, fifty cradles or four good mowing machines, and fifty helpers for binding the sheaves. Then the work of threshing and the rest would have to be done. The colony did not have a quarter of the necessary equipment. And where would they store 4,000 bushels?

The questions, all of which were raised several times, made Considerant ask Dr. Savardan to take charge of agriculture. However, Considerant could not be satisfied. According to Savardan, Considerant derided the "serial organization" that his own *Au Texas* and Fourier had advocated, the system that Savardan followed and had set up with colonist volunteers and was about to hold elections to cement in place. Was Considerant fearful of losing control after hearing the word "elections" proposed by Savardan?

Finally, Considerant's derision caused Dr. Savardan to resign his appointment to lead agriculture. According to the doctor, Considerant offered "no other views, advice nor incentive to the laborers. Nothing save barbed and sterile criticisms. His goal was purely and simply, with a lack of spirit or direction, the discouragement and voluntary return of nine-tenths of the persons gathered on the place. And he was loathe to spend company funds for their passage back to Europe."[26]

Letters of discontent especially critical of leadership reached Belgium and various parts of France late in September 1855. Jean Journet, a constant Parisian propagandist against Considerant's brand of Fourierism, published Fritz Colas's September letter to his friend in Savoy, a letter highly critical of colony leaders.[27]

However, letters to management from Cantagrel and Dr. Savardan during the same period still affirmed that the company of La Réunion was strengthening itself more and more solidly on its domain. La Réunion, they said, was showing a few hints of success. They were taking on the clearing of seven to eight hundred acres over the winter and wanted the management to send about sixty workers, either laborers or artisans, staggered from December to March. Families should as yet be held back.

Another 640 acres contiguous to the townsite were purchased. In western Dallas County, sometime in August, seven Swiss from Zurich were farming colony land. These seven, who chose not to enter the commune, settled on a tract between the forks of the river. They rented it from the company on a third share of the harvest on the ten acres already broken and on condition of ceding to the colony at the end of three years several acres in cultivation, of which the Swiss farmers would have had the usage during that time. Further, they agreed to build a road through woods owned by the colony from the farm to the river in the direction of the sawmill. The colony would then extend the road by the sawmill to the settlement site, opening the woods to productive exploitation. The sawmill onsite would reduce the cost of wood by 40 percent.

Based on this example of Swiss renters, the *Bulletin* was pleased to observe, "Texas seemed to offer a favorable place for all viewpoints, starting with that of a settler, of a merchant, or of an isolated worker, *up to* [emphasis added] that of an Association that combines and solidifies efforts. It also reported eighty oxen in late August, thirty-odd cows, twenty or so pigs, and one hundred chickens. They expected momentarily a herd of three to four hundred cows and heifers. With four hundred acres in cultivation and another eight hundred by next March, it foresaw a minimum of $20,000 from harvest by the end of the next year."[28] The company store was beginning to conduct business outside the colony, offering products not otherwise available in frontier villages, like brandied peaches. Dr. Savardan, the keeper of the labor books, reported with satisfaction sales of $200 to $300 a month.

Near the end of October Cantagrel reported that Charles Burkli was working like a madman to start a tannery, certain to be profitable. Burkli had arrived in early July leading twenty people from Switzerland. "As soon as he arrived Mr. Burkli became focused on the need for a tannery, of which he had made a special study in Zurich." He determined that the skin of a cow, fresh or dried in the sun, was worth one dollar in Texas but "worth eight dollars when it has been made supple and protected from the injuries of worms and insects by macerations in a bath of ashes and alum."²⁹ Finally, the same skin was worth from twenty to twenty-five dollars when it had been transformed into workable leather by the operations of a tannery. Since the raw material cost so little in Texas, and only poorly made shoes were available at great expense, Burkli's goal of establishing a tannery and later a shoemaker's shop made great sense.

With his own hands Burkli constructed a dam on a creek in the valley where he could wash the leather. He gathered ashes from the fireplaces in the colony to begin initial preparation. But he needed tannin. The source of tannin was the brushwood of the oaks and sumacs on La Réunion land. With no mill to grind the bark, "he slivered the slender branches of undergrowth and macerated them in water to produce a quite sufficient quantity of tannin." All Burkli lacked was a hangar, essential to protect the workers and their tools from the sun and rain. His request for a hangar was presented to Considerant. Not only did Considerant reject the request, but he made it known that he considered the use of the brushwood to produce the tannin "a destruction of property." In a few months Burkli left for Central America. Eighteen others who came with him from Switzerland also left La Réunion, discouraged by the "insulting conditions of existence" Considerant made for them.³⁰

Yet management proclaimed optimism all during the fall of 1855. The *Bulletin* reminded its readers that though the Texas legislature had co-opted for railroad baits the lands in North Texas that Considerant had hoped to settle, and there had been a highly unusual drought, land was still cheap, and the climate was healthy. Despite their proclaimed optimism, their concern grew, given the fact they still had received no communication from Considerant himself since he had been in Texas.

Concern had grown sufficiently in Paris by the middle of October that management dispatched a letter to its accountant, Simonin, in New York, asking him to go to Texas to review accounts, since he was already familiar with springtime equipment purchases for the colony. In New York on Monday, October 29, Simonin, thirty-three, received that first letter request. He was to regularize and render exact accounts of the colony's finances: "Give us your opinion." Two days later, Simonin received a second letter on the same subject, evidence of the seriousness of concern.

Still, the management followed Cantagrel's and Dr. Savardan's optimism, sending more colonists. From Le Havre, the ship sailed with Maximilien Reverchon, forty-five, and his son Julien, eighteen, with several others on the last day of October. Maximilien Reverchon had been head of the farm of the phalanx at Sig outside Oran nearly ten years previously.[31] With a grandfather who as a deputy had voted for the head of the king in 1792 and as an active participant in the revolution of 1848, he was a marked Republican under the regime of another emperor. For a second time he left France, this time with one of his four children, to pursue his passion for agricultural botany.

On November 1 from Guise, Godin, with still more anxiety, wrote accountant Simonin, explaining the need to send an impartial manager to the colony due to the lack of clear information from it. He spelled out the reality: even though the stock company had disengaged itself from responsibility for the administration of La Réunion, the future and monetary success of the parent company depended on the colony's success.

Godin also wrote the August Council of Seven, elected to run the company of La Réunion:

> You blame the management for many of your problems, but we work in the dark. If Réunion had been located on a large expanse of good land, which would have facilitated the development of industry and trade, the Society could have contracted with Réunion to build more farms and to develop outward from its center. Then, knowing what to expect, the Society could have encouraged emigration, etc. Réunion exists under different circumstances. But our resources are immobilized in it, so we must develop it. Unable to find large tracts of good land, find small plots of it. . . . Otherwise the Society must die while Réunion lives, for Réunion will devour it. I'm coming to find out what's possible.

At the same time, the directors in Paris were sending more ships from Le Havre across the ocean to New Orleans, bringing more colonists to arrive in January and then still more in the spring. They also planned for several later ships to satisfy the clamor of prospective colonists.

Meanwhile, readying the land for planting continued, and not without drama. Dr. Savardan, when on a visit to an American patient two miles from the colony, saw fire in the dark night. When the doctor left La Réunion on his medical call, the fire had been only a speck lit at sunset by Cantagrel and Karl Burkli to clear the high grass of an adjoining valley, as was the custom in the area. The small fire had now turned into a flaming sea, undulating, winding snakelike, rolling, either rapidly or slowly according to the impulse of the breeze, and forming finally the most marvelous illumination of which he had ever been able to dream of or to see even at the opera.[32]

In late October 1855 in Dallas, as well as all over Texas, everyone was organizing for the sixth session of the Texas legislature. After several meetings upstairs in the Masons' hall, the tiny new village was sending a delegation of "sundry citizens" to plea for incorporation; they drew up a formal petition to present to the committee responsible. All during the fall they plotted their lobbying with elected legislators.

At La Réunion, Victor Considerant wanted that empresario grant but seems to have been entirely uninformed about the legislative process. It was not until October 24 that Considerant, taking Edmund Roger for his translator and without so much as a handshake to a soul at Réunion, quietly slipped away from Réunion to go to meet the legislators.[33] In Dallas, the two caught the stage to Austin in order to be there for the session, which would begin on November 5. Arriving a week before the legislature met, even for seasoned lobbyists, would have been late in the process. There was no planning together by the townspeople and Victor Considerant at La Réunion nor early fall contact with Senate or House members by him. The Colonization Society had sent no lobbyists to Austin.

While there was no 1855 political mixing between Dallas and La Réunion, there was the beginning of another kind of integration. Four and a half months after Louise Dusseau from Aude reached La Réunion with Dr. Savardan's group, the marriage of this Gaelic colonist with an Anglo settler took place in Dallas. On November 1, a Thursday, Justice of the Peace Allen Beard united colonist Dusseau and settler Samuel Jones of Dallas. They met at a dance held at Réunion. The first formal social integration had begun.

18

Considerant and Texas Politics

That the citizens of the Southern States have the indefensible right to carry their slaves into any territory belonging to the United States, and there to enjoy and exercise all the rights of ownership and property, as freely and as fully as in the State from which they emigrate; and that any interference with, or obstruction to, the enjoyment and exercise of their rights as southern citizens, by the Government of the United States or of each territory, would be a violation of the rights of the southern States, which they possess as sovereign States, and co-equal members of the American Confederacy.

PLATFORM PLANK NO. 5 of the January 1856 State Democratic Convention

In late December 1855 the full Texas Senate met in its formal legislative chamber to discuss the question of Texas debt. To the astonishment of observer Amédée Simonin, the French accountant, "people were smoking, chewing tobacco and spitting in the spittoons or [on the] carpet. They sat in their armchairs, feet up on their desks, writing or whittling with their knives."[1] The cultured Simonin watched as a speaker stood and addressed the Senate, a quid in his mouth, which he spit out two feet in front of him.

> As he began, he had his two hands in the pockets of his waistcoat; when he became animated he took one out, with which he made a gesture from time to time, always the same, and from time to time put his hand back in his waistcoat, the other never coming out. He used the word "sir" two or three times in each sentence, in the manner that some soldiers sprinkle their tales with the words, "one says," "I say . . ." One had to have seen the room's carpet to know how it appeared, with tobacco juice [everywhere] and other crap. . . . As to the behavior and the dress of the senators, one must imagine that they came from the different counties of Texas.[2]

This was the milieu Considerant approached when he traveled to Austin to appeal for a land concession. Considerant wanted to found a "socialist state" analogous to the Mormons' Utah territory within which an "integral phalansterian community" might serve as a central locus for all kinds of social experiments. Two years previously he had described North Texas as "the flower of the United States," "the pearl of the world, blessed ground." He hoped the phalansterians could "make themselves the masters" of a part of this territory before it had been "deflowered" by settlers and speculators. He wanted to imitate the Mormons in opening the Southwest as a protected area for American and European socialism.

Considerant dreamed of himself as an empresario of his own land. What he failed to understand was that the legislature had taken from the executive branch the right of the president, later the governor, to execute such grants and had reserved that right for itself. Now instead of one person with whom to negotiate for land grants, as had been the case with Sam Houston under the republic, the French Fourierists had to contend with the entire state legislature. Considerant also knew that during the past decade the Germans had brought over five thousand settlers to receive land from the state. Why shouldn't the state continue that practice with the French?

When Victor Considerant arrived in Austin near the end of October 1855, legislators were to begin their biannual meeting the following week. He found a small one-story house to rent for himself and his translator. Committees, in preparation for the biannual session, were already meeting. He had only Edmund Roger, the twenty-nine-year-old unkempt Belgian who spoke with his teeth clenched, to translate for him before the committee members of the Sixth Legislature of the state of Texas.

> Roger was a small, thin man who looked about 23 years old. His hair was blond, but it was darkened by the dusty and dirty state in which he kept it. . . . He had sunken cheeks, flabby and hanging like an old person who no longer had teeth. He took no care of his person. His shirt, which he showed a lot because he was always either very disheveled or in shirtsleeves, was five-sixths of the time

black, not the black of a blacksmith's shirt, but the filthy black of the shirt of a French cobbler who's been wearing it for fifteen days.[3]

Roger, a medical student called "doctor," as Considerant introduced him everywhere, was hardly an effective representative of the stockholder corporation.

In New York the month before, accountant Amédée Simonin had received a long letter from the Paris stock company managers asking him to go to Texas to regularize and render exact accounts of the colony's finances.[4] Even though Considerant had disengaged the stock company from responsibility for the administration of La Réunion, the future of that company depended on Réunion's success. It was Cantagrel who had written Simonin to alert the accountant of the whereabouts of Considerant. Simonin, then, was in Austin because of Considerant, not the legislature, which convened on November 5.

Within a week, a member of the House introduced a bill for the relief of the German Emigration Company, which granted titles to that colony. Evidently, the creditors of the Fisher-Miller speculation were attempting to recover their losses from a bankruptcy declared two years previously. The bill was shortly read the second time and referred to the Committee on the Judiciary, a good sign of passage and a hopeful sign to other Europeans, like the French, waiting in the wings.[5]

Also within that first week in the House of Representatives among petitions offered by members, "sundry citizens" asked for the incorporation of the village of Dallas, which was referred to the Committee on County Boundaries. In contrast, Considerant fumbled his first attempt, only getting his bill written and presented a month later. His inability to speak English did not help. It would be January, two months after the convening of the legislature, before an actual hearing was first held for the European American Colonization Society bill.

Back at Réunion, Director Cantagrel persuaded architect César Daly, who had recovered from his trip north, to stop in Austin on his way to seek a ship in New Orleans rather than go a second time via Fort Smith. Cantagrel wanted him "to place himself without rancor" at Considerant's disposal to translate with the legislature.[6] "Without rancor" alludes to

Considerant having slighted Daly by ignoring him at Réunion for four months the past summer. Whatever caused the bruised relationship between the two old friends, Daly had invested twenty years in Fourierism and agreed to go help Considerant. He had recovered from Texas's seasons of allergies and left for Austin on November 23.

Like Victor Considerant, who had made his mark as an orator and writer in French, Daly, forty-four, was also gifted as a speaker, but in excellent English. To be more friendly to the Texan ear, he likely called himself Daley, his father's Irish pronunciation of his name, rather than his mother's un-Texan French one. With his father's Irish brogue, Daly supplied cigars and drinks at the bars and drank tea with the wives of the legislators while dressed to Beau Brummel standard. He understood their new milieu and went to work as a lobbyist to accommodate Fourierism to Texas. Daly's polish in speaking stood him in good stead in a southern society whose whole fabric was infused with politics and where oratory was universally cultivated. Daly was there to translate from the written word to the spoken Texas vernacular.[7] Writing was a deterrent to communicating Considerant's colonization society goals. Mississippian John Marshall in his *Austin Gazette* could pick and had picked apart Considerant's written words to the detriment of their cause. Marshall was therefore one of "Caesar Daley's" principal targets to influence.

Simonin had gathered some information on the Réunion accounts. En route to Texas, Simonin reached New Orleans on the evening of December 5 and over the next three days took summaries of accounts of the Réunion Company from Jules Juif and from the Bank of Louisiana.[8] He left the following Sunday for Galveston on the ship *Perseverance*. A thorough man, two days later he made himself a copy of La Réunion accounts. Then leaving the bayou water in Houston, he took a stagecoach on December 13, reaching Austin on Sunday, December 16. In Austin, Simonin found Daly, who evidently welcomed him as a teammate and invited him to share his room at the City Hotel. They had met before in New York the previous winter.

The next day Simonin sought out Considerant. He remarked in his diary on the slovenly state of the small, single-story cottage that he shared with the unkempt Belgian Roger, who forever lay on his bed, reading or dozing.[9] Considerant immediately wrote his wife, Julie, at La Réunion sounding relieved, saying that with Simonin and Daly in Austin, he was reinforced with two who spoke the language.[10] To the two men he said, "With you here, and since I cannot speak the language, you two run around and see as many legislators as possible. I have nothing more to do here, and perhaps will go to the west and then to Nicaragua." Still, his ambiguity about his own leadership caused him to stay in Austin throughout the first session.

Simonin, who was fourteen years younger than Considerant, was a personable, well-educated Frenchman. He was versed in business and knew how to mix in the business society of effective doers, immediately seeking out the persons who had already succeeded in the realm to which Considerant and the colonization society aspired.

In stark contrast to Roger, he was a polished representative for the management. Besides understanding business, he had read American literature, expressed opinions on the qualities of architecture and music, and in his comments understood the broad context of the colonization society's needs. He was polite, cultured, and able to read the motives of his contacts. He understood in what circles he needed to move to serve the interests of the society that he endeavored to represent. He received appropriate introductions before leaving New York and in Austin immediately found ways to meet and interview the effective leaders who had had similar experiences to those that the colony would have to undergo if it were to be successful. He was a pragmatist but with a subtle heart who attempted to help the colony's faltering leader, Considerant, and a conscientious man who carefully recorded the details of his interviews. However, much to the frustration of Simonin, Considerant avoided all small talk with him and evaded answering any questions about La Réunion accounts for the entire six months of Simonin's Texas trip. He cut short any idea Simonin attempted to express, sharply raising his voice, attempting always to demean him.

Considerant was in a dilemma. He needed translators who could communicate with the legislators, but, more important to him, he feared losing control of La Réunion. He knew he was out of his milieu, but he clung to his dream and could not suppress his ego to further the cause he had created. He was beginning to feel his age and clearly felt threatened by this younger man who could outcompete him in language and in connecting with important Texans. Considerant belittled the idea of Simonin calling on the governor, but Simonin ignored him, took his personal letter of introduction procured in New York from Major Merrill, and called on Governor Pease within three days of his arrival.[11] The Frenchman visited E. M. Pease at the governor's mansion, built two years previously on a knoll overlooking the generous grounds of the capitol.

Pease was friendly to the idea of the French colony. He was born in Connecticut, chose a Connecticut wife, and held a very long view and broad context for governing Texas, which made him an outstanding leader. In empty Texas, a group of educated persons with today's equivalent of many millions in cash promising education and industry would be a plum in the mind of a man of his aspirations for his new state. Pease had just laid the foundation for support of public education and the state university with the creation of the permanent school fund. He encouraged railroads and settled the public debt, which then freed funds to establish schools for the deaf and blind and a hospital for the mentally ill. Unfortunately, at the moment the French colonization society arrived in Austin, it appears that as a union sympathizer, E. M. Pease's political influence was beginning to slip.

Within two days in Austin, Simonin met Antoine Supervièle, state senator from Bexar County and one of only two foreign-born members of the Texas Senate.[12] Supervièle had arrived from France in 1843 at age thirty-five. He served as a precinct election judge in Houston in 1846 and moved to San Antonio in 1851. Less than two years later, he won a seat in the Texas legislature and was in 1855 beginning his second term as a state senator. He had been a lawyer in France and later practiced in Texas, but in this period he acted as a merchant in San Antonio and as a real estate agent selling headright certificates. He was, according to Considerant, "a fine type," perhaps because he spoke French, but more likely because the senator represented a vast county needing settlers to push Indians out of Texas. On Tuesday Supervièle took Simonin to see the tobacco-spitting, stick-whittling senators in session. By Friday, Simonin had begun interviewing principal merchants and land developers about business in Texas. Simonin drew out Antoine Supervièle to list and discuss the qualities of the ports of Texas, the chief importers in San Antonio, the value of their stock, where they bought, their honesty, and the types of products desirable for Texan markets for Simonin to record in detail.[13]

Considerant needed the votes of both the House and the Senate to pass his bill. His bill for the empresario grant was introduced in the regular session by House Member W. M. Cleveland, one of the three representatives to the legislature from Bexar County. Why did he not choose legislators from Dallas or North Texas to introduce it? Considerant had found immigrant Frenchman Supervièle, whom he thought could help him place the bill in the right political hands. He likely did not know that Supervièle was viewed as outside the mainstream of southern prejudice, and from the evidence of committees on which this Frenchman was appointed to serve, he possessed little power in the Senate, even in his second term.

While Simonin gathered information for Paris management, he also periodically commented with a trenchant rapier on the habits and ceremonies of Texans. Shortly after he arrived, a formal ceremony of the two chambers of the legislature welcomed the governor. A joint committee of senators and representatives called upon Governor Pease and led him down the hill from the governor's mansion and then up the opposite hill to the capitol with great solemnity and order. The accompanying band consisted of a bass, a flute, and two violins. When Simonin heard the music he thought they were Chinese. "The ladies were admitted to the halls of the Congress; the gentlemen chewed tobacco as usual; the Governor and the Lt. Governor each read a speech; they were both stammerers."[14]

Over four or five days after Simonin's arrival, he and Daly went several times with Considerant to the capitol or to legislators' homes to plead their case. They worked on the wording of the petition for their land grant. The accountant even lent Considerant $20 to pay the printing costs of the petitioner's bill to be put before the legislature.[15]

Why didn't Considerant have the petition ready the minute that the legislature convened, just after November 5? The reason may have been that he was engaged on two fronts at once, hedging his bets by quietly investing in land in a second frontier location even before the legislature acted on his plea.

Eighty miles west of San Antonio, in the empty frontier on the upper Leona River, near the site of Indian Fort Inge, one Reading W. Black pushed his plans to organize a county under the same legislature that Considerant lobbied. The same Senator Cleveland, the Bexar representative in the legislature who later introduced the French colonization society bill, also introduced one for Reading Black on Thursday, three days after the session convened. It received a favorable committee report in a month. This was enough to start the first real estate boom in Encina, Black's preferred county seat for Uvalde County. It was also enough to lure Considerant to begin buying land in the upper eastern corner of that county.

Black was a Unionist in an area that had few slaves. He had been attacked by John Marshall in the Austin press as an abolitionist and a socialist since February and throughout the summer. Between November 30, 1855, and March 28, 1857, Considerant acquired for his stockholder company forty-seven thousand acres in Sabinal Canyon, near present Utopia.[16] Considerant was likely either sold by or put in touch with a seller of lands by Antoine Supervièle. Frederick Law Olmsted, then a reporter for the *New York Times*, may also have recommended contacts to Considerant, since he had ridden through Black's newly laid out village eight months before he met Considerant in New York. Money did change hands that spring between Considerant and Supervièle. Was Considerant just buying headrights wherever he encountered them, or was he somehow already investing in Sabinal land apart from the legislature plea?[17] Was Considerant refusing to talk to Simonin about La Réunion accounts because he was concealing land purchases in a location three hundred miles from La Réunion?

What were the motives of the representatives and the senator from Bexar County as they aided Considerant in his plea and introduced his bill? Bexar County then contained an enormous semiarid and desert frontier extending to El Paso, distinct from smaller, less arid, and settled counties farther east that were capable of growing cotton and therefore of exploiting slaves. Were these gentlemen leading Considerant to invest not just to bring colonists to free land but also to free land in their political region? Did they introduce the Frenchman to DeCordova, who pitched and succeeded in borrowing funds from Considerant while in Austin?

Did Representative Arnold have similar designs for guiding French investment to his Comal and Gillespie Counties? These questions arise from Considerant's strange behavior. What had he been doing for the last nine or ten days of the year when he did not leave his house? Simonin continued to lobby and gather information for a Fourierist colony.

Simonin was either very astute or very lucky, or both, to find and engage so many major Texas figures of the period to give him advice. Henri Castro, a learned, wise, humane man, had become a U.S. citizen in 1827. He returned to France in 1838, then became a member of the Lafitte banking house. The Republic of Texas named him consul general in Paris because of the loan he achieved for the republic. Castro then became an empresario in 1842, chartered twenty-seven ships, and brought to Texas 485 families and 457 single men between 1844 and 1847. He was a role model for Considerant.

Castro, servant of his Alsatian colony, now sixty-nine as he talked to accountant Simonin, was as much German as French. He told Simonin of the Miller and Fisher colony, which obtained five million acres by grant. He told Simonin that they did not yet know where the greatest part of those lands was located. He commented that there were then only his and the German colony and that of Considerant in Texas.[18]

As he lobbied to establish rapport, Simonin interviewed Swante Magnus Swenson. In 1850 this immigrant Swede had established Swenson and Swisher, the only retail business in Austin, which he expanded to sell to distant forts. His holdings grew as he paid top dollar for headright certificates. In 1854 he invested in the future Buffalo Bayou, Brazos and Colorado Railway to run across Northwest Texas. He pointed out to Simonin that there was as yet only one railroad being built in Texas, the one that was chartered from Buffalo Bayou to Austin, and that line had only a small stretch completed. He discussed costs of freight, conditions of ports, sources where he bought wholesale goods, costs of building his own house, profits from land, and his view of the usefulness of white versus Negro employees.[19]

Swenson offered Simonin his view of the rising slavery controversy. He pointed out to Simonin that the slave naturally had no incentive to work. He professed to be opposed to the "peculiar institution," but he also owned several hundred black field hands. In 1854, the year before the Fourierists arrived, the German Catholics adopted a resolution opposing slavery. This then made the southern Protestant Anglos suspicious that the Germans (and all other Europeans) were neither Christians nor loyal to the South. This suspicion injected itself in the empresario grant issue, indeed, in all things European. Swenson, himself an immigrant, throughout his life encouraged Swedish émigrés by offering them indentures. He was a good politician. When he discussed these matters with Simonin, he already had served one term as Travis County commissioner and was about to serve another.

On Tuesday, Christmas Day, Simonin struck up a conversation with legislator J. F. Arnold, plying him with questions on costs of establishing settlements in the wilderness.[20] Ostensibly, Simonin was seeking information. However, he was also smart in communicating the society's business desire for land to a member of the subcommittee whose vote would help send their bill to the floor. From Arnold, Simonin learned the costs of acquiring land; building fences, cabins, and corn cribs; breaking prairie; and covering living expenses. He even learned how to make a profit. This man, state representative for Comal and Gillespie Counties, served on three standing committees, including the Committee on Public Lands. As a representative elected by German immigrants, he would not likely have been a secessionist. In the same meeting, M. L. Merrick, another of the three representatives from Bexar County, told Simonin his strategy on planting crops.[21]

Also on Christmas Day, architect and translator Daly, back at the hotel from a holiday party, told Simonin of a conversation, assuredly very witty, that he had with several ladies. These ladies tried to goad Daly; they claimed that "the socialists were not very amiable people since they denied differences by proclaiming equality, and asked him if he had known many women of the world who were imbued with socialist ideas." Daly responded, "No, ladies, I have known very few of them and I congratulate those few." He returned the thrust:

> You have a mission to transmit to posterity all that we have acquired of the good and the beautiful in our work and in our harsh experience

of 5,000 years—that is, grace, elegance, politeness, good taste, tact, in one word, all the fine and noble refinement which characterizes the distinguished woman. Preserve this treasure; it is useful to us and will be of further use in the socialist world. Do not involve yourself in our movement, which can only operate on a low level. Do not lower yourselves. We like you and admire you and we prefer to endure your disdain and even your contempt than to see you come down even by one degree from the place where you are, while we work arduously with our uncouth and rough limbs in the low layers of mass society.[22]

Simonin and Daly moved from a base very different from Considerant's. After a month of Daly's attention, Austin attitudes toward the colony began to change. Simonin observed that "under Daly's influence the press, hostile as it had been toward us, ceased to attack Mr. Considerant and our society." With "perfect knowledge of the English language, and his easy, witty and varied conversation, he knew how, with tact and conviviality, to attract all attentions, and to melt the superficial ice which muffles a great depth of gaiety and curiosity in this country [and as long as he was with Considerant, eased our path]. He was invaluable in our plea to the government."

Daly was trying to overcome southern fears of abolitionist voters, not something Considerant could overcome by writing treatises to this anti-intellectual society. Without language or a true ability to communicate a friendship tolerant of all and with a propensity to speak always of the colony as "his" rather than as the investor society's, Considerant appeared to be a snob. He lacked acumen in selecting those around him. Simonin, on the other hand, kept his own astonished views of the crude personal culture of the frontier private, though he recorded them in his diary. But there is little evidence that Considerant took the advice Simonin solicited from Messrs. Swenson, Castro, Pease, Arnold, and others about establishing a colony. Considerant was naive about the frontier, and his ego appeared to cause him to reject even information gained for the colony by those close to him, information about the practicalities of his dream.

On Thursday, December 27, 1855, Simonin again drew out Henri Castro, who defined how he would develop one hundred sections (at least) for settlement.[23] This scale was of interest to Considerant and the Réunion colony's European investors. Castro was much more generous and helpful to poor colonists than the Burnet County farmer whom Simonin encountered two days later. This elderly Texas farmer told Simonin of the practices of tenant farming, which offered a high return on investment. The tenant had to break one hundred acres and fence them in two years, and then he had to begin paying rent of $400 a year. The third year he also had to begin paying 10 percent interest on the original $800 cash extended to him as a tenant.

On Monday, 1855 ended. The Fourierists were learning that gaining an empresario grant was not easy. As the new year began, there were at least three problems they had not foreseen. First there was slavery, a belief and a seeming requirement for them to gain the confidence of the Texas government. Next, a great swath of land they had hoped for was now reserved for railroads. Third and even more important was their leader's seeming ambivalence about what he had created at La Réunion and where the colony should be instead.

Just after New Year's, Henri Castro explained to Simonin the business of investing in land development, including how to loan capital to a farmer family and reap profits in five years.[24] But on the same day, Mr. Alexander, a speculator who later in the month sold Considerant some 9,200 acres of headrights, took César Daly and Amédée Simonin to see the Supreme Court room in the capitol: Simonin again expressed his revulsion at Texan behavior, counting forty-five visible spittoons, with more hidden, all of which did not prevent the men from spitting on the carpet. Mr. Alexander told Daly and Simonin about loan practices and the fluctuating interest rates over the year: interest had risen to 25 percent in August when there was no cash. To their dismay, he also pointed out that land prices had increased 18 percent a year for several years. He concluded with a discussion of wood chopping and of course the cultivation of grape vines, which the colony had already begun.[25]

Then to the surprise of Daly and Simonin, Vincent Cousin arrived from La Réunion on the first Saturday of the New Year, summoned by Considerant.[26] Considerant wanted his own man by his side. He knew that Simonin would soon go to La Réunion and that Daly would be departing for New Orleans, leaving him with Roger, who was not useful with legislators. Thus Considerant sent for Cousin, a known quantity and follower. His excuse to the others was that Cousin would bring him a pair of pistols.

On being introduced to Cousin, Simonin was appalled. Like Roger, Cousin "has the air of one who does not pay attention to his intimate toilet, wear clean underwear, or take care of his person." Cousin's physique reminded Simonin of the blacksmith Hollingsworth in Nathaniel Hawthorne's *Blithedale Romance*.[27] Supervièle was mystified at Considerant's choice of companions. He told Daly and Simonin that after several days around Roger, he could not restrain himself from asking Considerant, "Of what use is Doctor Roger; how can he be helpful to you? It seems to me that if you were in need of someone this is not the man you would want." There was about his person "evidence of an old filth, a quality of which almost all those who have been in Considerant's house have hinted to me."[28]

In Houston, the Galveston and Red River Railroad, another new line, began laying track toward Cypress City, twenty-five miles north. This was good news for French investors in the colonization society, as the rails were aimed for North Texas. However, on January 8 the Senate offered a caution to future impresarios when it considered prohibiting the issuing of land patents as a penalty to the Texian Emigration and Land Company (the fourth name given to the Peters Colony by its latest investors) for lands lying in the Peters Colony. At issue was a reward of 1,700 acres to the colony contractor, for which he had done little or nothing. Finally, after a month of waiting, also on January 8, legislators held the first meeting of the subcommittee to which Considerant's business had been submitted. The meeting was not long, but legislators let the Réunion representatives see that they responded favorably. Two days later, the chairman of the subcommittee gave them an appointment for 3:00, but Simonin had been overoptimistic. They all waited two hours for him; he did not come. Later in the week, a great number of the senators and representatives got drunk. When the Speaker of the House did not appear in the chamber, his vice president substituted for him. This meant that, following all this, Daly and Simonin did not have another meeting with the subcommittee. On the next Saturday, Simonin attended an evening meeting of the committee. The chairman promised to make his report to the colonization society very favorable. One of the three supplicants wrote to the Paris office, announcing this sign of pending success. Latham's House subcommittee, appointed to examine the exceptional demand of free lands, did make a favorable report, and the Frenchmen's hopes for success revived.

Then the following Monday, Simonin brought J. D. Arnold, representative from Comal County, to a meeting at Considerant's house to discuss the manner of presenting the bill to the Senate.[29] Senator Supervièle and Jean Goetseels, an important Réunion investor, were there. With a continental railroad company charter about to be confirmed by the legislature, the approach to the French plea for land had to be reevaluated. Rail access, water transport, Indians, markets, soil and climate, prior settlement and impresario agreements, competitors—all affected the plea and the response to the plea. Most of all, growing slavery politics and antiforeign sentiment claimed attention.

To the astonishment of the Europeans, on Tuesday evening legislative business suddenly stopped in order to convene the Democratic State Convention in the House chamber, making a further complication to the French society's plea for land. The convention vehemently opposed any but its own view of slavery; that is, slavery must be allowed in every state. Almost immediately a delegate moved to expel the Galveston delegate for supporting the Union and unanimously condemned Sam Houston's recent vote for the Union. Foreigners were not exempt from this hysteria. "Every anti-Know-Nothing patriot who could speak in public was urged to do so . . . during the ensuing campaign."[30]

Simonin could point Considerant to this bloodletting partisanship and remind him of the number of times back in New York during the editing of the English version of *Au Texas, The Great West*, that he had cautioned Considerant to suppress any mention of individuals known to be abolitionists. Now the accountant turned lobbyist found, after he carried five hundred copies of the society's statutes to Austin to use with legislators, that he could use none of them because the list of investors included famed abolitionist and New Yorker Albert Brisbane, the man who brought Considerant to Texas.[31]

All during this session, new positions were being forged and hardened. J. W. Latimer, editor of the *Dallas Herald*, became a member of the State Central Committee of the Democracy of Texas and thus an influence in North

Texas toward southern positions. Perhaps this new status changed his written positions from the year before toward the Réunion colony's pleas for land.

Simonin was frustrated. Once again the session stopped in order to convene the Democratic State Convention in the House chamber. Nothing was accomplished from January 15 to 21. "The political assembles and a torrential rain prevented any kind of consensus in our favor."[32] The rain must have come from a warm Gulf weather front colliding with arctic air. The temperature fell to 13 degrees. "Unheard of. . . . Hard to work in this cold," said Considerant. He was getting his introduction to the dramatic alternating pendulum of Texas winters.

At Bottonley House on Sunday, a cattle rancher gave Simonin a lesson in the economics of cattle husbandry. Then on Tuesday Simonin quizzed Pete Nickles of Brownsville and the representative from Hidalgo and Cameron Counties on the sheep and wool economy in the Far South.

Tuesday the cold front retreated enough to turn the Gulf wind into the frequent morning fog that Austin is known for and to envelop Considerant in a gray depression. Simonin records in his diary Considerant's tempest in a teapot made over the burning of some past issues of the *Courier des États-Unis*.[33] In Simonin's view, the huge quarrel Considerant made over five or six old issues he claimed had not been returned to him showed that he was mentally declining, growing senile, perhaps due to the weight of responsibility. The energy necessary for him "to deploy in order to make the project succeed, paralyzes him with terror. This is why he clings to stupidities and trifles—to cover up somewhat and excuse in his own eyes his laziness and incapacity." Simonin feared their leader would "never do but half well, if he does not spoil the thing, if he doesn't lose all."[34]

Simonin was treading water while waiting on Considerant to live up to his promise to answer questions for his report to the managers. He went back to a man for fence costs. They also discussed labor costs.

At Considerant's house the next morning, Simonin found his leader overwhelmed again as he had almost always seen him there. Considerant spoke of the manner in which the Paris management had thwarted his plans, sending more people than he had asked for since the first spring, and even sending Simonin to Texas without consulting him.[35] He then spoke to Simonin of the state of mind in which he found himself in New

York last spring when he saw that he was snowed under by the number of emigrants the Paris office was sending him.

He confessed to an idea he had in New York that Simonin did not even want to write down. Should we speculate? Cancel the whole business? Before Considerant left Europe he had approved the lists of people of the "pioneer avant garde" to be sent in the first ships. Bureau in Paris and the management had followed those lists. Cantagrel had followed Considerant's instructions in land purchases and in hiring Americans to prepare a receiving site. It seems Considerant, only in reaching New York the second time, learning of the railroad reserve, and now realizing the growing prejudices of the South and the true climate he had failed to investigate on his first visit, was grasping at finding excuses to divert blame from himself for misguiding his many Fourierest followers. There was no grand Utah valley, a place remote and, as he said, unspoiled and as yet not deflowered by settlers and speculators to which this Moses could lead his flock.

In the afternoon, when Simonin returned to Considerant's house, the leader asked Simonin to keep to himself what he had told him that morning, showing the same sadness of thought and of face. Since the two were alone in the house, Simonin pushed the bayonet into Considerant's flanks. Simonin tried to raise Considerant's morale as energetically as he could, saying to him, "You have not lost anything," and "in spite of the bad results of the first campaign, a clever player like [yourself] could regain the game and all the time and land lost." Simonin urged, "You still have all the means and all the resources." He gave the most energetic oaths that he had ever given in his life. It is in this regard that he saw the "strangest phenomenon ever presented" to him.[36]

As they talked for about an hour, little by little Considerant's face lightened and regained its color. When Simonin left him Considerant was laughing and had a charming expression, happy and beaming, as Simonin had not seen on him since his first trip to America. He spoke, appropriating Simonin's ideas and words by degree, interrupting to tell the accountant, "But yes, this is what I think, what I do, what I say for all eternity, and I will never have other rules of conduct," never admitting that Simonin was right and taking as his own all that Simonin was telling him. Considerant smiled confidently. Finally, seeing that his strategy had worked, Simonin ended amicably with this outburst: "Well, what are you complaining about if such are your views and your ideas? All will go well, all will be given, and all will work. Leave off this mask of melancholy that you wear unceasingly and which lengthens your nose by six thumbs, and be gay, courageous and confident in the cause, in the business, and in the future."[37] Considerant was wound back up.

Simonin sought absolution from Daly for his work on Considerant. He deplored the effects of icy Cousin and Roger on Considerant:

> Considerant is entirely wrong in choosing two intimate counselors like those he has. These two men are two ice cubes, as cold as two Americans. The two men offer nothing of what would have been necessary to Considerant. He has spent his life in the midst of people full of blood, of heat, and of affection, which they have shown him unceasingly. To not fail here, it would have been necessary that he find some true and devoted friends, full of warmth and generosity. . . . He needs to have around him warm persons with affectionate natures and with devotion of which he is certain, because no one more than he feels or is sensible to the evidence and marks of true devotion and of true affection.[38]

Again on a Wednesday, two weeks after the Democratic Convention, the legislature stopped for a second convention. This time the assembly of the Know-Nothings took place. As Daly reported to Simonin on his return from the convention, that "General [Hugh McLeod] said in his speech to the gallery as an argument in favor of the principles of the Know-Nothings that foreigners attached less importance to patriotism than was generally thought, and the proof was that he had heard attributed to Victor Considerant himself that if one left after twenty-one years of residence, that this would not prevent him from settling in Texas, because it was not for him an essential question."[39] A few minutes later Considerant entered the convention to the murmur of the Democrats. Daly later asked Considerant, "Did you say this?" Considerant responded, "I do not think so. I do not remember."[40] Daly wrote a protest in English from Considerant addressed to General McLeod, which Considerant signed and which they showed those most devoted to the cause. "But the blow was no less spoken of, and it could well have contributed to [their] failure."[41] This seemed almost merited by the visit made to the editor of the Know-Nothing newspaper by Daly, Considerant, and Simonin.

In spite of their talents and accomplishments, Considerant, believing he could get along without Daly, who had overshadowed him, did not show any desire to see him either remain or leave. There was something in his character that prevented him from understanding that "a leader grows in the eyes of the world in proportion to the grandeur of the ministers whom he employs." Simonin vented his frustration in his diary: "Considerant arrived here six weeks before me, and four before Mr. Daly."[42] He had himself presented everywhere he could.

> The position he had assumed since my arrival was this: each person here, in speaking to us, said Mr. Considerant, or Mr. Considerant's colony, so that everything [was] personified in Mr. Considerant, and that only Mr. Considerant remains. How was this done? Why don't they say the European-American Colonization Company, or at least, the French colony? I know absolutely no reason why. . . . And this fact has importance and influence; because those who are going to carry out our business, that which we do, Mr. Daly and I, have the aura of little clerks, or of little I-don't-know-whats, who cannot operate as equals in relation to the representatives and cannot obtain from them important things, cannot in sum exercise a great deal of influence. I have nevertheless done all the errands and solicitations that I could do, in spite of the bad conditions in which I found myself.[43]

Then there was the day Simonin went to Considerant's house to discuss Arthur Young, mentioned in a letter Simonin received from the Paris management written on November 29. Simonin opened the letter in front of Considerant, placing it between his two thumbs and index finger. Immediately, Considerant started to tear the letter from Simonin's hands. As Simonin's face reddened, he held on tightly to the letter and read it. Considerant did not listen. Then Simonin got up and left the letter on the table, turned to the door, and said, "Read it if it suits you."[44]

In the eyes of Simonin, Considerant was not worthy of representing the colony. Unknown to Daly and Simonin, Considerant was working against the best interests of La Réunion. He bought 9,210 acres of land from speculator Alexander on Saturday, January 25, 1856. This amounted to two leagues and labors of headrights for $2,302.50.

The following day, Sunday, Simonin continued to fill his free time for the benefit of the stock corporation by lobbying House members while waiting to question Considerant on the financial books of the society. Finally, unable to pin down Considerant, he resolved to leave Austin the following day. That last day, he persevered in quizzing Mr. Studer on particulars of vegetables that grow well in Texas. They discussed weather and watering, the threat of insects, the hearty trees to bring to Texas, and cultivation in a climate of intermittent, unpredictable rains. That evening Amédée Simonin wished César Daly well on his travels and packed for the 4:00 a.m. stage.

On Monday, Simonin left Austin for La Réunion.[45] The question before the legislature was in the hands of the Committee of Public Lands, which Simonin thought would make its report before adjournment. While Dallas's petition for a corporate township passed, Daly had not gotten the empresario bill out of committee. As the legislature's members focused on the political trades of getting their own bills passed, with only Bexar and Comal County members' support for an empresario grant, the European-American Colonization Society's interests were awash in the session's final-week frenzy. Hugh McLeod's Know-Nothing sally against Considerant and John Marshall's *Gazette* editorials over nine months still left a black cloud over the society's petitioner bill. Daly had not been able to do enough. Victor Considerant had been given a lesson in Texas land speculators' bait-and-switch techniques in making claims for a golden investment in the future. Simonin could do no more.

The relations between the "sundry citizens of Dallas" who successfully petitioned the legislature and the representatives of La Réunion, three miles away, whose petition remained in limbo, are not recorded. Certainly, the gulf between them was growing wider as positions on slavery began to harden.

In Austin, Considerant wrote his wife, Julie, "I leave in two days for San Antonio with César Daly and Antoine Supervièle, a fine type I have met here."[46] Daly was reverting to research in his profession as an architectural publicist, no longer acting as a Fourierist emissary while treated as an errand boy by Considerant. He wanted a couple of days to look at San Antonio's Mexican heritage before he went to the Gulf to find a ship.

Considerant, departing Austin with his man Cousin at his side and his pistols, was guided by a state senator on his home territory of Bexar County. In the new year still no one around him knew Victor Considerant's secret that on November 18, within three weeks of his arrival in Austin—before he even had a Réunion petition printed seeking an empresario grant to give to the legislature—he had bought land with Réunion funds at a new unseen site far away from La Réunion in North Texas. This new land was in distant Bexar County, in the Canyon de Uvalde.

Considerant had not discussed the purchase with anyone. He knew what Godin would have to say about the purchase. Earlier, Considerant had reported his encounter with the then newspaperman Olmsted and the idea of a purchase in the Canyon de Uvalde in a letter to Godin. In his reply, Godin had frowned on the idea, saying that in locating a site, they should stick with potential water routes to get products to market and certainly not go to a western frontier where they would have to add fighting the Indians to their other problems.

Just as Considerant and Daly were leaving, the legislature approved incorporation of the Memphis, El Paso and Pacific Railroad Company on the final day of the session. This railroad bill might have seemed good news to Fourierist investors, as the reserve lands from the thirty-first to the thirty-third parallel meant that the railroad route to the west coast had a good chance of passing through Dallas County, along the northern border of the reserve lands, and where the French stockholder society was already invested in some thirteen thousand acres of land. The reserves between the latitudes took on new meaning; now they were real reserves for a railway that would likely come. What was the reality now for Considerant's dream? Lands north of the thirty-third parallel, between it and the Red River, were too close to Indian Territory and still dangerous.

From Austin, Daly's and Simonin's departures meant there would be no skilled speaker in English addressing members in the adjourned session, scheduled to be reconvened next July. No one would remain to advocate their pleas for giving the colony an empresario land grant. Victor Considerant now had an excuse to ignore Godin's strictures against buying land west of San Antonio. He would set his sights on the land south of the thirty-first parallel.

19

Downward Slide

In January Jean Goetseels, the investor from Belgium, pushed on to La Réunion after only four days in Austin. He had seen enough. Once at La Réunion his first mission was to extract his seventeen-year-old stepson Philippe from what he considered a morally corrupt splinter group led by a prescript newspaper writer named Sauzeau. They were living at what they called Mutuele.[1] Next, Goetseels demanded his $30,000 investment back. Cantagrel gave him certain items of La Réunion stock and equipment. Goetseels bought the land where the splinter group was squatting, located on beautiful Mountain Creek, a virginal tributary of the Trinity River West Fork, and kicked the squatters off. He then tried to found New Leuven in competition with La Réunion. He lured some of the Réunion young architects from his hometown in Belgium to come build a house for him and his family. La Réunion now had splinter colonists.

When accountant Simonin arrived from Austin, he was greeted by Cantagrel, who showed him a bunk in the big hangar, where he would be staying while he reviewed La Réunion's paperwork.[2] Simonin took one look at his sleeping quarters, shook his head, and said, "No! I will not be treated as a lowly bookkeeper. I demand personal quarters!"

Simonin settled down at his desk in his private quarters to extract the detailed information he wanted for his report while recording his impressions of the colony members and leaders. He smirked at Cantagrel's pile of little papers that had been handed to him; they did not suggest business order or adequate records. He was impressed with Dr. Savardan, who sometimes worked seventeen-hour days to develop accurate labor records. Dr. Savardan's cooperation made Simonin a friend. Simonin wrote in his diary, "It is fortunate that Dr. Savardan is in the middle of the colonists. He gives them the example of abnegation, of frugality, of activity, of work, of gaiety and liveliness. Considerant could gain some great advantages, it seems to me, from the presence of this doctor at Réunion."[3]

While the accountant admired Dr. Savardan's style of leadership and record keeping, he found that Director Cantagrel was ignorant of accounting. Cantagrel saw no need to close quarterly accounts. Others helping with record keeping could not do addition without mistakes.

Maximilien Reverchon and his son Julien arrived in January as well. Dr. Savardan looked forward to having the benefit of their expertise. The senior Reverchon had spent three months in the 1840s in North Africa at the Algerian Union de Sig phalanstery in charge of horticulture. He had also researched plants grown by irrigation, hot-weather beans from India, pistachios from Persia, and warm-weather grape varieties in his large garden on the Rhône south of Geneva. Dr. Savardan had hoped for a third competing garden with the arrival of these two experienced horticulturalists, but Reverchon refused to participate. He told Simonin that after watching François Cantagrel manage the colony, he wanted to take a stick to him.[4] To Dr. Savardan's dismay, the most experienced horticulturalist not only did not want to garden at La Réunion but also did not want to participate in the commune at all. He chose to live alone on Coombs Creek and build a garden for his personal use. Now La Réunion had another splinter group.

Dr. Savardan sniffed that Reverchon's isolation furnished few evidences of his capacity: "His conversation is that of an educated man; his mind is ornamented, but his character appears to resemble very much the Texas climate of extremes and sudden variations."[5] Savardan wrote sarcastically that Reverchon's great knowledge was proven by his having spent $300,000 of his own fortune in agricultural experiments. His son Julien was already writing letters to Asa Grey at Harvard and sending him specimens of plant species unknown in cooler climates. Charles F. B. Bussy encouraged Reverchon to write to France that North Texas would someday support grape culture. He had tasted a bottle of wine made from wild grapes harvested the fall before: the climate would be good for wine production. La Réunion had still another splinter colonist.

Extreme February cold set in as the colonists argued about the acceptance of paper money, which was illegal in Texas. A few members of the

14. Julien Reverchon. From *Memorial and Biographical History of Dallas County, Texas* (Chicago: Lewis Publishing, 1892). Courtesy of DeGolyer Library, Southern Methodist University.

failed North American Phalanx came to La Réunion. A few left the colony, writing notes back from New Orleans warning not to put another sou into the enterprise as long as Considerant was the leader. But despite all the negatives, since Considerant left for Austin in October, things had settled into a routine and were improving, with Cantagrel's construction and Dr. Savardan's organization.

After the harsh winter, they were building homes to escape the disadvantages of dormitories. One was a wood-frame home, and the other was made of mud brick, each to hold eight households.

Exploring science on the ground, Dr. Savardan wrote his friend at the Jardin des Plantes, "We immediately had to create cesspools for toilet waste, and found thereby beetles that are friendly helpers in the disposal of feces. They are social insects who help each other carve and round portions into balls, and then roll them away to store in their burrows."[6]

Since the constitution of the corporation, the company of La Réunion had cleared and now cultivated 430 acres of land, two-fifths of which were enclosed. A herd of sheep and a pigsty had been enlarged. They now had six hundred head of cattle, all branded. "During the rigors of one of the harshest winters in Texas memory [they] lost only two oxen and a horse." They constructed "fences and a cattle water hole, a well and a building for the processing of tallow and the manufacture of candles and soap, shelters for a tannery and the laundry, a kitchen, a bakery, a grocery store, a shelter for honey-bees, a henhouse, a smokehouse, and a forge. A building housing the office now [kept their] papers dry." And at last an infirmary was being built, the infirmary Dr. Savardan had requested on arrival at La Réunion.[7]

"Sunday [was] consecrated to the regular reading of the Gospels, to the general elucidation of the social aim and of common faith, to higher education and freedom of the soul in accordance with general ideas and the religious feeling of the population."[8] Two hours were consecrated for singing on Sunday mornings under the guidance of Charles Capy. Considerant had criticized the effort before he left for Austin, saying, "How was that general culture as important as the fields and gardens?"[9] Considerant never came to hear a concert of those singing, nor did he ever honor its professor with a single word of encouragement. Julie

Considerant criticized the chorus for what she called its exclusive use of the Galin-Paris-Chevé method of music notation. Dallas neighbors at first came to hear Capy and his singers but lost interest when the participants' numbers dwindled. And there were the Sunday dances when weather permitted.

Gifts of books made to the colony by phalansterians had remained stacked pell-mell in a storehouse, contrary to the promise of reading rooms in *Au Texas*. Now the books were at least shelved on some low bookshelves where they could be found when colonists wished "to cultivate their intellect."[10]

During the previous months, the doctors attended to the health of the colonists. A few colonists died. Abel Bossereau, the strong, able-bodied man of twenty-eight who was one of Savardan's choices from La Sarthe, died of typhoid. A teenage daughter of Jean-Baptiste Louckx, just arrived from Belgium, died. Dr. Savardan treated a young man named Mique, who was sheltered in an abandoned cabin in the Dallas hamlet after Considerant banned Mique from La Réunion because he had not been given permission to come.

Dr. Savardan, with some hesitation, ended a report to Paris describing the progress to date with this remark: "The truths that I have to tell have many proofs and many witnesses; yet because of my age and the peculiarities of my style, I may fail in calmness as well as in power to tell them. I hope nevertheless to possess sufficiently the characteristics of justice and impartiality that one has a right to expect from a contemporary historian, an actor himself in its history."

New colonists from France were arriving every day. Doderet, a notary from Burgundy, possessed a knowledge of agriculture and rural construction, as well as an independent fortune. He arrived that cold winter. He spent the first night at La Réunion in the middle of the prairie outside in the cold without food or fire. The next night he was provided with a pallet on the floor of the windy attic instead of the furnished room he had been promised on departure from Europe.

After an absence of five months, Considerant, Roger, and Cousin returned by stagecoach from San Antonio on March 24. As Considerant and his men walked up the eastern trail to La Réunion from Dallas, they passed the garden in the eroded side of the caprock begun by Savardan and Nicolas. On that day, volunteers were attending the garden, as were the doctors. The garden had flourished with eight months of care, something impossible not to notice. Considerant walked only a few feet away from the two doctors. Though he had not seen them in five months, he did not say a word to them. He did not even acknowledge their presence with a tip of the hat. His silence spoke louder than any of his oratory to the crowds in Paris.[11]

Simonin, who was also present that day, was astounded at Considerant's behavior toward the two doctors: "This fact proves, like so many others, that Considerant does not any more understand how to direct souls practically than to direct the other affairs of his enterprise."[12] Considerant's conduct toward two respected elderly men astonished another onlooker, Mr. Doderet, who had just arrived in January. He had never before seen Victor Considerant. He could not and would not believe so rude a man was actually he, the great Fourierist leader so famous in Europe. Doderet believed the others were mistaken when they told him Considerant himself with his two aides-de-camp had just passed. He maintained that it must have been some Americans. "It was thus that Considerant acted in order to disappear from the minds of all the other colonists."[13]

Was Considerant seeing this progress at La Réunion to be a threat to his new land purchase for a different colony? Why was he so rude? In Simonin's words, "He showed a petty vanity like small people with narrow minds. He has scraped himself with his own fingernails off the angel's pedestal of the colony on which his friends had placed him, and he had fallen flat on his stomach. He is at the bottom now, and will never raise himself back up on his pedestal again."[14]

Before the executive director had traveled to Austin, he left François Cantagrel in charge of La Réunion as director. On his return, Considerant took back control and interfered in management. He obliquely announced change by sending his Belgian friends Cousin and Roger to lay out and stake individual parcels of society land, hitherto a noncommunal practice that was frowned on in this utopia. The colonists feared that Considerant intended to privatize the land of La Réunion, that the land would be bought and sold. When Dr. Savardan and others asked why he was surveying the land, Considerant reminded the nervous people, "Has not the council asked that a map of the property be made?"[15]

Cantagrel became concerned with Considerant's behavior and the prospect of having the land divided into parcels. Finally, he became so frustrated that he resigned on April 4.[16] Alarmed, Considerant rode out onto the prairie with Cantagrel and told him, "I will blow my own brains out if you persist in resigning."[17] Considerant promised Cantagrel more authority and autonomy. Cantagrel relented.

Rumors among the colonists about the breakup of La Réunion began to circulate. Esprit started to lag, and production sagged. However, two weeks later the colonists held their annual celebration in honor of Charles Fourier's birthday, organized by the workers, not the *gros-bonnets*.[18] Considerant was asked to speak at the event. He stood in front of the stalwarts of Fourierism, the colonists who had come from so far away to establish his dream of a utopia in Texas, and sounded conciliatory, admitting his own mistakes and proposing harmony. Esprit seemed to be restored.

On April 8 Cantagrel wrote to management in Paris that he would continue as director only until Paris sent his replacement. When Considerant abrogated his agreement to cede power, Cantagrel resigned again. Cantagrel would wait no longer under Considerant's leadership for a replacement from Paris.

The rumor persisted that Considerant's purpose in having the land surveyed was to sell the land. Dr. Savardan asked Considerant repeatedly to explain his actions, but Considerant would not hear him out. Seeing no other avenue for communication, on April 15, 1855, Dr. Savardan wrote Considerant a letter. He implored him: "We all want to keep Association. I cite important things achieved by working together in groups as Fourier has advocated. However, since the day of your return, these goals have begun to falter. I remind you, Victor, of your moral responsibility and duties." Dr. Savardan went on to enumerate the accomplishments to date, as well as the expenses the colony faced due to Considerant's exorbitant spending, such as the $3,000 or $4,000 spent on Bardot's garden. He reminded Considerant that the society "voted unanimously for revision of the article in the statutes defining an advance on the price of labor. Currently that wage is really insufficient for the necessities of the laborer. It asks also for revision of the article concerning the reserve dividend, the distribution of which cannot fail to be completely illusory for several years."[19]

In response to the letter, Considerant invited Dr. Savardan to join him and Cantagrel that night at Considerant's home. Once the three took their seats in Considerant's dimly lit living area, Considerant raised the issue of the dissolution of the society. Dr. Savardan protested the idea, again pointing to the accomplishments of the colonists in such a relatively short period of time despite the challenges. He reiterated the opportunities Considerant had vetoed that would certainly bring income to the colony from the locals and elsewhere: potential profits in utilizing the sawmill equipment, building a tannery, a soap-making business, a candle-making business, a distillery, a carriage business, and an irrigation system for the valley. His arguments fell on deaf ears. Dr. Savardan and Cantagrel stood up and walked out the door.

Dr. Savardan and Considerant continued to discuss the dissolution of the colony, but only by Considerant's preferred method of communication: exchanging notes. Neither man changed his position.

Meanwhile, Simonin was still taking notes for his employers in Paris. Too many people from Europe were descending on the colony, and they were not the farmers who were really needed. Facilities had not been prepared for so many. In mid-April Considerant, Cantagrel, and Simonin met to discuss how to close La Réunion. Considerant could not answer the basic question posed by Simonin: What are you going to do with all these people and all that equipment and all those big ox carts full of materials shipped from Europe now at the Réunion site? La Réunion was a commune with communal land, housing, tools, farm equipment, animals, bakery, and kitchen.

In late April Considerant wrote to the colony's way station at its Houston farm with instructions to discourage new arrivals from coming north to the Réunion site. The executive director sent Edmund Roger to New Orleans and Europe to discourage immigrants. Roger was instructed to stop all those traveling to La Réunion and urge them to return home, head for San Antonio, or remain on the prairies in the center of the yellow fever districts. Roger carried with him a letter from Considerant blaming others for his own failings.

Along the trail well north of Houston, Roger met the Santerre family, a family of eight who had sold their farm near the Loire River in France. Roger informed the Santerres that they must turn around and return home. They would not. They felt they had no choice but to continue on to La Réunion, especially after their treacherous journey.

Marie Catherine Santerre, traveling with six children, had waited two weeks for a ship at Le Havre while nursing her five-year-old, who caught red measles there. On the ship she faced an epidemic of black measles that broke out among the children, one that infected all of hers. After forty-two days at sea, food gave out, and for five days passengers ate only molasses. In the middle of the night in a great thunderstorm, the Santerres were dumped without a guide on the bank of Buffalo Bayou to seek the colony way station. As they walked north, Marie Catherine and her teenage daughter had to carry a three-year-old on their backs the entire three hundred miles. In the heat, clouds of dust from the oxen covered them, and rains forced them to wait for weeks at stream crossings. The teamsters deserted. At rainy campsites, the children's shoes floated away. They bid Roger farewell and headed to their new home, La Réunion. They finally arrived, but their travails had not ended. The family of eight was assigned to keep house in two eight-by-eight-foot rooms without doors or window glass in one of the colony's big, barnlike shelters.

Simonin penned a note to himself in his diary that Considerant's treatment of immigrants was dishonest.

In late April abundant rain cured thirty-eight days of dryness. Then, soon after, a torrential rain under a north wind turned gardener Barbot's company-sponsored garden into a lake. At the Réunion central courtyard, water "rocked like the sea." Rather than calming the colonists after all of nature's chaos, Considerant exaggerated it.

On April 26 Considerant finally admitted the truth. He at last told Cantagrel and Dr. Savardan that he was definitely leaving for "the west," taking two colonists he wanted with him to start another establishment that would be in the "proximity" of La Réunion. He claimed that it would be easy to maintain relations between the two colonies, that communications would not be an issue. Considerant failed to explain that the two colonies would be 350 miles apart and that the only available transport would be by horse across active Indian trails.

Considerant again urged the privatization of La Réunion. Cantagrel's conscience made him argue against Considerant's proposed dissolution of the Proprietor's Society, which was organized to control shares of La Réunion funds and the privatization of its land and resources at the expense of the laboring colonists.[20] Dr. Savardan's view remained unchanged.

In early May Considerant finally relented to Dr. Savardan's request a year earlier to open a school, even though the number of children to be taught remained the same. What had changed was the teachers. The Bar family of teachers, who had been assigned low-paying jobs, had left La Réunion for Dallas. They had been unable to earn a living at the utopia. They eventually returned to New Orleans, nearly ruined.

In May, just as the spring foliage had leafed out, Réunion was hit with an unseasonable ice storm so severe that the river froze for three days. Their crops were ravaged. Thirty new colonists arrived from their long, cold journey just about the time the management of La Réunion passed a resolution to dissolve the society of La Réunion, a resolution Dr. Savardan resoundingly rejected.

In late May Simonin gave up asking the executive director for fund details and gave up altogether. He left La Réunion to return to New York and France, still without answers on specific accounting practices in order to close the books and with no specific knowledge of Considerant's actual land purchase elsewhere in Texas. From Simonin's perspective, Victor Considerant, the hero proponent of Fourierism, became a secret saboteur of his own and his faithful adepts' dreams of utopia.

In June, after a month of raging arguments with Considerant over the value of their stock and over the value of the labor they had put into the colony, some three hundred colonists who had paid their own way across the ocean to participate in Considerant's dream brought the issue to a head. Part of the dispute was over the colonists' share of the reserved dividends. The colonists demanded a one-half share; Considerant offered a one-third share. Considerant scoffed: Wasn't the food the colonists had received sufficient compensation? Had they not been fed?

Cantagrel, who deplored Considerant's refusal to recompense colonists who had contributed to the community, resigned as director without equivocation. Cantagrel left with his family to return home to Europe. Dr. Savardan resigned his role of keeping company labor records and his role of treasurer for both the company of La Réunion and the general stockholding company.

Considerant announced that he had found a replacement for Cantagrel: Alexandre Duthoya, an accountant who had come to La Réunion to replace Simonin as the bookkeeper. Dr. Savardan argued against making Considerant's replacement nominee, Duthoya, both treasurer and a director, as they were conflicting roles. In response, Considerant unilaterally approved Duthoya's titles.

Considerant was left to personally take over bargaining with the colonists. As negotiations continued that summer, the relentless drought killed the few crops that had survived the May ice storm. The wheat, oats, barley, and garden vegetables were decimated. There was unrest among the colonists. Artisans were eager to seek a more comfortable lifestyle and paying jobs in their skilled trades.

Despite the discontent and turmoil, La Réunion paused for a July 4 celebration, attended by locals and colonists. The *Dallas Herald* reported the 1856 Fourth of July celebration:

> Others, and among them some of the fair portion of God's creation, spent the day at "Réunion," the French settlement of Messrs Considerant & Co. where, we are informed, a handsome dinner was served up to a large number of invited guests, and at night a dance enjoyed. Those who spent the day . . . returned highly pleased with the entertainment. Among the exercises of the day was a target practice in the morning, and a national salute at 12 o'clock. The grounds were tastefully arranged, particularly the place assigned for the dance. This was an arbor built on a level piece of ground, hung with handsomely designed lanterns, and from the

top streamed numerous small national flags, the predominant ones being American and French. By the way, we were much pleased to see a large American flag floating from the top of the principal building. We understand that a number of national songs were sung by the French, among them, of course, the "Marseillais" [*sic*]. Altogether, the day passed off to the entire pleasure and satisfaction of the assembled company.[21]

A month and a day later, on August 5, Considerant reached an agreement with the laborers. They would receive one-half of the reserved dividends, as they had requested. The agreement was to be written up in a formal document for signatures the next day. But on August 6, instead of honoring the compromise agreement and giving the colonists half their wages, previously withheld, Victor Considerant sneaked away from La Réunion, headed to San Antonio under the dark of dawn and accompanied by Cousin.

He left without signing the final paper hammered out with the colonists the day before. He left without a good-bye. He kept his empresario dream, even if it was reared on the backs of some three hundred unpaid immigrants, as well as the others still to arrive at La Réunion. The colonists would not be compensated for their efforts. Many more small investors would lose their savings in Europe. Dr. Savardan deemed Considerant's departure a "flight"—a flight from his own inability to lead.

Victor Considerant later wrote from San Antonio that he would have no more to do with the colony, claiming he was ill. He never returned to La Réunion or North Texas. The great Fourierist leader abandoned his utopia and the people who had followed his call into the wilderness.

20

Demise

In late August, a letter arrived from management in Paris designating Dr. Savardan the acting leader until Allyre Bureau, the kindly corporation leader in Paris, could reach La Réunion and assess the situation. Duthoya was to remain as the bookkeeper. The letter, however, was addressed to Dr. Savardan in care of Considerant. Julie Considerant intercepted the letter and sent it to her husband in San Antonio. Considerant sent the letter back to La Réunion. When Dr. Savardan finally received the letter on November 7, he handed the letter, without reading it, to Director Duthoya, who proceeded to hand Dr. Savardan his resignation as director. Dr. Savardan, knowing Bureau was soon to arrive, asked Duthoya to continue his duties.

Bureau arrived on a freezing cold day in mid-January 1857, having just spent a few days with Considerant in San Antonio. At dinner, Bureau shared with Dr. Savardan the substance of his discussion with Considerant. Considerant had told him to give up on La Réunion. Dr. Savardan made clear his wishes to continue the association. After dinner, Bureau paid a visit to Julie Considerant, then went to sleep that night on planks in the ice house. Director Duthoya had neglected to prepare a room for him.

A few days later, Dr. Savardan and twenty other colonists walked to the large meeting hall in the cold to meet with Bureau. All gathered around to hear Dr. Savardan in a clear voice read a report he had written on the state of La Réunion and a view of the future. Bureau listened carefully, then said, "I was in accord with the views expressed in your report when I left Paris. Today, having spoken with Considerant, I believe the society of Réunion should be dissolved."[1] Bureau was still under the sway of Considerant.

But the weight of it all was heavy on Bureau, who was out of his element. He could not sleep. He confided in Dr. Savardan that he was tired and confused and "would be much happier if he were sleeping in his grave."[2] Dr. Savardan urged him to return to Austin, where Bureau's beautiful wife, Zoé, and their children were waiting for him. Bureau refused to leave. Instead, he called a meeting of all the members of the colony. Again, they all gathered in the large meeting room. People were angry, enraged, disappointed. The laborers who had negotiated with Considerant for additional money had not received a penny. Some colonists shouted threatening demands. Bureau tried to respond but could not handle the situation.

Bureau became melancholy and preoccupied with suicide. At this point, he had moved into Considerant's home with Julie. The archives of the colony were moved there as well. Dr. Savardan met with Julie and requested she tell Considerant to return and take control of La Réunion. She refused, so Dr. Savardan wrote Considerant requesting his return.

The next day, Bureau prepared but did not post a placard signed by him stating, "The Society of Réunion Is Dissolved." An advisory committee was formed. Director Duthoya and Dr. Nicolas prepared to leave. A few days later, committee members gathered for a meeting, presided over by Bureau. In the meeting the committee proposed that Bureau grant the laborers half the reserve dividends as negotiated with Considerant. Bureau agreed. Now the decisions needed to be carried out, but the next day Bureau failed to post his placard announcing the dissolution. Some committee members suspected that Julie Considerant played a part in the delay. That evening, several members met with Bureau to remind him of his obligation to post the sign.

Bureau posted the sign that evening. By morning the sign had disappeared, but the restaurant was full of people spouting "menacing stump oratory."[3] The next day everyone lined up for their money. They were given work tickets, which could be used as money at La Réunion to buy land or tools or equipment then owned by the commune. Work tickets were of value to those who sought to remain and buy land at La Réunion and work for themselves, but they were of no value to those who had no means of making a living there and wanted to leave and seek their income elsewhere. What could those people do with a work ticket? The laborers demanded money from Bureau instead of the work tickets. They threatened him. Bureau might have been in physical danger had Julie Considerant not protected him in her cottage.

The advisory committee allowed colonists to rent equipment and tools using their work tickets. Land was sowed and cleared. Equipment was rented to the farmers. Workshop tools were shared. The forge was rented to Louis. Carpenter tools were rented to Charles Auguste Capy. Tin plate equipment was rented to Dailly.[4] Formal leases were drawn up and signed by Bureau.

In mid-February, Considerant's aide-de-camp Vincent Cousin arrived at La Réunion, much to the displeasure of Dr. Savardan. When asked why he had returned, he said he had come to take Julie Considerant and her mother to San Antonio, where Considerant was waiting. Cousin handed a note to Julie that said, "Tell Dr. Savardan that I thank him for having written, but that I cannot return to Réunion."[5] According to the letter, by mutual agreement with management in Paris he was no longer to be involved in the affairs of the colony.

Cousin, who clearly had not returned just to take the ladies to San Antonio, soon made his intentions clear. He placed his bed next to Bureau's and forbade him to speak with others. Cousin had an agenda.

Dr. Savardan decided Zoé Bureau needed to know of her husband's distress. He wrote her a letter on February 20, telling her that Bureau was mentally distraught and that she should come for him. When Zoé received the letter, she rode the stage for three days to Dallas. Three days later, Julie Considerant and her mother left La Réunion without Cousin. Before she left, Julie informed people at the colony that she was going to prevent Zoé from coming to La Réunion. When they met Zoé en route to Dallas, Julie warned her against going to La Réunion. Zoé ignored Julie, sent for her husband to come to Dallas to meet her, and eventually convinced him to return with her to Austin, leaving the arguments over the remains of the colony to others. Bureau fought her request. He did not want to be deemed a coward.

Dr. Savardan wrote Bureau a note, signed by all the committee members, saying he was sorry Bureau had left, but perhaps another day they would all be under his direction. Wrote Dr. Savardan, "You are the man for harmonious times."[6]

Once Bureau was gone, Cousin implemented Considerant's agenda. He disbanded the advisory committee, placed all functions under himself, and refused to honor the leases drawn up but not yet executed. Cousin wanted to sell, not lease, everything, even though the people had no money to buy. To make matters worse for the colonists, Cousin unilaterally set high prices.

In the case of Dailly, he had no interest in purchasing the tin plate equipment at so high a price. At this point, he wanted to save for his return to France. In response, Cousin had the equipment removed from the workshop and piled up in the store, rendering it useless to anyone. Colonists were then forced to go to Dallas for repairs and purchases.

The Dailly family joined the mass exodus that spring and summer when the majority of people at La Réunion fled the destruction of their dream of utopia. Half returned to France, as did the Dailly family. Bardot turned over the gardens to individual management and headed to Houston. The garden soon turned to a field. Fifteen others soon followed on the same route. Ten had preceded them. Doderet and Dr. Nichols left to first explore Venezuela before returning to France. Former bookkeeper and director Duthoya soon followed them. Many of the younger generation remained in Dallas.

Guillemet, who had a wife and three small children, was like many others who had no financial means of returning to Europe. When Bureau was still in charge, he had approached Dr. Savardan and several friends with the idea of purchasing the Horton property together—320 acres and the home. Guillemet would farm the land. They all approached Bureau to buy the land as a "collective reimbursement and offered to pay eight dollars an acre," which would realize a profit for the society. Bureau's response, "Wait until Considerant returns."[7] When Cousin arrived in lieu of Considerant, Guillemet presented the offer to Cousin, who rejected it. Cousin insisted on fifteen dollars an acre, despite letters from management in Paris stating that it had no intention of benefiting from members of La Réunion. Guillemet, Dr. Savardan, and the others had no other choice but to pay the price. They moved in and lived together in association, with Reverend John Allen's son teaching English.

Perhaps the ultimate petty action on the part of Cousin had to do with Dr. Savardan's medical case, which included surgical instruments and medicines that he had so carefully gathered before leaving France. Dr. Savardan had for two and a half years cared for over three hundred patients using the equipment and supplies held in that case.

Cousin approached him and demanded, "Give me the box of surgical instruments and medicine!" "By what authority?" Dr. Savardan replied. Cousin handed him a note from Bureau stating that Bureau delegated his management authority to Cousin. Dr. Savardan responded, "That paper has no value without the signatures of the managers of the company! What's more, Considerant had no power of attorney to give to Cousin since by mutual agreement, Considerant is no longer involved in Réunion matters!" Cousin persisted, saying, "I will have you put in prison." Dr. Savardan did not budge.[8]

Then on March 24, Cousin came to Dr. Savardan's home with two young men. When Dr. Savardan opened the door, Cousin demanded the return of the medical bag, still standing outside the doorway. When Savardan again declined, Cousin commanded the two men, "Seize the bag!" Neither man moved. The older of the two removed his hat and said to Cousin, "Had we known your intention, we would not have come. We did not come to America to be policemen." Cousin then bellowed, "I will enter myself!"[9] "At your own peril," responded Savardan. "You will respect my home!" With that, Cousin turned around and left the premises.

Cousin returned about two weeks later. He made another attempt to take the bag under false premises, but again Dr. Savardan persevered. Dr. Savardan wrote a letter to Cousin saying: "I will not be long, I hope, in ridding the administration of Réunion of an old, honest face."[10]

By April, "instead of a prosperous cooperative community, [they] had the old colony disorganized and more and more deserted and Cousin's city with three log cabins inhabited by unhappy people."[11] Tools and equipment and workshops had now been suppressed, as was the communal kitchen. The remaining residents had to install a kitchen in their home or create another situation for meals. Cousin created a boardinghouse. Eight people rented rooms. But the first proprietor gave up the enterprise, complaining of the high charges fixed by Cousin for the beef and utensils. Another man in Cousin's good graces received lower rates. He continued serving meals. Ultimately, the boarders found that even the lower price did not make it worth boarding there. Four left.

Dr. Savardan, having no interest in breaking bread with Cousin, proposed to twelve friends that they continue to run a common kitchen. They rented the infirmary space and installed a kitchen and dining room. Dr. Savardan saw patients there as well. They divided general expenses and paid for what they ate, and each did their share of work. The Horton farm provided eggs, milk, and butter. The small group created their own association, sharing the ideals that had brought them across the ocean.

Young Allen, who had been teaching, left to return home to Reverend Allen in Patriot. A few others left their small association as well. With so few people to support the association, Dr. Savardan and the others remaining were faced with the possibility of renting or buying slaves to assist with the work. But this was not an option, given their morals and values.

Adding to the atmospherics, Considerant and Cousin were called to appear before a grand jury in Dallas County. No one knows what precisely transpired at the hearing, since it was held in secret, but Dr. Savardan learned that "severe and threatening remarks were addressed to Cousin on certain details of his administration which might compromise the interests of the colony and neighbors of the colony." The good reputation established by Cantagrel in Dallas had been tarnished.

So, given the situation at hand and "not expecting anything more in the effecting of ideas, hopes, and promises" that had brought him to Texas and "resigned to add up as a loss the three years Considerant caused" them to lose, Dr. Savardan decided it was time to leave. He put his affairs in order, renting his property; the agreement included a clause requiring the renter to plant a certain number of trees each year and to build a fence enclosing the property. He packed his trunk, wrapped the painting of his wife, and prepared for the trip back to Château Gaugain.

Dr. Savardan took his leave on August 18 at 8:00 a.m. The remaining residents surrounded him to wish him well that warm summer morning. Dr. Savardan climbed into Considerant's pretty gig. Haizé, at a charge of

$80, had offered to drive him. They headed to Dallas for Savardan to say his good-byes to locals and former members of the commune and then on to Preston, where he waited at the hamlet on a sunbaked afternoon.

Cicadas buzzed in the oppressive heat. Sitting in the shade on a porch on top of a hundred-foot-high bluff whose south side had been cut into red and white bands of soil by the river, Dr. Savardan looked across from Texas into Indian Territory to the north. The river below was the red for which it was named, but it seemed shrunken, with many of its meanders dried up or reduced to pools. Its wide floodplain wove among strands of giant primeval sycamores, their trunks white against its red waters. He thought of the twenty-five chestnut trees he had grafted that also had big, bright green, water-filled leaves. He had personally planted and labeled each one for an orphan whom he had helped shelter many years ago. They would have grown tall enough now to harvest as a down payment for a village school at La Chapelle-Gaugain.

Waiting to be poled across the red waters below, Dr. Savardan saw a group of Indians sitting at the other end of the porch. They were also waiting for the ferry, visible in the distance. It would be a while before the ferry returned to load the two mules, carriage, and wagon lined up on the ramp below. Dr. Savardan commented in French on this to his driver, triggering attention from the others sitting in the shade.

Hearing Dr. Savardan speak French, the storekeeper became excited. He had never before seen a Frenchman. Wanting proof, he led Dr. Savardan to the back of the store and stood him opposite two illuminated engravings. With a professorial tone, he asked, "Do you know who they are?"

"Why, yes," Dr. Savardan answered him, "the three Napoleons and Lafayette. I have seen all four of them."[12] The doctor did not reveal that the police of one of the four had ordered him to remain under house arrest for six weeks while Louis-Napoleon became Napoleon III.

"Oh!" replied the shopkeeper and then added, "Are they not four great men?" "Oh, certainly," said Dr. Savardan. Savardan's memory flickered back to the age of fifteen in La Flèche, when the small one with the tricorn hat with his hand pushed into his vest had passed in a carriage

15. Allyre Bureau's family, photographed at La Réunion by son Gustave. From left to right: father-in-law Guillaume Rey, Allyre Bureau, son little Allyre, daughter Alice, wife Zoé, and son Paul. Courtesy of Gabrielle Cadier-Rey.

16. Bureau cabin. Courtesy of Gabrielle Cadier-Rey.

through Place Neuve on the way to make Savardan's old Jesuit convent school into the Prytanée Militaire.

This memory was interrupted by one of the Indians, who was charmed by Dr. Savardan's foot-long beard. Encouraged by the Frenchman's smile, Choctaw John took advantage of his own age and dignity to ask permission to touch it. Dr. Savardan smiled and said yes. Choctaw John ran his hand over it and passed his fingers through the combed white hair, testing its thickness. He smiled at Dr. Savardan and said, "Beautiful! Oh! Beautiful!" Then Choctaw John rubbed his own stubble and made a face, as if to say, "Not so beautiful."[13]

The ferry arrived. Men and goods were loaded, and all settled in for the ride. The slaves were poling Dr. Savardan back toward France and his home, which he had left over two and a half years before.

Back at La Réunion, the bits and pieces of utopia continued to be reorganized and swept away. Efforts were made to sell whatever possible in order to defray the losses of investors while at the same time Considerant in San Antonio tried to establish a new utopia at Canyon de Uvalde. He approached the Fourierists in Paris to invest in his new dream, but no one would take the bait. He took Bureau, who was still living in Austin, to see the land, and then they returned to their separate homes.

The following spring, Bureau, his wife, Zoé, and their family returned to La Réunion, where Bureau purchased the doctors' east-side garden park. He ran the land company and a store, trying to salvage the stockholders' investments in the colonization society. They brought a piano, and Bureau composed. Their twenty-four-year marriage ended when Zoé received a letter saying Bureau had died of yellow fever on his way back to her from Houston, a trip he made to restock the store. Zoé, with scarce funds, asked Considerant for monetary assistance for the passage home, but he refused to help her. Zoé booked passage on an old wooden boat and took her family back to Paris in poverty. She blamed Victor Considerant as the instrument of her loss and never forgave him.

21

Endings and New Beginning

On the first morning of his return, Dr. Savardan summoned two work-ers to unpack his trunks, reshelve his books in the library, and return the painting of his beautiful wife to its former prominent place on the wall in Château Gaugain. Then he saddled his horse for a ride through the village on this cool winter morning. The village had not changed in any real way, as he suspected would be the case. The stability was somehow reassuring.

He rode past his wife's grave. He rode past the village hall, where so many foundling babies had been left by desperate mothers. Past the twenty-five chestnut trees he had planted and labeled with the name of each of those orphans he had sheltered. There was work to be done. He would renew his efforts to improve the lives of these foundlings. As he rode along, he thought to himself, I have not changed. Certainly, my beliefs in Fourier's teachings remain steadfast. There is no change in me, he thought, except for my faith in certain men, which was too big, too blind.

Before he could renew his efforts on behalf of the children, he knew he must respond to the book sitting on his desk in the library, *Du Texas: Premier rapport a mes amis*, written by Considerant and published that year, 1857. That book was "an unfortunate web of insinuations and bombast!" With that thought, he turned his horse around and headed back home.

He pushed aside the rich green wool curtain near the salon fireplace and opened the concealed door that led to his library. The books were back in order. Fourier's stern visage still looked at him from the cor-ner of the room, hands folded across the top of his cane. Savardan sat down at his desk and pulled out a sheaf of blank paper from the desk drawer. On the top of the first piece of paper he wrote, "Un naufrage au Texas" (A shipwreck in Texas). He began: "I find on returning to France a pamphlet of M. Considerant entitled *Du Texas* in which he complains bitterly of having seen squandered under his very eyes, in spite of his efforts during the two years, the greatest part of the funds that had been entrusted to him . . . and in which finally he expresses regret for not having dared to send back to France nine-tenths of the persons gathered on the place!" He put down his pen. Dr. Savardan was incensed by Considerant's accusation that during the two years of the colony its funds had been squandered by unnamed persons, leaving suspicion suspended over all. He continued: "I believe I owe, both to you and myself, the story of those three years." He also said that he owed his response to the interest of the École, since "the men who have committed these mistakes persist in remaining in the government of our company, and the general assembly of stockholders, insufficiently enlightened, gives authority to them and bestows civic crowns on them."[1]

He paused again and reflected on why the envisioned utopia failed. Yes, friend Henri Fugère's warning had proven true. Savardan should not have placed himself under the leadership of Considerant, who knew nothing about commanding men, and, yes, Considerant's temper had exacerbated all their efforts.

Dr. Savardan wrote of the persistence on the part of Considerant to pose as the perpetual and omnipotent leader of a company of stockholders governed by a general assembly and by management of which he had been the founder, without doubt, but of which he was nothing but the executive agent. Dr. Savardan described the day Considerant cried at him, "You do not realize, then, that the management is nothing, absolutely nothing, in Texas, and that I, I alone, am everything!"[2] Then he wrote of the inexplicable attitude of Considerant, who for two years assisted in squandering the greatest part of the funds entrusted to him, a man who now says he did not know how to stop it other than to feel the death rattle in his throat, thunderstruck, crushed, overwhelmed as a living corpse, as Considerant states in *Du Texas*.

For page after page, the doctor methodically described the history of La Réunion, only occasionally veering from his factual account to an emotional venting. All had started well. Savardan assumed increasing responsibility for management of the new community directed by

Cantagrel. In August he was named a member and secretary of the nine-member council of the Society of Réunion and treasurer of the stock companies. Willingly and without pay, the doctor had cared for 228 patients. He had established the general inventory.

He described the efforts of the earnest colonists, the obstacles of nature, and the hardships, as well as the delights. He wrote of an idea for ventures proposed to Considerant that would have brought income to the society or enriched the lives of the colonists, ideas ridiculed by him. And in the end, Considerant failed them all, the doctor wrote, "by bringing us to Texas, where the political constitution created more difficulties than the climate, by denying the promises made in the spirit of association, and by throwing us violently into the difficulties of private establishment."[3]

The colony had failed, in his view, not due to any flaw in Fourier's vision or to the colonists but through the failure of leadership, namely, Victor Considerant. "I remained until the last bond had been broken," he wrote. The colonists' work had been "unappreciated, impeded, unrecognized, or destroyed by him."

The book was sent off for publication. That chapter of his life ended, Dr. Savardan began researching the first of several books to come arguing the necessity of caring for all children, rich or poor. Dr. Savardan never lost his focus on the cause or his moral compass, despite the shipwreck in Texas.

And what of Considerant? Julie and Victor remained in San Antonio and farmed in Bexar County, unable to raise funds to start a new utopia and unable to return home, since he was banned from France by Napoleon III. When Napoleon lost power in 1869, friends paid for the Considerants' return to Paris. They settled on the Left Bank, where Julie sold her paintings of flowers on the street and Victor, dressed in a serape, could be found pontificating and posturing as a socialist sage.

Afterword

La Réunion's Influences on Dallas

In 1855 two groups of people were assembling in the region of what was to become the city of Dallas. One group clustered around the county courthouse square, a few stores, and the two-year-old Masonic Lodge a quarter mile off the knoll to the north. The town's founder had left for the California gold rush, then come back and sold most of his headright along the brow of a bluff carved by the meandering river, along with the right to operate a ferry. Alexander Cockrell bought the headright land and ferry rights in 1853.

Entrepreneur Cockrell had wrestled a steam-powered sawmill from the nearest river port, 150 miles east, and was now building a covered bridge over the Trinity River. Five years before, the county of Dallas had held two elections to settle the location of a county seat. It was Dallas by a margin of twenty-eight votes. The next January 1856, the nascent villagers got a charter for the town of Dallas from the state legislature. Later that year, ninety-two people voted to establish a city government. Currency was in land deeds, headrights, and a market of headright scrip. Land, animals, and slaves were the only mediums of exchange. It would be another thirteen years before a bank opened in Dallas.[1]

Suddenly into this sleepy, remote river crossing arrived a stream of people ignorant of the frontier and bent on curing European social ills in a new utopia. This group had amassed $400,000 in Europe and hoped for an empresario grant from the Texas legislature to do what the group led by William S. Peters had partially done a dozen years previously: bring people to settle. This second group had opened bank and credit accounts in New Orleans and Galveston. They had organized a stock company and had people in Europe clamoring to come. They had paid American workers to prepare a site, found oxen drayage to haul mechanical plows, and shipped communal kitchen and laundry equipment, greenhouse glass, and even a library to the chosen site. Waiting along Houston's Buffalo Bayou were more equipment and thousands of plants and fledgling trees from French nurseries to be hauled north to this site. They named the new colony La Réunion. Why did the cultured Europeans of La Réunion not succeed over a few dozen yeoman farmers, who had depleted the region of bear and buffalo and who continued to look westward to fresh land and meat, in building a community?

In 1855 the thirteen-year-old hamlet of Dallas consisted of a sprawling dirt-pathed, one-story village of log cabins and a few frame structures standing on bois d'arc stumps, as much to avoid snakes and tarantulas as rot. It was peopled with yeomen farmers, primarily from the South, a few merchants, and a feverish breed of lawyers, "land men," and surveyors consumed with cornering free or cheap prairies.

Across the river to the west, there may have been almost seven hundred Europeans, including children, who came in dribbles between 1855 and 1857. They were bakers, ceramicists, masons, and brickmakers, skilled cabinetmakers and a metalsmith, cobblers, a lithographer, meat processors in the skilled European meaning of that term, and sophisticated market gardeners. They included new professions never seen on frontiers: architects, educators, two civil engineers, a man trained in astronomy, even a botanist and a poet. They included doctors with competing European medical ideas, a veterinarian, bookkeepers, notaries, accountants, and two watchmakers.

Kalikst Wolski, a Polish engineer, exile, and translator with the earliest group of Europeans attracted to utopian La Réunion, saw few signs of "civilized" specialization. Seeing Dallas in April 1855 through the eyes of the thirty-nine-year-old Pole brings the rawness of the thirteen-year-old settlement to life:

> For meat we have to go to town, since there are not enough of us so far to make our own slaughtering practical. In town, market opens at four in the morning and closes at six, lasting two hours, as after this it is too hot. Here in Dallas, market is not held every

day of the week, as there is no butcher here. When some colonist or other person slaughters a bull, he brings it to the town square very early in the morning and cuts it up with his meat axe, selling the pieces as he cuts them off, by the eye, without scales. The meat must be disposed of by six, and those who buy it must bake or fry or boil it at once, as it would spoil in a very short time. The people here for nine months of the year (March to November) eat only cold meat dishes. The swift spoilage of meat here may be ascribed not only to the heat, but also to the custom prevailing of killing cattle by shooting them.[2]

Onto this remote prairie, the French, Swiss, and Belgians brought their own cultural traditions. These contrasted with summer sectarian revival meetings, held in the shaded defiles near water where the air was ten degrees cooler than on the prairie tops. There was no celebration of the Fourth of July in the village of Dallas, but at La Réunion there were decorations for an evening dance and invitations to Dallas visitors. Especially the French and Swiss demanded different foods and a different standard of food preparation. To preserve perishables, they dug a cave in the escarpment hill. They introduced the first specialization of food processing as a component of a civilized society.

But in spite of their culture, it was La Réunion that failed in creative leadership. Considerant's intransigence to improvisation and blindness to the reality of ideas needed to fund costs on the ground drove Swiss leader Karl Burkli away. The manpower assembled was not put to good use. Considerant laughed at Savardan's proposal to irrigate crops from the river; he frustrated François Cantagrel by micromanaging. Considerant refused to divulge his actions to accountant Simonin, made extraneous loans unrelated to the colony, hoarded funds, and did not know how to lead men. Sadly, Jean-Baptiste André Godin, principal stockholder, failed to cross the ocean because of illness. His pragmatism was sorely needed.

Lacking strong leaders of their own, not many months after the group arrived, the Europeans began to integrate themselves into the frontier town. Jacob Nussbaumer, disillusioned with communal life, moved across the Trinity River in 1857 to establish an abattoir east of Dallas on Mill

Creek and on what became Swiss Avenue. Henrey Boll, Nussbaumer's future brother-in-law, listed as "charcutier, chasseur, et pecheur" (pork butcher, huntsman, and fisherman), was soon joined by parents and siblings, who after the Civil War established a family grocery. Advertisements in the *Dallas Herald* suggest that it may have been the first grocery store that was not a general store. Possibly the first recorded prepared foods for sale in the village were bread and pastries that Salomée Michael baked when she moved to the village from the commune.[3]

Along with food specialization, the Europeans brought a new view of agronomy to the area. Of the thousands of fruit trees, grains, and plant slips of all kinds that were contributed by a nursery in the French Finistère, many survived the ocean crossing because the colonists had the good sense to rest them in New Orleans, then purchase land on the Houston ship channel and leave a few of their group to immediately plant the cases of budding stock rather than risk killing them in a further month-long trip to Dallas. Later, cuttings were transferred to La Réunion, where most were lost to a seven-year drought, a plague of grasshoppers, and a freak spring ice storm.

While Victor Considerant dreamed of formal gardens and greenhouses, the Reverchons, Santerres, and others conquered the heat to create dairies and the La Réunion Fruit Farms, as well as other food enterprises. And gardens did come later, from which colonist Julien Reverchon was noted often to appear with armloads of flowers.[4] Maximilien Reverchon experimented with heat-resistant varieties of beans from India and immediately instituted deep plowing as a defensive technique in the first years of drought.[5] Ten years before, his short experience as the head of farming for the Fourierist commune Sig in Algeria, at a latitude closer to that of Dallas than France, was preparation for Texas.[6] Perhaps it was his brandied peaches that the La Réunion store sold, an item reputedly much in demand.

A Réunion colonist was the first to contribute to an important scientific endeavor. Maximilien's son Julien collected thousands of Texas plant specimens for the great taxonomists Sereno Watson and Asa Gray at Harvard. Numbers of them were named for Reverchon. St. Louis today benefits as the custodian of Julien's own important plant collection because after his death no place could be found in Dallas to house it. To contribute to the beginning of the Dallas Public Library in 1900, he solicited serious tomes from his learned friends in other places. The Reverchon legacy of interest in plant biology lived on in Maximilien's descendants Marie Caillet and Shirley Lusk. Caillet was a national authority on a group of five species of natural hybrid iris growing in the South, Midwest, and Texas and the coeditor of the major and definitive publication on the subject. One may see the continuation of Maximilien's and Julien's gardening tradition in an article on her garden in San Francisco in *Country Home*, published in February 1990. Lusk, an authority on rare native Texas plants and flowers, worked in nature conservancy to save disappearing species.

Before the early war against "varmints" was won, another Boll son, Jacob the naturalist, collected crustaceans, spiders, reptiles, butterflies, and numerous other insects as examples of Texas fauna for Louis Agassiz at the Museum of Comparative Zoology at Harvard.

Réunionists must also have contributed the first designed building to the community. Young architects, just out of school in Louvain, were among the early arrivals in 1855. Of course they came to build the ideal phalanstery, or commune, which they had seen pictured as a grand, Versailles-like image decorating the walls of architectural schools of their day, just as a romantic space station might adorn such a school today. But the only building of any size constructed on the Réunion site was built in the spring of 1855 before they arrived: an oversized structure of four spaces with verandas and a dog run but no doors or windows. Everyone came to inspect this wonder because no one in the area yet lived in anything but sixteen-by-sixteen-foot log cabins or their accretions. The building—thrown up by local labor to receive a hundred colonists—was no phalanstery to impress the young architects. Rather than camp in such primitive quarters and erect equally crude structures, architects soon departed for cities more hospitable to building.

But not the yeomen settler bred on the frontier for several generations. "Looking toward the future and always westward, he seldom felt himself permanently enough located to improve his dwelling, dig a well, or build fences, except as a requirement for headright ownership.

And he was ever ready to sell his holdings or to make an advantageous trade. The average Texan could see no point in improving property he might soon leave."[7]

Before intern architect Josse Vrydagh left, Alexander Cockrell, the chief entrepreneur of the hamlet, had Vrydagh design a new hotel of modest but pleasant design with Greek Revival details to eclipse the reigning Crutchfield House, an accretion of logs.[8] But life and culture were fragile in any frontier society. Cockrell was murdered in the street in front of the St. Nicholas Hotel before it was completed, and the building itself lasted little more than a year, until the fire of 1860. Vrydagh came back from greener architectural pastures in 1890 to submit an entry in the competition for the design of the present 1893 Dallas County Courthouse. Another Belgian trained in fine cabinetry, twenty-six-year-old Jean Louckx, saw there was no place on the frontier for his craft and became a contractor; later he served on Dallas's first school board. Charles Capy, a twenty-four-year-old Parisian painter and ship joiner, became a carpenter.

Another contributor to the building of Dallas, Émile Rémond, applied his background in ceramic engineering to identify clays worthy of a brick plant, which the colonist Frichot brothers built. Ironically, his knowledge of argillaceous compounds led in the twentieth century to the Réunion townsite itself being strip-mined for cement.

An early personal service trade was begun by Antoine Gouffe, who opened a tailor shop at Main and Lamar in Dallas; he became successful enough to make regular visits between Dallas and France in his later years. Jacob Charpentier, leather goods designer and shoemaker, opened a shop in 1857.

In 1855–56 Dallas was not ready for education, although the Swiss Bar family was ready to provide it. Thirty-six-year-old Kaspar Bar had learned from Pestalozzi, the great Swiss educator of children during the nineteenth century, and came to La Réunion filled with the best and latest thinking, planning to teach its children. Discouraged from staying by Considerant, he and his two talented young musician daughters could find no employment in Dallas. Before retreating to Louisiana, the family of six nearly starved trying to farm.

Everyone brought their own cultural habits. The Indians left theirs, as Reverend Allen and Roger found when they lost their horses and had to buy them back. There had been an Indian village on the southeastern corner of the tract later sold to Émile Rémond, which he mined for artifacts.[9] The orderly Swiss continued to keep order. Seventeen-year-old Benjamin Lang (later Long), a member of the first Swiss group arriving in 1855, soon adapted to Dallas. After the Civil War he twice was elected mayor and in 1870 returned to Switzerland to convince others to come to Dallas. While serving as federal marshal in the roaring railhead days of the 1870s, Long was killed attempting to settle a brawl.

The other arts, as well as architecture, had to wait until Dallas had grown enough to appreciate them. Yet the Réunionists practiced some of their skills. Allyre Bureau's bucolic view of his residence at La Réunion is the earliest known extant example of a spontaneous sketch made in Dallas by a European. Although he was reputed to have done so, did Bureau also really bring the first piano to Dallas? There is a story that in 1849 James Lattimer brought the first one and that his wife gave an impromptu concert on the square while the instrument was still on its wagon. Pianos were certainly symbols of culture, and many such stories may be apocryphal. Still, Bureau was an accomplished musician who had composed and played in Paris, and he did write at least one song used by Texas children. The colonists also imported the Galin-Paris-Chevé method for teaching the untutored to read music while singing in their a cappella group: the method had been much admired by the democratic workers' movements in France.

Finally, the Europeans brought a tolerance for humankind that was considered a threat by the Texas slavery-advocating frontiersmen. Indeed, with New Yorker Albert Brisbane and Reverend John Allen, conspicuously well-published in the North as abolitionists, linked with the colony, it would have been hard to escape that suspicion. Although one bitter critic accused Réunionists of asking settlers to lease slaves to them to improve their chances of acquiring free land from the legislature, there is no evidence that they ever used or owned slaves. Most likely, the legislature determined not to give Considerant free land in 1856 at least partly from suspicions of abolitionist sentiments among the "socialist" colonists. Later, when attempts were made to conscript La Réunion colonists into the Confederate army, most of them, particularly the French, barricaded themselves and fought to remain neutral from yet another war; they had left Europe to be free from further wars. A few Swiss did show their acculturation by enlisting for the South.

The colonists, both political republicans and socialists and therefore anticlerical, tended to reinforce a suspicion of the Roman Church in a period when a mass had not yet been said in Dallas and when less than 1 percent of the populace were of Roman Catholic faith. Dissident Colas reported that the Fourierists had their own doctrinal police: Cantagrel supposedly scolded a colonist for reading the rival doctrine of Alphonse Toussenel, *Work and Idleness*, because Toussenel had slid into communism. Criticized by Calvinists for holding dances on Sunday, the colonists explained that they worked all other days and hence only had Sunday for such pursuits, thus bringing another point of view to the narrow religions of the frontier.

Even before La Réunion, Dallas benefited from that earlier failed idealist experiment, Icarie, which was founded in Denton County in 1848. Adolphus Gouhenant, who led the sixty-nine men onto the plains of Texas in June in their uniform black velvet doublets and gray felt hats, escaped the ire of his followers to stay in the Dallas / Fort Worth area, where the next year he is said to have trained the Fort Worth garrison in fencing, taught French, and educated Commandant Arnold's children. Before Considerant visited Dallas in 1853, Clarksville's *Northern Standard* had commented on the Art Salon built by Gouhenant facing the courthouse square in up-and-coming Dallas. Victor Considerant was impressed that Gouhenant slept on bed sheets. These sheets and the Fort Worth commandant's napkins were evidently the only two items of civilization unique enough to comment on in Considerant's letters home.

Gouhenant also introduced advertising art to Fort Worth. When his friend Ephraim Daggett needed to lure customers to the dining room in his new hotel (improvised from the departed garrison's stable), Gouhenant, an artist by training, painted a great marquee that depicted the victuals served within.

The mature colonists who had already prospered in Europe—the intellectuals Burkli and Daly, the professionals such as Nicolas and Savardan, the dyer and witty poet Leray, the teachers, and the architects who wanted to practice their profession—soon left. Without strong communal leadership, the colony could not support individual intellectual and professional pursuits. Those depended on accumulated wealth.

The milieu was a place for pragmatists, for manually skilled persons in basic—not fine—crafts who had the energy to answer the frontier's demands. The foremen, farmers, carpenters, meat processors, cobblers, and tailors stayed. Lawyers and bankers who were in Dallas in this period before the Civil War lived off real estate and land-related dealings, not arguing fine points of law before appellate courts.

The Fourierists who stayed were mostly too poor to leave, although they also had to learn the peculiar blend of entrepreneurship and frontiersmanship needed to survive. Whereas the Anglos, bred for several generations to live on the frontier, preferred the independent life of living off nature and remained distant from most people, the Europeans at once set to work sharing their skills. After all, one of the chief tenets of their philosopher-mentor, Fourier, was to share the drudgery and therefore spend less time working. One senses that this more relaxed, worldly, tolerant view of life brought a slight leavening to the Calvinist work ethic of the frontier settlers. Not much, but a little.

One wonders if the colonists contributed to the twenty-first-century emphasis in Dallas on appearances and added to the demand for imported quality. Why did fairs begin in Dallas as early as four years after the utopian Fourierists arrived? Perhaps learning what was the latest was more than usually important to this village; people came to a fair to see what was new. The frontier ethic alone did not embody that inquisitiveness. From the extant evidence of connections maintained by colonists with Europe, one senses that a hunger for the world was early a factor in the Dallas psyche and a component of its competitiveness.

In 1850, on his odyssey to the gold rush, Maxime Guillot stopped off and discovered that Dallas needed a wagon and carriage maker. He returned home for a wife but returned to water the elms he had planted along a future center city street that took his name. Street names are another legacy of La Réunion. Cantagrel, Boll, Reverchon, and others have been remembered in street names and a park.

Most importantly, the colonists brought a civilizing view of collective specialized life, as practiced in cities, to this frontier yeoman culture where each person was judged on his ability to function completely independently of anyone else. For the first time, city dwellers, fresh off the boats from Europe, provided services that had been lacking in this nascent community. They were watered-down services, diluted by the demands of the frontier, which dictated all actions for survival, but in most cases they were the first such services, and Dallas was the beneficiary.

Appendix

Persons and Places

This list is compiled from all the bibliographical data used in this research, including the census reports of 1850 and 1860. See the author's La Réunion collection, as well as colonists' and correspondents' biographies. The last names of colonists or related immigrants are shown in capital letters.

Aisne, Department of: In northeastern France, containing the town of Guise and, after 1859, Jean-Baptiste André Godin's Familistère.

ALLEN, John (1814–58): Universalist minister born in Massachusetts, he was a conspicuous American reformer in the 1830s for a ten-hour working day and a temperance abolition and Fourierist advocate in the 1840s. He was also a fundraiser for Brook Farm and the participant whom Victor Considerant credited with a major role in the formation of La Réunion. Father of Fred, who joined him at the colony. (Fred was noted as the infant who carried smallpox to Brook Farm.) Allen's second wife, Ellen Lazarus Allen, and three children awaited him in Patriot, Indiana, when he went to Texas. Daughter Mary Catherine became an important Shaker leader in the twentieth century.

Associationists: The American name for the followers of Charles Fourier.

Aude, Department of: In eastern France; supplied eleven colonists to La Réunion in 1855.

Austin, Texas: The capital of the state of Texas, where Amédée Simonin, César Daly, Victor Considerant, Vincent Cousin, and Edmund Roger on behalf of the European American Society of Colonization in Texas lobbied the Texas legislature for an empresario grant of land for the colony in 1855 and 1856.

BAR, Kaspar: In 1845 Bar wrote an important biography of educator Heinrich Pestalozzi after studying with him. Bar brought his wife and musical daughters to La Réunion to establish a school on the famous man's principles but was refused by Victor Considerant. His family suffered great hardship before returning east.

Bell, Peter Hansbrough (1812–98): U.S. congressional representative from Texas (1853–57), a Virginian by birth who fought in the Battle of San Jacinto for Texas independence, and a Texas Ranger. He participated in the Battle of Buena Vista. He was the governor of Texas from 1849 to 1853 and was the senator whom Victor Considerant would have sought out on his trip to Washington in early 1855. He later served as a Confederate colonel in the Civil War.

Besançon: Seat of the Department of Doubs. Early Fourierists resided there, and Victor Considerant attended secondary school there.

BOULAY, Domanique: Brought his family for a second time to the New World to participate in La Réunion, having earlier gone to Brazil to be a part of Doctor Jules Mure's communities in the 1840s.

Bourdon, Émile Jean Baptiste: Member of the editorial staff of the Paris daily *Démocratie pacifique* from 1845 to 1851 and a writer for the newspaper. He was also a functionary in the Paris office of the École Sociétaire and named head of the stock company in 1855.

BOURGEOIS, Lucien (1817–85): Born in Cannes, Alpes-Maritimes; he migrated to Paris, where in 1841 he signed the protest of workers against dueling. He became a Cabetist who led sixty-two people to Denton County, Texas, in 1848. After that failure, he settled in North Texas on a headright grant of land but moved to Dallas before 1853, when Considerant found him settled there. In 1855 he became a commissioned pilot or guide for François Cantagrel while the latter sought land for La Réunion. He was the second man to blend Anglo and French culture in July 1856 by marrying Louisa Sampson, a widow from Massachusetts with a seven-year-old daughter. He remained in Dallas for the rest of his life.

Brazil (1840–44): A Fourierist experiment under the leadership of the French doctor Jules Mure took place in the province of Santa Catarina, first on the off-shore island of São Francisco, then on the peninsula of Sai and at nearby Palmital. At least one family, the Boulays, from this attempted phalanx came a second time to the New World to join La Réunion.

Brisbane, Albert (1809–90): Scion of a real estate / lumber fortune from Batavia, New York, who carried Charles Fourier's message to the United States after he had been a student of Fourier. He was the French connection of Associationists in the United States. In 1842 Horace Greeley gave Brisbane a byline column on the front page of the *New York Tribune* that stimulated some thirty attempts at Fourier-inspired communes. He figured in the transformation of Brook Farm into a Fourierist phalanx and helped to create the North American Phalanx. He persuaded Victor Considerant to visit the United States and led him to Texas. Brisbane was married three times, twice bigamously, and the father of Arthur Brisbane, national columnist of the twentieth-century Hearst newspaper chain.

Brook Farm: The Transcendental community and later Fourier phalanx (1841–46) in Roxbury, Massachusetts.

Buffalo Bayou: A channel flowing into Galveston Bay, Texas, and connecting to the village of Houston. In March 1855 colonists on the first ship carrying plant materials from France bought a site along this channel where they could put their plants in the ground to rest from the ocean crossing before later shipping them to La Réunion.

BUREAU, Alice (1836–?): Eldest child of Zoé and Allyre Bureau. She kept a diary of her travels with her family between Europe and Texas from 1856 to 1860.

BUREAU, Allyre (1810–59): Son of a French army officer from Cherbourg, graduate of the prestigious École Polytechnique in Paris, and a student leader in the Revolution of 1830, for which he received the Cross of July. Fourierist convert of Victor Considerant at the army artillery school in Metz. Later in Paris he supported himself as a musician by teaching, playing in the Théâtre-des-Italiens orchestra, and writing light opera. Allyre was a three-star general in Considerant's army of Fourierists; he was jailed in four prisons for five months in 1849 by Louis-Napoléon. He administered the École Sociétaire in Paris and formed the corporation for Texas land investment, Bureau, Guillon, Godin et Cie, known as the Société de colonisation européo-américaine au Texas. He oversaw the sending of emigrants from Europe to Texas. In 1856 he was sent to Texas with his family and was forced to dissolve the commune in 1857. He operated the colonization society as a land company from the site of La Réunion and died of yellow fever in Texas. Married to his mentor's daughter Zoé and father of five.

BUREAU, Antoinette Zoé, née REY (1813–?): Wife of Allyre BUREAU and daughter of Allyre's mentor, Antoine REY. Mother of five. Blaming Considerant for her husband's and family's vicissitudes, she appears to have burned all correspondence between her husband and Considerant after her husband's death. Considerant would not loan her money to help her family return to France.

Burford, Nathaniel Macon (1824–98): Lawyer who came to Dallas in 1848 and established a partnership with John H. Reagan. He was elected district attorney in 1850 and 1852. He and partner John Good defended the European American Society of Colonization in Texas in suits brought against it by colonist Jean Priot et al. Burford drafted the first Dallas city charter in 1856; was the first occupant of the Sixteenth District Court judgeship in 1856; enlisted in the Confederate Army in 1861; was Speaker of the Texas House of Representatives in 1866; became a Dallas County judge in 1875; was judge of the Fifth District in 1876; became U.S. commissioner in 1879. He was one of the three founders of the Dallas Masonic Tannehill Lodge in 1849.

BURKLI, Karl (1823–1904): Swiss member of the École Sociétaire; leader of twenty-five colonists to La Réunion in the spring of 1855. Burkli was a tanner and later became a banking reformer in Switzerland.

BUSSY, Charles François Bernard (ca. 1803–?): An accountant and former subprefect from Avranches, a village on the inner Gulf of Saint-Malo in the Department of Manche. He left his wife and two children in France to try his luck in Texas. He traveled with a manservant, Robert Martin, as a cabin-class passenger on the *Nuremberg* and acted as an entrepreneurial man of ideas at La Réunion, although his ideas were ignored. He left the colony in November 1855.

Cabet, Étienne (1788–1856): Lawyer from Dijon, Côte d'Or; director of the Carbonari, a leader who participated in the Revolution of 1830. He served as *procureur-general* in Corsica under Louis-Philippe. He was elected to the Chamber of Deputies but was exiled for five years in 1834 as an extreme radical. In England became an ardent disciple of Robert Owen. Author of histories of the revolutions of 1830 and 1789 and in 1840 of *Voyage en Icarie*, a social romance that attracted to him labor idealists of Paris. He figured in a landmark case of French jurisprudence that established in 1843 the right of the defendant to legal counsel, which propelled him to national prominence. He established a journal in Paris called *Le populaire*. As leader of the Icarian movement and on the recommendation of Robert Owen, he treated in London with the William S. Peters Company to bring a contingent of his followers to settle on a branch of the Elm Fork of the Trinity River in southwestern Denton County, Texas, in 1847. After the Texas frontier defeated them, he led them to occupy the Mormons' abandoned village Nauvoo in Illinois. He objected to Victor Considerant calling Adolphus Gouhenant "brave" in *Au Texas*.

CANTAGREL, François Jean Feliz (1810–87): Engineer, architect, lawyer, columnist for the *Démocratie pacifique*, editor and author, and collaborator of Victor Considerant. Jailed in the 1840s. With Considerant, he was pictured in engravings of the Paris salons of the 1840s. Author of *Le fou du Palais-Royale*; socialist-Republican member of the Chamber of Deputies from Loir-et-Cher in 1848 with the help of Alexandre Raisant's Comité des Travailleurs. He was a Montagnard who was condemned in perpetuity but escaped into exile with Victor Considerant to Belgium in 1849. He was the three-star general in Considerant's army who came to Texas in 1854 to buy land and begin La Réunion. He left the commune for Switzerland in 1856 and returned to France after the 1859 Amnesty, although he was again accused and jailed for a few months in 1871. He served as vice president of the General Council of the Seine in 1872 and was elected deputy of Paris's Thirteenth Arrondissement in 1876. In the 1870s he bought the residual land interests of the La Réunion stock company, including lands in Uvalde and Dallas Counties. Married to Josephine Conrads and father of a son and daughter, the latter of whom died at La Réunion.

CANTAGREL, Josephine, née Conrads (1830–1909): Wife of François Cantagrel and mother of two, one of whom was born at sea. This daughter later died as an infant at La Réunion.

Canyon de Uvalde: A verdant, unique, and mountainous frontier canyon covering an area of twelve by twenty-four miles. It is eighty miles west of San Antonio, Texas, in then Bexar County. Victor Considerant bought forty-seven thousand acres of inexpensive land there beginning in November 1855. It was also a major watering place for the Comanches on their trips to Mexico. The county has been renamed Uvalde County.

Capy, Charles Auguste (1829–1920): Son of Auguste Capy and Albertine Debeufles; he arrived in Dallas County in 1855 to join La Réunion colony. He started out as a ship joiner and painter, but he eventually became a carpenter in Dallas.

Citeaux, Department of Côte-d'Or: Site of a Fourierist trial in 1834 that was funded by Englishman Arthur Young.

Cockrell, Alexander (1818–58): Tennessean and 1845 immigrant to Dallas County; one of the first entrepreneurs in the village. He bought founder John Neely Bryan's residual headright land in and around the village of Dallas. He erected a steam sawmill and built the first bridge, which was partly covered, across the Trinity River in 1855. He commissioned the design of the St. Nicholas Hotel by Belgian colonist Josse Vrydagh.

In 1860 the U.S. census showed five former La Réunion members living in this hotel. He married Sarah Horton, born in Virginia in 1821. Following her husband's murder in 1858, she became Dallas's first effective businesswoman.

COLAS, Fritz (ca. 1828–?): An exiled journalist who was not a Fourierist but who came with the first arrivals and worked in the colony for some three months before moving to New Louven. Wrote a critical letter about La Réunion that was published in Paris by Jean Journet, a rival Fourierist and militant critic of Victor Considerant. A single man.

COMPANY OF RÉUNION (August 8, 1855–January 27, 1857): The Texas Fourierist experimental commune set up within the European stock company to operate thirteen thousand acres of land in western Dallas County, much of it purchased with headright options bought from sellers of scrip.

Condé-sur-Vesgre: A village sixty miles west of Paris near which a Fourierist phalanstery trial association was attempted on Dr. Baudet-Dulary's land in 1832 and toward a revival of which funds were raised for a second attempt by Auguste Savardan in 1852–53. Architect César Daly advised on the project and lived on the site until 1836.

CONSIDERANT, Julie Josephine, née VIGOUREUX (1812–80): Daughter of Clarisse Vigoureux. Victor Considerant married Julie in 1838. A devoted follower of her husband, she was reduced to painting flower pictures for income after her husband spent her financial resources on Fourierism. They had no children.

CONSIDERANT, Victor Prosper (1810–93): Son of a town hero in Salins-les-Bains, in the Jura. Graduate of the École Polytechnique and a career army officer, he resigned his commission to prune Charles Fourier's writings into a coherent dialectic and became the leader of the Fourierist movement in Europe. A gifted orator, he wrote numerous books, including *Au Texas* and *Du Texas*; established a Paris daily newspaper, the *Démocratie pacifique* (1843–51); became a member of the Chamber of Deputies after the 1848 Revolution; and exhorted the Montagnards against the future Napoleon III in 1849, for which he was proscribed and fled to exile in Belgium. He was the onsite director of the European American Society of Colonization in Texas. Married to Julie Vigoureux and without issue.

Coombs, Leven G. (1824–?): A miller from Kentucky who was married to Millea from North Carolina. Sold his 640 acre headright land to François Cantagrel; it became part of the colonists' first land purchase. It included what became the La Réunion townsite. The creek running through his land still bears his name.

COUSIN, Philippe Vincent (1822–?): A Belgian born in Mons, an architect in Brussels, and Victor Considerant's confidential agent; he was a principal stockholder and leader of a group to help begin La Réunion. In 1857 he was appointed by Considerant in his absence as director of the colony, much to the displeasure of Auguste Savardan. He later moved to Austin and then to San Antonio before returning to Belgium. A single man.

Crockett, John M. (1816–87): The Dallas law firm Crockett and Guess represented Jean Priot and others as plaintiffs in suits against the colony leadership in the district court in November 1855. Crockett was one of three founders in 1849 of Dallas's Masonic Tannehill Lodge. He was born in South Carolina.

Dallas, town of, and Dallas County, Texas: Established on the North Texas frontier in 1846, seven years before Victor Considerant and Albert Brisbane first visited it. Contained the site of La Réunion. The European American Society of Colonization in Texas bought over thirteen thousand acres of land in the western half of Dallas County. The land in La Réunion was incorporated into the county in 1860. The village of Dallas, which was chartered in 1856, at the time contained some three hundred persons. It lay three miles to the east of the La Réunion village site.

DALY, César Denis (1811–94): Natural son of a French émigrée who was a member of the Bernard de Calonne family and a well-off British naval officer from an important Irish family. His early life was spent in London. One of his grandfathers had been a page in Marie Antoinette's court. Daly was a gifted speaker, architect, publisher of the prestigious *Revue d'architecture* (1839–86), and conservator of the Albi Cathedral (1847–77). At heart an aristocrat and monarchist, he was intellectually a socialist who developed visual images of the ideal phalanstery in the 1830s and financially supported and collaborated in writing for *La Phalange* and the *Démocratie pacifique* (1843–51). He accompanied Considerant to Washington and La Réunion from New York in 1855 and treated with the Texas legislature for free land in 1855–56 on behalf of the colonization society. He was made an honorary member of numerous European architectural societies and the American Institute of Architects. He received the Legion of Honor and was awarded the Royal Institute of British Architects gold medal in 1892. A single man at the time of the colony, he married at age forty-seven.

Dana, Charles (1819–97): Member of Brook Farm (1841–46) and early writer on the *Harbinger*, a weekly magazine that examined social and political issues. He was correspondent-observer of the 1848 Revolution in Paris. Dana later became a major figure in journalism, first with the *New York Tribune*, where he propounded its antislavery policy, and later with the *New York Sun*. During the Civil War he became an important behind-the-scenes arbiter of functioning government, called the "eyes of the administration" by Lincoln. He developed an early "cyclopedia" with George Ripley.

DE GUELLE, Philippe (1837–56): Son of exiled Republican member of the Chamber of Deputies from the Jura. His father was persuaded to send his young son to La Réunion, where he died of tuberculosis.

Demeur, Adolphe (?–1892): Belgian lawyer and Fourierist who hosted Victor Considerant in Brussels.

Démocratie pacifique (1843–51): The daily Paris newspaper founded by the École Sociétaire in 1843 to expound Fourierist principles. It was funded by English Fourierist Arthur Young; edited by Considerant, Cantagrel, Bureau, Daly, Bourdon, and Guillon; and published until 1851.

Desutter, Désirée (ca. 1830–?): Shipmate of Adolphe Leray on the *Lexington* from Belgium. A dyer by trade, he was a cultivator at La Réunion.

Doubs, Department of: In eastern France; its capital, Besançon, was the cradle of support for Charles Fourier's philosophy.

DUSSEAU, Louise (1830–73): One of eleven from the Aude who traveled with Auguste Savardan to the colony. Within six months of her arrival, she married Dallas man Samuel Jones, with whom she had a daughter. She later went back to France. The daughter married a Cockrell, fully integrating herself into Dallas.

École Normale Supérieure: Paris university holding a portion of Victor Considerant's Texas-related manuscripts.

European American Society of Colonization in Texas (Société de colonisation européo-américaine au Texas): Legally first named Bureau, Guillon, Bourdon et Cie and later changed to Bureau, Guillon, Godin et Cie. It was a stock company registered in Belgium in 1854 and in Texas in 1856 that ended twenty years later.

Familistère: Jean-Baptiste André Godin-Lemaire's coined name for his manifestation of the Fourier phalanx in Guise, Aisne. Built in 1859, it was legally owned and operated by the workers in Godin's next-door factory until 1969. (Available to visit as Familistère de Guise.) A two-story block of apartments built around a covered courtyard, a library, food commons, nursery, laundry, and gardens were all part of the enterprise. La Réunion colonist Pierquet joined it.

Fisher, James T.: Boston supporter of Brook Farm and other American Associationist enterprises.

Fourier, François Marie Charles (1772–1837): French utopian socialist philosopher from Besançon whose ideas created the Fourierist movement in France, Brazil, and Algeria in the 1830s and 1840s, as well as the Associationist movement in the United States in the 1840s and 1850s.

Fourieristes: Name applied in Europe to followers of Charles Fourier.

Galveston, Texas: The largest city in Texas at the time of La Réunion, containing seven thousand people. A port through which all La Réunion colonists passed on their way from New Orleans to Houston.

Godin-Lemaire, Jean-Baptiste André (1817–88): Founder of a major manufacturing industry in cast iron and steel products in the 1840s. Godin invented, manufactured, and distributed the equivalent of the Franklin stove in France when railroads first made distribution feasible; the company now makes iron-and-enameled Le Creuset ware. Godin was the chief funder of La Réunion and later builder of the Familistère in Guise, Aisne. He was the author of many letters of advice to the École Sociétaire.

GOETSEELS, Jean (?–1868): Wealthy Louvain Belgian investor in La Réunion stock who married the widow Devleschoudere and brought their combined large family to Texas. He withdrew his support of the Fourierists in order to establish an alternate village of Belgians called New Louven.

Good, John J. (1827–82): Born in Mississippi, lawyer, organized the Dallas Light Artillery for the Confederate army. Elected to the bench in 1866 but was a prejudiced judge who brought no grand jury indictments to trial during Reconstruction. Sam Jones, a Unionist and married to colonist Louise Dusseau, gave his opinion of Good to John Horton, a Freedmen's Bureau agent; Horton therefore removed Good from office in 1867. Good later had Horton removed as a "military tyrant" in about 1872.

Gouhenant, Adolphus (ca. 1805–72): A painter, entrepreneur, and friend of Étienne Cabet and Victor Considerant from the Haute-Saône. He was one of twelve defendants in an 1843 sedition case that was a landmark in French jurisprudence, allowing the accused to have right of legal counsel. The case propelled Gouhenant with lawyer Cabet onto the national stage in France. In 1848 Gouhenant led a group of sixty-two men to settle on Peters Company land in Denton County, Texas, some twenty-five miles northwest of the later La Réunion. In 1849 he participated in the life of the frontier army Fort Worth and after 1850 established and operated the Art Saloon in Dallas. A land speculator, he was accused in a Dallas court of "squandering the resources" of eleven dead Icarian colonists. In Dallas, he acted as host and frontier counselor to Considerant and Cantegral. In 1855 his son Ernest from France joined him and first worked for the La Réunion Stock Company in building shelters to receive colonists. Gouhenant died in a train accident while on a trip.

Greeley, Horace (1811–72): New York publisher of the *New York Tribune*, for which he wrote articles in support of La Réunion. He was a supporter of Brook Farm, an investor in the North American Phalanx, and a candidate for president after the Civil War. His name prejudiced southerners against the colony.

Guillon, Charles François Ferdinand: Fourierist administrator in the Paris office of the École Sociétaire; editor of the *Démocratie pacifique*.

Guise, Aisne, town of: Where Jean-Baptiste André Godin built the successor to La Réunion, the Familistère, in 1859.

HAECK, Fredericus Wilhelmus (1825–?): Belgian Fourierist accountant who spoke English and German; colonist at La Réunion. A single man at the colony.

Hautes-Alpes, Department of: In southeastern France. Home of Dr. Jean Nicolas and three other La Réunion colonists. A particularly leftist and socialist-leaning department.

Horton, John W.: Military commander of Dallas under Reconstruction—to the southern Anglos, a tyrant. He appointed several colonists from La Réunion to office, including Swiss colonist Benjamin Lang as mayor.

Houston, Sam (1793–1863): Texas leader of its army of revolution and first and third president of its republic. Earlier a governor of Tennessee; U.S. senator from Texas who probably told Victor Considerant that the state policy on free land in North Texas had changed the year before Considerant's visit to Washington. He was a Unionist, and he was removed from the governorship in 1861 by Confederate sympathizers.

Houston, Texas: Town at the head of Buffalo Bayou. La Réunion colonists transshipped from boat to horse and oxen in Houston. In 1855 it held five thousand people, the second largest town in the new state of Texas.

Jones, Samuel S. (1829–63): By marrying Louise Dusseau in November 1855, he and Dusseau became the first to integrate La Réunion and Dallas cultures. In the first Dallas city election of 1856, he was elected recorder with ninety votes unopposed. A Union sympathizer, he was appointed Dallas City clerk by John Horton during Reconstruction.

Jura, Department of: In eastern France, containing the town of Salins-les-Bains, birthplace of Victor Considerant.

Keechi Creek: A tributary of the Brazos River in northern Palo Pinto County, Texas, which was considered as a site for La Réunion.

La Chapelle-Gaugain: Village in the Department of Sarthe, southwest of Paris, and location of the Château de Lesseps, home of Auguste SAVAR-DAN and four other colonists.

LANG, Benjamin (1838–77): Swiss colonist from Seegraben (Zurich), Swit-zerland, who changed his name to LONG. He was appointed mayor of Dallas during Reconstruction and then elected. In 1861 he fled to Mexico to avoid the southern draft. In a double wedding, he married Belgian col-onist Eugenie Devleschoudere in 1862. He returned to Switzerland in 1870 and led a second group of Swiss back to Dallas. He was murdered while attempting to quell a brawl in the raw village of Dallas soon after the rail-roads arrived.

Lattimer, James Week (1820–59): Newspaperman who arrived in Dallas in 1849 to begin the *Cedar Snag*, later renamed the *Dallas Herald*, which he published until his sudden death in 1859. Unlike newspapers farther south in Texas, his editorials at first welcomed the Réunion colonists to Dal-las County but changed as passions flared over slavery and the flood of immigrants to the United States.

LAWRIE, Arthur (1829–1902): Young New Yorker living in Indiana who substituted for his brother John as a factotum to guard François Canta-grel carrying gold on his trip to Texas. Wrote a memoir in the form of a diary of his experience between November 29, 1854, and January 20, 1855. Returned to his Indiana farm in the spring or summer of 1855. His sister Mary married Marx Ellsworth Lazarus, John Allen's brother-in-law, Brook Farmer, and La Réunion investor. His brother Alexander was the artist.

LAWRIE, James (1830–1913): Younger brother of Arthur Lawrie. James collected machinery ordered for La Réunion in Cincinnati and led a group of Ameri-can workers hired to help Cantagrel and Allen prepare for the colony.

LAZARUS, Marx Ellsworth: One of the very few American investors in La Réunion; Brook Farmer and brother of Ellen Lazarus, who was the wife of John Allen. He married Mary Lawrie, sister of Arthur and James Lawrie, New Yorkers farming in upper Ohio who were hired to build a receiving area for La Réunion colonists. He did not come to the colony.

LERAY, Adolphe Joseph (1810–85): Witty poet and printer from Tournai. He was one of the early "pioneers" who helped build shelters to receive colonists at La Réunion. In 1845 he may have been to Santo Tomas on the coast of Guatemala, where Belgian king Leopold I established a colony. He was so revered in Tournai that a statue of him was erected in a public park. A dyer by trade, he left the colony the first fall and worked his way back to Belgium in New Orleans and New York.

Marshall, John: Editor of a publication with a southern bias who held Reverend John Allen in disdain.

McCoy, John C. (1819–87): Lawyer who built the first office on the Dallas town square.

McCracken, Anson W. (1806–79): Born in Tennessee, he and his wife, Mahala, set a new real estate price benchmark for Dallas by selling their 640-acre headright section, the southernmost of the La Réunion parent site, to François Cantagrel for $4,800.00, or $7.50 per acre, when land was generally selling for $1.00 to $3.00 per acre.

Metz: Location in eastern France of the artillery school to which Victor Considerant and Allyre Bureau were posted after they graduated from the École Polytechnique in Paris.

Mountain Creek, Dallas County: A large, well-watered valley tributary of the Trinity River, three miles west of La Réunion, where dissident colonists leased land to start a village called Mutuelle.

Muiron, Jean Claude Just (1787–1881): Journalist and employee of the prefecture of Doubs. He was from Besançon and the original organizer with Clarisse Vigoureux in the 1820s of support for the theories of Charles Fourier. Senior leader of the École Sociétaire.

Mutuelle, village of, Dallas County: A split-off group of the La Réunion colony that attempted to settle on land in Mountain Creek Valley. They were kicked off by Jean Goetseels when he bought the land the following year. He employed young Belgian colonists who then built a home there for the Goetseels family.

Napoleon III (1808–73): Charles-Louis Napoléon Bonaparte, at once the nephew and stepgrandson of Napoleon. He capitalized on the popularity of his name, the myth of a Napoleon who was a democrat, a soldier, and a revolutionary hero. Between 1848 and 1852 he sedulously acquired power until his coup of December 1851. Aligning himself with the Monarchists and Catholics, the party of order after the industrial riots of 1848 and the attempted Montagnard revolt of June 1849, he put down the press, cleared the administration of all Republicans, suspended the right to hold meetings, dismissed the Assembly, and returned education to the church. There was no longer any place for communists, socialists, Republicans, or Fourierists in France. He proclaimed himself the "beneficent motive force of the whole social order" in the 1852 Constitution. Conspicuous Fourierists such as Auguste Savardan and Jean-Baptiste Godin were put under house arrest at the time of the coup, and even foreigners such as Albert Brisbane were under police surveillance. He lost power in 1869, whereupon Victor Considerant, with financial help, returned to Paris from Texas.

New Louven, Dallas County: A community established by Belgian investor Jean Goetseels some six miles southwest of Dallas.

NICOLAS, Dr. Jean (1799–1887): A medical doctor and Republican from St. Bonnet, Hautes-Alpes, who made an archaeological discovery in the south of France in the 1840s and ran a losing political race in 1850. He then became a La Réunion colonist. A widower, he left one married daughter and five grandchildren in France to come to La Réunion. He left the colony to explore Venezuela before returning to France.

North American Phalanx: The longest-surviving Fourierist phalanx, from 1843 to 1855, at Red Bank, New Jersey. Four members were hired by Victor Considerant, two of whom drove a party of *gros-bonnets* in a gig from Houston to La Réunion. A few others followed to help establish the new colony.

NUSSBAUMER, Rupert (1807–55): Swiss Fourierist from the Canton Soleure who had been the proprietor of a leftist café and center of Fourierist politics in Paris. He left his wife and son in Paris, organized the colony's Buffalo Bayou plant nursery, and died of typhoid at La Réunion in September 1855.

Olmsted, Frederick Law (1822–1903): Noted American journalist, author, and later landscape architect who toured Texas in 1850–54 and who probably gave advice on locations for settlement to Considerant in New York in the spring of 1855.

Patterson, James Martin (1812–1906): With J. W. Smith, he established the first general store in Dallas in 1846; he became chief justice (or county judge) of the Dallas County Court in 1854–68. He opposed the appropriation by the county commissioners of $7,000 voted to buy arms for the Confederates.

Peak, Jefferson (1801–?): Born in Scott County, Kentucky; married, farmed, became a merchant and the postmaster for ten years in Warsaw, Gallatin County, on the Ohio River. Formed a company for the Mexican War in 1846 and fought in the Battle of Buena Vista. Member of the Kentucky legislature in 1847–48. At age fifty-four, "Captain" Peak brought his family to Dallas in May 1855 as La Réunion was forming and rented land for a year from Henry BOLL.

Peters Colony: A vast area of North Texas that included from Dallas westward through Tarrant and other western counties; subject of an empresario land grant in 1841 under the administration of President Sam Houston on behalf of the Republic of Texas, contracting with a group of investors led by William S. Peters of Louisville, Kentucky. The lands of La Réunion had originally been surveyed under the Peters Colony in one-mile-square quadrants. These were headright sections of land for which a family was eligible to receive one section free if they cleared and farmed fifty acres of it, built a cabin, and lived on the land for three years. Persons who were entitled to apply but did not wish to establish themselves on the land sold their rights as headright scrip, for which there was a secondary market. La Réunion lay within this area.

Pryor, Samuel B. (1820–66): Medical doctor and scion of a Virginia family; in Dallas Anglo society he was noted for both his social and intellectual skills, as well as his professional ability. Came to Dallas from Virginia in 1846. First mayor of the city in 1856–57; Masonic Worthy Master of the Tannehill Lodge in 1863. He confirmed Auguste Savardan's practice of cupping and bloodletting. Savardan noted that Pryor had the only garden in the village of Dallas.

RAISANT, Alexandre (1812–70): Born in Honfleur, Calvados, of independent means. He was a militant revolutionist close to Blanquism and secretary of the Society of Families; condemned to transportation in 1838 for clandestine fabrication of munitions in the Affair Raban. One of the founders and then the treasurer of the Company of Industrial Unions. He was again arrested in 1846 as chief of one of the secret communist societies issuing out of the Society of Families. Influential in the Second Republic. Spent two sojourns in America. One of the eight founders of the Company of Réunion in August 1855. Correspondent of *L'Association* in 1865. Invaded the Palais-Bourbon in 1870 to proclaim the Third Republic. A single man at the time of the colony.

Reagan, John H. (1818–1905): Texas State Ninth (later Fourteenth) District Court judge who presided over several suits brought by colonists against Considerant and Cantagrel. Reagan came to Texas in 1839, helped President Mirabeau Lamar force the Cherokee Indians to leave Texas in 1839, studied law, and became county judge of Henderson County and then district judge of a region including Dallas County until 1857. He was then congressman for two terms (1857–61); postmaster general of the Confederacy and briefly secretary of the treasury; imprisoned in Boston; again in Congress from 1875 to 1887; U.S. senator from 1887 to 1891; first chairman of the Texas Railroad Commission in 1891.

RENSHAW, James: A member of the North American Phalanx who moved to La Réunion.

REVERCHON, Julien (1837–1905): Botanist who collected plants in several parts of Texas for Asa Gray at Harvard and for whom many plants were named. Author of a diary describing his travels across the ocean and of his bag from hunting. Son of Maximilien, whom he accompanied to La Réunion. A teenage youth at the inception of the colony, he later married colonist Paul Henri's daughter Marie; their two sons died as youths. His plant collection resides in St. Louis. He solicited books for the Dallas Public Library, built in 1900.

REVERCHON, Maximilien (1810–79): Journalist correspondent of the *Paris Globe* from Marcigny, Saône-et-Loire; freethinker who married his wife after she had delivered their third child; ardent Republican and Fourierist who lost his fine farm at Diémoz, Isère, when it was mortgaged to fund the phalanx attempt at Sig in Algeria. He was in charge of the farm at Sig and came to La Réunion with his son Julien but lived apart from the commune on the McCracken section. Father of five, three of whom eventually came to Texas. He was a Saint-Simonian propagandist in 1831. His grandfather was a deputy who voted for the execution of Louis XVI. His wife and two sons remained in France.

REY, Antoine Guillaume (1793–?): Father of Antoinette Zoé Rey Bureau and mentor of Allyre Bureau. As a widower, he accompanied his daughter's family to La Réunion.

Ripley, George (1802–80): Unitarian minister from 1826 to 1840, one of the founders of Transcendentalism, and leader of the Brook Farm phalanx in Roxbury, Massachusetts (1845–47). He was a literary critic for the *New York Tribune* and an author. Developed an early "cyclopedia" with Charles Dana.

ROGER, Edmund: Belgian medical student from Louvain who argued against cupping and bloodletting. Translator for Cantagrel in the formation of La Réunion. He was a sycophant devotee of Considerant and much disapproved of by Augustin Savardan and Amédée Simonin, who called him a "dirty little man." He was sent back to Europe in 1856 by Considerant to stop immigration to La Réunion. A single man at the time of the colony.

Rusk, Thomas J. (1805–57): U.S. senator from Texas whom Considerant probably sought out in his quest for free land on his trip to Washington in February 1855.

Salins-les-Bains: Town in the Jura department of Bourgogne-Franche-Comté where Victor Considerant was born.

SANTERRE, François (1809–89): Republican born near Blois in the Orléanais who carried the heritage of being the great-nephew of the general of the Army of Orléans and battalion commander who had guarded and accompanied Louis XVI to the scaffold platform and ordered the executioner to drop the guillotine blade. He brought his family of six to La Réunion in 1856 and remained in Dallas. Granddaughter Eloise in 1936 wrote a master's thesis on La Réunion, translating Auguste Savardan's *Un naufrage au Texas*. This first history of the colony preserves photographs of colonists who remained in Dallas.

Sarthe, Department of: North of the Loire and southwest of Chartres, containing the village of La Chapelle-Gaugain. Contributed five colonists to La Réunion, including Auguste Savardan.

Sat, Santa Catarina, Brazil: A peninsula on the southeast coast of Brazil where French doctor Benoît Jules Mure attempted to create an industrial phalanx.

SAUZEAU, Louis Alix (ca. 1805–?): Democrat and author who ran his own Republican-socialist newspaper in Niort, Deux-Sèvres, for which he was jailed the first time in 1850. He used his time in jail to write *La démocratie: Études philosophiques, économiques, politiques et artistiques*, for which he was again jailed just before the 1851 coup d'état and exiled. In Belgium he met the Fourierists and was persuaded to accompany the first group of Belgian colonists to La Réunion. When the commune was established at La Réunion in August 1855, he abandoned it for Mutuelle. He was later expelled from Mutuelle by Jean Goetseels. He was a single man at the colony whose wife stayed in France.

SAVARDAN, Auguste (1793–1867): Medical doctor who practiced phrenology, cupping, and bloodletting as the normal practices of his day. Fourierist, reformer, author of several books on medicine and social issues, and mayor of the village of La Chapelle-Gaugain, Sarthe, who led a group of forty-three colonists across the ocean. At La Réunion he headed a group who wanted to live communally in opposition to Considerant's leadership. He returned to France in 1857 and wrote *Un naufrage au Texas* (A shipwreck in Texas), detailing his experiences at the colony. A childless widower at the time of La Réunion, he claimed as his own his wife's sister's children, having formally adopted the sister in 1844.

Sears, Charles: Wealthy reformist, investor in the North American Phalanx, and leader of the NAP's Raritan Bay schism. As the NAP foundered in 1854, he proposed that the European American Society of Colonization in Texas buy it as a way station for immigrants going to Texas.

Sig, Algeria: Fourierist experimental colony outside of Oran created in 1846 and at which Maximilien Reverchon was head of farming.

SIMONIN, Amédée: French immigrant accountant and agent for the European American Society of Colonization in Texas in New York who was sent to the colony to audit the books and report on the colony's financial condition in 1856. Wrote a diary (November 26, 1855–June 12, 1856) describing his findings and left an important cache of papers concerning the colony at the Library of Congress. A single man at La Réunion.

Spring, Marcus: Investor in the North American Phalanx.

Supervièle, Antoine (1808–42): Born in France, he was a lawyer/merchant in Houston (1845–50) and then a merchant in San Antonio (1850–?). Senator from Bexar County in the fifth and sixth state legislatures who guided Victor Considerant politically and may have led him to land purchases in Uvalde County.

VESIAN (or VAISIAN) (ca. 1830–55): Decommissioned lieutenant of the French African Army from Marseilles who had come to the United States to make his fortune in business. Sent by Considerant from New York as an advance man and to buy headright scrip in Texas in the spring of 1855; traveled as translator with Savardan to La Réunion. A single man, he arrived at the colony with typhoid fever and died in three days (the first colony death).

VIGOUREUX, Claire-Charlotte-Dorothée (Clarisse), née Gauthier (1789–1864): Early supporter of Charles Fourier who introduced Fourier's theories to Victor Considerant while he lived in her house as a student in Besançon in the 1820s. She later became his mother-in-law and traveled with him to La Réunion. Author of *Paroles de Providence*, a point-by-point response to Félicité de Lamennais's *Paroles d'un croyant*; her book was then placed on the Index Expurgatorius. She supported Morize and Daly in the late 1830s as they developed images of the ideal phalanstery.

She was a widow and the mother of Julie Considerant and two older children; she lost her and her children's inheritances after investing them in her brother's steel business in 1841. She died in San Antonio.

WOLSKI, Kalikst (also Kalikxt) (1816–55): Genteel Polish expatriate from the province of Lublin who was forced to flee to France in 1831 after participating in the aborted revolt against the czar. He trained as an engineer in France and participated in various railroad projects, including one from Bordeaux to Besançon and Mulhouse. He was a Fourierist and a Republican, and when Louis-Napoléon consolidated power in the fall of 1852, Wolski left France for the United States. He learned English in New York and Buffalo and made himself at home in New York. He was dispatched by Considerant to meet the ship *Uriel*, the first carrying colonists, in New Orleans and accompanied Vincent Cousin's group across Texas to La Réunion in the spring of 1855. He remained at La Réunion until November 1855. Author of a reminiscence written as a diary published in Poland in 1876. A married man at the time of the colony, he became a father at sea coming to America in 1852 but boarded his daughter in a New Orleans convent while at La Réunion.

Young, Arthur: Wealthy Englishman who backed the first "practical" trial of Fourierism at Cîteaux, Côte-d'Or, in the 1830s and in 1843 gave Victor Considerant 400,000 francs to begin the Paris newspaper *Démocratie pacifique*. Having spent much of his fortune, he arrived from Australia in New York in early 1855 to help with the colony. His health and depleted resources prevented his going to Texas.

Notes

Being able to visit the château, which was just as Savardan left it, eat lunch on his dishes, and go through his papers in his attic meant that I could re-create my hero's actions within his home with unusual confidence. Similarly, my interviews of La Réunion descendants, beginning with the Countess de Lesseps, answered many research questions. With the years of research by myself and funded professionals in France, Switzerland, Belgium, and Dallas, I gathered hundreds of contemporary accounts—the French were voluminous letter writers—including pamphlets and books, which I had translated both for my own convenience and so that I could cite them in English. Much of the most vivid material came from the books and diaries written by leaders of the colony after they returned home to vindicate their own behavior, such as Simonin's description of Roger or the picture of Considerant with a cigar in his mouth, lolling in one of his two hammocks. As the saying goes, "I couldn't make up this stuff!"

1. THE DOCTOR'S COMMUNITY

1. Savardan was deeply troubled about the future of foundlings and raised the problem in many of his writings. See, for example, Savardan, *Défense des enfants trouvés*. In addition, he was inspector of the work of children in his Department of the Sarthe from 1841 to 1848. See Brémand, "Auguste Savardan." The abandonment of children on the streets, in doorways, and in churches was widespread in nineteenth-century Europe. For a comprehensive account, see Fuchs, *Abandoned Children*.
2. Schama, *Citizens*, 146.
3. Savardan, *Avenir*, 461.
4. Fourier, *Traité de l'Association agricole et domestique*.
5. Savardan, *Avenir*, 401.

2. A BETTER SITE

1. Savardan, *Asile rural*.
2. Savardan, *Défense*.
3. Savardan, *Avenir*, 403.

4. Savardan, *Avenir*, 392.

5. "I have inspected for a year in the departments of Indre-et-Loire, of Loir-et-Cher, of Eure-et-Loire, of Seine-et-Oise, of l'Aisne, of Pas-de-Calais and of Nord."

6. Savardan, *Avenir*, 401, 405.

7. Savardan, *Avenir*, 405.

8. Schama, *Citizens*, 5.

9. Savardan, *Avenir*, 404.

10. Albert Brisbane had been instrumental in the establishment of Brook Farm in Massachusetts and the North American Phalanx in New Jersey, among others. He had paid Horace Greeley for a front-page byline in the *New York Tribune*, in which he led a propaganda effort for Fourierism under the American banner of "Association."

3. FIRST EMISSARIES TO THE FRONTIER

1. Gibbon, "Lawrie's Trip." This diary fragment by Arthur Lawrie covers the period from November 29, 1854, to January 20, 1855.

2. U.S. Census, 1850, Posey Township, Switzerland County IN.

3. They entered Texas at a ferry crossing north of Clarkesville, probably at Mound City or perhaps Pecan Point, to reach their stated destination at B. H. Epperson's house.

4. Fort Worth, the fort, was decommissioned in September 1853. The town eventually became officially Fort Worth.

5. Codman, *Brook Farm*, 122–23.

6. Record of the Newton and Watertown Universalist Societies, minutes of meeting, November 1837.

7. Cobb, *Autobiography*, 273–74. A Mainer come down to Malden, Massachusetts, to lead the Universalist Society, Cobb had shown Allen a model of dedication to a mission. He preached a full load to a Universalist Society while at the same time teaching a group of fledgling ministers such as Allen and devoting three days and evenings a week as agent of the Middlesex County Temperance Society. Cobb's change of profession coincided with Allen's seeking his own first pulpit.

8. Record of the Newton and Watertown Universalist Societies, minutes of meetings, April 8, 1839, and April 19, 1839; John Allen to "Zilla" (Matilda Eastman), October 1, 1845, Abernathy Library of American Literature, Middlebury College, Middlebury VT.

9. Allen, *An Occasional Sermon*; Miller, *The Larger Hope*, 601; *Christian Freeman*, June 25, 1841, 29.

10. Record of the Newton and Watertown Universalist Societies, *Universalist Register* (1839), 17; *Universalist Register and Almanac* (1840), 25; *Universalist Register* (1841), 59; *Universalist Register* (1842), 50; *Universalist Register* (1843), 51; *Universalist Register* (1844), 48; *Universalist Register* (1845), 35; *Universalist Register* (1850), 35; *Universalist Register* (1851), 52; *Universalist Register* (1852), 51; *Universalist Register* (1853), 50; Babson, *History*, 524.

11. Rozwenc, *Cooperatives*; and Noyes, *History*.

12. Ellen's letter to her uncle at this same time does not reveal that she was about to move to Texas, but all her actions earlier and later in her life suggest the passion for association that she shared with her husband, John. See Ellen L. Allen to George W. Mordecai, Mordecai Papers.

13. At reform assemblies throughout New England and New York in the early 1840s, John Allen had met Albert Brisbane, the self-proclaimed messenger who had brought Fourierism from France to the United States. Brisbane's articles on Association in the *New York Tribune*, the front-page column for which he personally paid, had sparked a rash of phalanx attempts. It was at the height of this fever in 1845 that Allen joined Brook Farm.

14. John Orvis was John Allen's companion lecturer and fundraiser at Brook Farm.

15. John Allen to M. Dwight, March 9, 1846, Abernathy Library of American Literature.

16. Minutes of the Religious Union of Associationists, October 10, 1847, Fisher Papers.

17. Considerant to Mes Amis, May 3, 1853, 10AS28(9), Archives nationales (France). (Hereafter cited as AN.)

18. Considerant to Julie (Considerant), May 7, 1853, 10AS28(9), AN. See also École Normale Supérieure, 8, II, 1.

19. Switzerland County Deed Records, Vevey, Indiana, show the extent of Allen's holdings. The magnitude of his viniculture business in 1854 is glimpsed in Ellen Allen's letters to George W. Mordecai in the Mordecai Papers.

20. *Cincinnati Daily Commercial*, November 30, 1854, 1, col. 6. This was an announcement of the Texas colony just after Cantagrel had passed through Cincinnati.

21. Marx Lazarus, another Brook Farmer, as well as Allen's brother-in-law, contributed $2,500. Ellen L. Allen to George W. Mordecai, October 28, and November 2, 1858, Mordecai Papers.

22. A letter from Ellen to her uncle in January said that John and Fred were in Texas. However, there is no evidence of Fred's presence in Lawrie's

diary. As Fred was often shuffled for long periods to relatives by John, it is likely he went with John to Cincinnati to meet Cantagrel and stayed with Benjamin Urner or James Lawrie, brother-in-law of Allen's brother-in-law, Marx Lazarus, or with his uncle Simon in Oxford, Ohio, until the equipment ordered was ready for James Lawrie to transport. See Swift, *Brook Farm*, 182–84. Fred had also carried a product to Brook Farm. Swift called it "fanatical carelessness" that Allen did not believe in vaccination, which led Fred as an infant to acquire smallpox from a runaway slave at his aunt's Grahamite Hotel and underground railroad in Boston. Brook Farm's school and finances were decimated by the epidemic, and Fred was severely pocked for life. The epidemic added to the farm's financial woes. See also John Allen to Matilda Eastman, November 2, 1845.

23. V. E. Gibbon, inferred from Arthur Lawrie's diary ("Lawrie's Trip").
24. François Cantagrel to Allyre Bureau, May, 5, 1854, 10AS36(2), AN.
25. It is my supposition that the trip may have prevented the baby from being carried to term. The infant, named for her mother, Josephine, died at La Réunion.
26. *Bulletin*, May 2, 1855, 2.
27. Cantagrel to Lavardant, April 15, 1852, 10AS, AN.
28. Cantagrel to Bureau, June 11, 1852, 10AS37(2), AN.
29. Simonin, Diary, January 10, 1856, 45a.
30. Savardan, *Un naufrage au Texas*. All citations from this work are from Santerre's English translation.
31. *Bulletin*, January 18, 1855, 8, lists 1.4 million francs from 725 subscribers.
32. François Cantagrel to Allyre Bureau, June 11, 1852, 10AS37(2), AN.
33. Wolski, *American Impressions*, 173. Coleman cites Ollendorff as having written a new method for reading, writing, and speaking English in six months; it was published in Paris in 1848.
34. *Bulletin*, January 18, 1855, 6.
35. Author's supposition. Slaves were often used in the South for such tasks, as documented farther up the Red River near Preston.

4. VIEW FROM PARIS

1. Bureau to Savardan, November 1854.
2. For a biography of Bureau, see the thesis by his great-great-granddaughter: Rey, *Le Fouriériste Allyre Bureau*.
3. Considerant to mes amis, October 21, 1854, 10AS28(09), AN.
4. Bureau to Considerant, June 3, 1854, 10AS36(12), AN.
5. Rey, *Le Fouriériste Allyre Bureau*, 254, 296.

5. VIEW FROM GUISE

1. See Rabaux, "En prélude," 4–6, for a chronology of Godin's life. Godin established his first workshop in 1840, inventing the French equivalent of the American cast-iron Franklin stove. This invention was economically dependent on railroad drayage for its success. Today his factory is known for its enameled iron Creuset ware.

2. Marie Howland, letter to the editor, *Winston (CT) Press*, February 15, 1883. She cited Godin's being inscribed in a police book as "Homme dangereux d'autant plus dangereux qu'il est honnête." He was offered the cross of the Legion of Honor and refused it. From that time he was considered an enemy by the imperial government. He later accepted the cross from the republican government.

3. A January lung infection threw off Godin's timing for going, and messages from Texas thereafter discouraged him from making the trip.

4. Godin to Considerant.

5. Adolphe Gouhenant, the leader of the Cabet colony, and Lucien Boisonnas stayed in the Three Forks after that colony failed. They were living in Dallas when Considerant first visited in 1853.

6. Godin to Cantagrel, April 1854, 10AS, AN.

7. Marie Godin, September 2, 1854, vol. 1.

8. Godin to Considerant, May 1854, 10AS38(13), AN.

6. VIEW FROM BRUSSELS

1. Just Muiron in Besançon to mon cher ami, August 12, 1854, 10AS40(7), AN, on the manuscript's first page.

2. Charles Fourier's birthday, April 7, was still celebrated annually by his followers on both sides of the Atlantic after his death in 1837.

3. Godin to Considerant, November 2, 1854, 10AS31904, AN.

4. *Bulletin*, January 18, 1855, 2.

5. Considerant in Brussels to Bureau in Paris, December 1, 1854, 10AS28(9), AN.

6. Considerant in Brussels to Bureau in Paris, December 2, 1854, 10AS28(9), AN.

7. Albert Brisbane, an American from Batavia, New York, had brought Fourierism to America in the 1830s. In the 1840s, in the reaction to the depression created after the Panic of 1837, working people flocked to the ideas expressed in his front-page column in the *New York Tribune*. The column sparked some thirty attempts at "association."

8. This twelve-year-old, most successful of the utopian socialist experiments in the United States was then expiring in Red Bank, New Jersey.
9. James T. Fisher was a Boston supporter of Brook Farm.
10. George Ripley was the reverend and founder of Brook Farm. By this time he had been reduced to writing for a living in New York.
11. See Coleman, "New Light."
12. See Becherer, "Between Science and Sentiment," xii. Becherer's otherwise thorough chronology of Daly's life slights his time involved with Considerant on the East Coast in the spring of 1855, at La Réunion, and with the Texas legislature through January 1856.
13. In this era, the École Polytechnique assumed the top in the pecking order of institutions of learning. The Industrial Revolution was large in the public imagination and was flexing its muscles. Engineers from the Poly were its chief apostles.
14. Becherer, "Between Science and Sentiment," xi–xv. Daly began the annual publication in 1839, and it ran until 1886.

7. VIEW FROM LA CHAPELLE-GAUGAIN

1. *Bulletin, Société de Colonisation Européo-Américaine au Texas*, January 18, 1855. The meeting was held on December 26 at the École offices, rue de Beaune 6, Paris.
2. Condé-sur-Vesgre was the earliest attempt to establish a phalanx on Charles Fourier's principles; it was sixty miles west of Paris (1832–33). In a second attempt to create a commune there, Savardan and his friend Lavardant in 1852–53 raised 100,000 francs to buy its land. They aborted the project after Considerant discovered Texas. *Bulletin*, January 18, 1855, 2.
3. Savardan, *Un naufrage*, 25.
4. Countess O. de Lesseps, owner of the château, interview with the author, May 30, 1981.
5. Savardan, *Un naufrage*, 1. According to Savardan, Dr. Baudet Dulary, former deputy, devoted his entire fortune to establishing a phalanx at Condé and was ruined by its failure. This is the first of a large number of failures on four continents over a span of twenty-two years leading up to La Réunion.
6. Savardan to Très cher ami, November 13, 1852, 10AS41(14), AN.
7. Bureau to Savardan, December 24, 1852, 10AS41(14), AN; Savardan, *Un naufrage*, 1–18.
8. The Archives de La Sarthe confirm that Savardan was born in 1792, and his death certificate supports that. I remember his grave stone at La Chapelle-

Gaugain showing 1793. The *Bulletin* of May 3, 1855, lists him as two years younger.

9. Savardan, *Un naufrage*, 8. "The Emperor in 1852 honored that project with a word of benevolent attention." But this comment was written in 1857–58, after he had returned to France, six years after his arrest had cooled, and when he had to make peace with the regime.

10. "Une décision de la Commission departementale 5ᵉ catégorie prononce l'interdiction de sejour d'Auguste SAVARDAN en Sarthe et Loir-et-Cher du 2 mars au 1ᵉʳ avril 1852. Une décision du Président de la République du 23 avril 1852 lui fait grace de l'internement" (A ruling by the 5th Category Departmental Commission pronounced a prohibition on Auguste Savardan visiting Sarthe and Loir-et-Cher from March 2 to April 1, 1852. A decree by the President of the Republic on April 23, 1852, thanked them for the internment) (Archives.Sarthe.fr, Department of La Sarthe, France).

11. Or, as Savardan would have written in French, "Charles Burkly."

12. Savardan, *Un naufrage*, 25–28.

13. Savardan, *Un naufrage*, 9.

14. Savardan to mes amis Bureau, Brunier, Bourdon et Guillon, May 14, 1854, 10AS41(14), AN. Fie was the second of some two hundred who wrote saying they wanted to go, and he had replied within a week of the publication of *Au Texas* to have his name enrolled. See also Savardan, *Un naufrage*, 19 ff.

15. Catherine and Abel Bossereau are listed in a letter fragment of the École's records of persons wanting to go to Texas (10AS, AN).

16. Savardan, *Un naufrage*, 24–25. H. Fugère was, according to Savardan, a wise, early adherent to Fourierism. He signed himself "graveur-estampeur" on an 1848 placard championing a model commune on Fourier's principles.

17. Savardan, *Un naufrage*, 19–20.

18. Considerant, *Au Texas*, 106–10; and Savardan, *Un naufrage*, 20.

19. Savardan, *Un naufrage*, 20–21.

20. *Bulletin*, January 18, 1855, 3.

21. Savardan, *Un naufrage*, 63. That was the equivalent of $1.4 to $1.6 million in 1854 value.

22. Savardan states that he left the army after six years at the age of twenty-eight, which would have been in 1820. Thus, he would have entered the army before Waterloo. An 1860 book by Savardan states that he wrote a medical tract in 1822. Countess O. de Lesseps in a letter to me dated June 15, 1979, states that Savardan married in 1827 and was mayor of his village from 1836 to 1848.

23. Photocopy of a handbill advertising Nicolas's run for office in the author's files.
24. Savardan, *Bulletin*, May 3, 1855, 6. Savardan actually led forty-four persons, including himself, across the ocean and added a few in New Orleans.
25. Savardan, *Un naufrage*, 28; *Bulletin*, May 3, 1855, 6.
26. *Bulletin*, May 3, 1855, 6. Renier was born in 1824, son of a mason on the estate. Archives, Departement de La Sarthe; Countess O. de Lesseps, interview with the author, May 30, 1981. Renier's descendants in 1981 still lived on the estate in the same compound from which he had departed and to which he returned after his sojourn in Texas.
27. *Bulletin*, January 18, 1855, 3.
28. Savardan, *Un naufrage*, 26.
29. Considerant, *Au Texas*, 74, as quoted in Savardan, *Un naufrage*, 32: "The figs, oranges, lemons, dates, pineapples, olives, and other tropical fruits, with the peaches, melons, grapes, and other fruits of temperate climates, abound in the southern parts of North America."
30. Savardan, *Un naufrage*.
31. Countess O. de Lesseps to the author, June 15, 1979. The very beautiful lithograph became a principal icon of the Fourierist movement in the 1840s. According to the countess, it had been "tirée par V. Considerant au moment de la souscription a remplacer la revue *La Phalange* par un quotidien" (drawn by V. Considerant at the time of subscription to replace the journal *La Phalange* with a daily newspaper). That would have been in 1843, some six years after Fourier's death. It has usually been attributed to Jean Gigoux. However, a recent catalog (no. 270) of Paul Jammes attributes the lithograph to Francisco Cisneros after the engraving of 1846 by Luigi Calamatta.
32. Besides the numerous artifacts belonging to Savardan in the house, in the attic the countess pointed out an armoire containing the letters of Ferdinand de Lesseps, the engineer of the Suez Canal and her husband's grandfather. In her words, "Nous avon depuis, six generations, gardé de nombreux souvenirs de l'epoque qui vous interesse" (For six generations we have held on to many mementos from the period you are interested in). May 30, 1981, during the author's visit to the Château Gaugain.

8. VIEW FROM NEW YORK

1. R. Brisbane, *Albert Brisbane*, 6–7.
2. Albert Brisbane, *Democratic Review*, September 1842, 302.
3. R. Brisbane, *Albert Brisbane*, 172, 187.

4. R. Brisbane, *Albert Brisbane*, 292. It is not clear how early the École Sociétaire took possession of the rue de Beaune property. Certainly, they were in it by the 1840s on several of Brisbane's trips there, as he here describes it, and R. Brisbane, *Albert Brisbane*, recorded it. Brisbane's assertion that these meetings were unprecedented is questionable, if one remembers the gardens at the Palais Royale used for political harangue. Perhaps he means a physical setting for interchange on socialist matters.

5. Buffalo City Directories, 1835, 1836, 1837, and 1838. The theater venture appears to have turned sour after the Panic of 1837. Brisbane hired new management every year.

6. In 1995 terms that would be $2.5 million, with an annual income of $200,000 to $250,000. "The stream is but seldom in good boating order, rapid and full of shifting shoals, making a very tedious ferriage."

7. By 1868 Olmsted reported 140,000 per square mile in Liverpool and life expectancy there of only seventeen years.

8. Charles Sears to James T. Fisher, July 23, 1853, Fisher Papers. Brisbane wrote his wife from Fort Worth that he, Brisbane, "would adhere."

9. Motto in the heading of *The Future* 1, no. 1 (January 30, 1841) and used in practically all subsequent periodicals of the Fourierist movement, as well as on the title pages of such pamphlets as Brisbane's *Concise Exposition*.

10. This is my assumption. Both men, close in age, were from towns in Genesee County, New York. Considerant states in letters before leaving New York that Brisbane was going to take him to Fort Worth in Texas. Brisbane had a quick direct itinerary there, without stopping in other states or looking anywhere at other property. It was almost as if he was already convinced of the place and was only going to perfunctorily show the place to Considerant. An article in the *San Antonio Press*, November 12, 1932, states that Merrill and Brisbane were friends. When Considerant was thrown in jail in August 1854, Brisbane apparently had Merrill write the Belgian authorities that Considerant's gun purchases were only for American friends.

11. Considerant, *Au Texas*.

12. Marie Godin, letter alluded to in January 1855 by Jean-Baptiste André Godin in a reply to Paris.

13. Ellen L. Allen to her uncle George W. Mordecai.

14. Noyes, *History of American Socialisms*.

15. Considerant, *The Great West*.

9. FINDING LAND

1. Considerant, June 6, 1853, 10AS, AN.

2. Guillot had been in Dallas off and on for five years, having first arrived there in 1850 on his way to the gold rush and stayed. Later he returned to France and collected a wife to share his frontier life. He planted the trees in front of his house on the site of the famous School Book Depository that gave Elm Street in downtown Dallas its name.

3. Wolski, *American Impressions*, 179, maintained there were no speakers of French in Dallas County.

4. Dallas County Deed Records, 1852, 53, 54, Dallas TX.

5. Considerant, *Au Texas*, on keeping animals out of the garden.

6. George Rottenstein married them in 1856.

7. Jn. M. McCoy, May 12, 1872, defines the time it took to ride a horse to Fort Worth. Archives, Dallas Historical Society.

8. *Dallas Herald*, December 8, 1855, 4.

9. Long Bottom became West Dallas, and the trail became modern Singleton Boulevard.

10. The cleared land lay between modern Hampton and Westmoreland; the trail followed Fish Trap Road.

11. The earliest name of Sowers, which became the twentieth-century Irving.

12. Gibbon, "Lawrie's Trip," 248.

13. Miller Scrapbook, vol. 1, 73, Dallas Public Library; undated newspaper clipping by W. S. Adair, "Reminiscences of W. W. Glover, First White Child Born after County Organized," 6.

14. J. Beeman, "Memoirs."

15. Not to be confused with Bird's Fort.

16. Later Veal's Station in northeastern Parker County.

17. Isaac Healey was one of two who surveyed Parker County the following year, 1856.

18. Marcy, *Thirty Years*, 89.

19. Lawrie's diary is ambiguous as to the town being Gainsville, but logic suggests it.

20. Bowie, *Gay as a Grig*, 33.

21. Big Fossil Creek rises about a mile north of Calef in northeastern Tarrant County and flows sixteen miles southeast to join the West Fork five miles northeast of Fort Worth.

22. Twenty years later, Cook called this area "the American hunter's paradise."

23. Probably in what is now Wise County.

24. Savardan comments on Allen's preferring land they had seen on the Brazos.

25. W. Beeman, *Pioneer Tales*, 179.

26. *Bulletin*, May 2, 1855, 1.

27. Godin to Amis, 10AS38(13), AN, refers to a letter from Cantagrel to Considerant on January 28 and a second letter from Cantagrel to the Gérance on January 31.
28. *Bulletin*, May 2, 1855, i.
29. *Dallas Herald*, December 8, 1855, 4, third-column advertisement. The line ran via Waco, Belton, and Georgetown and connected to Houston; to the northeast it ran to Clarksville.
30. Wolski, *American Impressions*, 187.
31. *Texas State Gazette*, February 10, 1855; and *Northern Standard*, February 24, 1855.
32. They might have seen the German architect drawing plans for a new land office, which began construction that year; it stands restored at the southeastern corner of the capitol campus.
33. *Cincinnati Daily Commercial*, November 30, 1854, 1.
34. Savardan, *Un naufrage*, 37.
35. The Keechi valley provided a major north–south aboriginal route to and from the Brazos. Keechi Creek rose in East and West Forks in south-central Jack County, united in northern Palo Pinto County, and continued to flow south to the Brazos River about seven miles northwest of Mineral Wells in northeastern Palo Pinto County.
36. *Northern Standard*, February 24, 1855, quoting the *Dallas Herald*.
37. Gard, "Trinity River."
38. Probably on modern Coombs Creek. La Réunion colonist Émile Remond later bought the tract.
39. *Bulletin*, May 2, 1855, 2.

10. SAILING TO AMERICA

1. Renaud in Le Havre to Bureau et Cie in Paris, February 6, 1855, in author's collection. See also letters of Renaud of February 5, 7, 10, 15, and 19, 1855, concerning the sailing of the *Nuremberg* and Savardan's comments on the crossing in *Un naufrage*.
2. Letter from Lisa Halttunen, reference librarian, August 13, 1980, G. W. Blunt White Library, Mystic Seaport Museum, Mystic CT. This ship was built by William Hall in 1847.

11. EXPECTATIONS

1. Morrison, *History*, 411; and Smith, *Passenger Ships*, pt. 1, 16.
2. In April 1853, when Victor visited Oneida, Martin had written an excellent description of his prowess as a fly fisherman in competition with four others. Martin died from overwork in June 1854.

3. *Le Courrier des États-Unis* had covered Considerant's trip in 1853.
4. Jules Juif's name appears on a single-sheet undated flyer advertising La Réunion.
5. Inferred from Juif's letter to Considerant. Aimée Beucque pointed out that Juif was the lawyer in charge of the interests of a powerful French company (the baron de Pontalba); see Beucque to Clarisse Vigoureux, February 16, 1855, 10AS36(5), AN.
6. Considerant to Julie (Considerant), May 7, 1853, 10AS28(9), AN.
7. Houston signed the Peters Colony Agreement in 1841.
8. Coignet, *Victor Considerant*, 26.
9. Just Muiron to Considerant.
10. Coignet, *Victor Considerant*.
11. *Bulletin*, May 2, 1855.
12. Nichols, *Franklin Pierce*, 540.
13. *New York Daily Times*, February 5, 1855, review of a book by Helen Dhu, *Stanhope Burleigh—the Jesuits in Our Homes* (New York: Stringer & Townsend): "Of this book we have already spoken freely in our editorial remarks. . . . We have little to say in addition. In plot it is old, threadbare and puerile—in its style, loose,—in its love-scenes, sickening. The characters, however, will save it. 'Hubert' is but another name for Bishop Hughes; Loveblack for GREELEY; Fouché for THURLOW WEED; Woolsey for Senator SEWARD; and Counselor Donnell for CHARLES O'CONNOR, Esq. The *Herald* and BENNETT it puffs by name. A copy of this 'powerful production' has been sent to every member of the Legislature; and it has the endorsement also of SAM. We make this appeal to our Brethren, because we feel confident we are doing an American Work, in asking your early and especial attention to a publication which promises to be so powerful in arousing the jealous vigilance of AMERICA'S FREEMEN."
14. Considerant met Henri either between March 5 and 19 or between April 4 and 13.

12. STORM CLOUDS

1. Nichols, *Franklin Pierce*, 375–76.
2. *New York Daily Times*, February 5 and 6, 1855.
3. Nichols, *Franklin Pierce*, 539–43. Pierce and his counselors thought in terms of Jackson and Polk. They were honest, consistent, laissez-faire Democrats who made no concession to the importuners. General Pierce had limited imagination and did not see his domestic job as that of a creative statesman, only as a defender of the strict construction of the Con-

stitution and "Union." His abysmal political sense and his poor choice of advisors left real leadership, such as it was, with the Congress.

4. Considérant to Chère petite, February 20, 1855, 2, 1, 6, École Normale Supérieure, Archives Victor Considerant, author's collection. (Hereafter cited as ENS.)

5. ENS, 2, 1, 6.

6. *New York Daily Times*, February 1855.

7. James, *The Raven*, 304.

8. Bell moved permanently to North Carolina in 1857. Rusk shot himself that year. Smyth served in the Confederate army. Only Houston defended the Union.

9. *Mississippi Valley Historical Review*, XH, 17–18:379; H. Doc. No. 91, 33:2 (791).

10. ENS, 2, 1, 6, "We will stay here several days. It's very important, by the way, if Daly arrives before I have sent a notice to the contrary, to make him leave at once to come join us here. There are several departures daily, morning and afternoon. He only has to take an overnight bag to have two or three shirts with him, and to have his head on his shoulders, his intelligence in his head, and his tongue in his mouth. . . . Instruct Charles Brisbane to see that Daly, on his arrival, will be able to find us quickly."

11. ENS, 2, 1, 6.

12. Dana appears to have left Fourierism long before this date. He may have been collecting items for his *Household Book of Poetry*, which D. Appleton published in 1858. He and Ripley were completing their *Cyclopedia* that year. James T. Fisher, August 1848, MS E.4.1.69, Boston Public Library.

13. Johnson stayed at least to the end of the summer of 1855, as his name appears on the August 27 work list.

14. Considerant, *Son Compte*, 2.

15. Milton, *The Eve of Conflict*, 155.

16. Coignet, *Victor Considerant*, 26.

17. Nichols, *Franklin Pierce*, 389–90.

18. Milton, *The Eve of Conflict*, 206–7.

19. César Daly to James T. Fisher, March 29, 1855, Fisher Papers.

20. Considerant, *Son Compte*, 2.

21. *Bulletin*, May 2, 1855.

22. New York Customs Records, SS *Baltic*, February 22, 1855.

23. In April 1853, when Considerant was waiting for Brisbane, he paid a short visit to Oneida; the *Oneida Circular* wrote a charming description of Considerant with four others fishing.

24. Considerant, *Son Compte*, 2.
25. Considerant, *Son Compte*, 2.
26. Godin to Considerant, April 5, 1855, 10AS38(13), AN.
27. Godin to Considerant, April 5, 1855; and Moët, *Veuve*, 1:436–37.
28. Considerant to Chérie petite, ENS, 2, 1, 6.

13. FROM SAILS TO STEAM TO FEET

1. Savardan, *Un naufrage*, 32.
2. *Bulletin*, January 1855.
3. Wolski, *American Impressions*, 141.
4. *L'Abeille de Nouvelle Orléans*, February 27, 1855, 1.
5. They were hospitable in part because Wolski was already known to them. He had arranged for his daughter to stay with them.
6. The number grew in New Orleans as people from other ships joined the group. Juif to Considerant, April 6, 1855, 18, 160, Simonin Papers.
7. *Bulletin*, May 2, 1855.
8. *Bulletin*, January 20, 1855.
9. Wolski, *American Impressions*, 152.
10. Wolski, *American Impressions*, 153; *Bulletin*, May 2, 1855, 8; *Bulletin*, June 13, 1855. The *Bulletin* appears to have exaggerated the purchase: "Our friends have taken possession of a house that can lodge 30 people, with 45 acres of land."
11. Wolski, *American Impressions*, 154.
12. Wolski, in *American Impressions*, says twenty pairs, but Jean Louckx, who wrote soon after the event, seems more accurate than Wolski's reminiscence twenty years later.
13. Wolski, *American Impressions*, 155.
14. Wolski, *American Impressions*, 155.
15. *Bulletin*, August 5, 1855, 4.
16. Hutchins, *An Historical Narrative*, 34–36.
17. Savardan, *Un naufrage*, 39, quoting an 1850 description of the riverboat *Hecla*.
18. With this small incident began the manifold failures that, in Savardan's eyes, Considerant perpetrated. But sailing ships had no scheduled arrival dates, and though Considerant assuredly had knowledge of their departure date from Le Havre, he would have had only general information on arrival. He may have thought he and Daly would be present for their arrival, but he missed by two days. With his state of mind and stated ill-

ness, as commented on by others, he should not be held accountable by nitpicker Savardan.

19. The cathedral had been redesigned and enlarged in 1851, and the baron de Pontalba's investments in the buildings facing each other across the square were five years old. Juif had a major management responsibility for the baron's investments.

20. Savardan, *Un naufrage*, 40.

21. Godin to Considerant, April 5, 1855, 10AS38(13), AN.

22. Godin to Considerant, April 5, 1855, 10AS38(13), AN.

23. Debenham, *The Victor*, 257.

24. See Juif to Considerant, April 6, 1855: "The good words [of your coming] made my heart rejoice and helped me spend one of the best moments I've had in my life."

25. In Galveston Considerant bought headright scrip at 22.5 cents per acre for three thousand acres. *Bulletin*, June 13, 1855, 2. And later, "Nos correspondants à Galveston ont commission d'acheter 25,000 acres de headrights" (Considerant, *Son Compte*, 2).

26. The department in southeastern France that we know for its ski resorts.

27. Savardan, *Un naufrage*, 33.

28. Savardan, *Un naufrage*, 45–46.

29. Savardan, *Un naufrage*, 34.

30. Neither Houston nor Austin had banks in 1855.

31. Savardan, *Un naufrage*, 47.

32. Savardan, *Un naufrage*, 48.

33. Savardan, *Un naufrage*, 41, 50.

34. Savardan, *Un naufrage*, 50–51.

35. Savardan, *Un naufrage*, 52.

36. Beucque to Vigoureux, February 16, 1855, 10AS36(5), AN.

37. Savardan, *Un naufrage*, 52–53.

38. Savardan, *Un naufrage*, 53–54.

39. Savardan, *Un naufrage*, 55–56.

40. Savardan, *Un naufrage*, 56.

41. Savardan, *Un naufrage*, 56.

42. Savardan, *Un naufrage*, 41–42.

43. Savardan, *Un naufrage*, 52–53.

44. *Bulletin*, June 13, 1855, 2.

45. The state of Texas had quadrupled its size since independence had been declared but still had fewer than 250,000 inhabitants; the Réunion colo-

nists had just seen its two largest cities. Its third, San Antonio, could only boast four thousand persons.

46. Wolski, *American Impressions*, 54.

47. Though the Houston and Texas Central Railroad received a franchise on February 7, 1853, the Civil War delayed backing until 1872.

48. Savardan, *Un naufrage*, 56.

14. FROM HOUSTON TO THE THREE FORKS

1. Wolski, *American Impressions*, 164.

2. Savardan, *Un naufrage*, 57.

3. Translation by Jimmy Phillips, 6.

4. *Bulletin*, June 13, 1855, 4.

5. Savardan, *Un naufrage*, 59.

6. Vesian to Simonin, May 13, 1855, Simonin Papers.

7. Wolski, *American Impressions*, 163.

8. Raisant to Mon Ami in Paris, April 22, 1855, 10AS31(4), AN.

9. *Bulletin*, August 6, 1855, 2.

10. Savardan to his adopted children, June 9, 1855, author's collection; *Bulletin*, August 6, 1855, 5.

11. They probably got beds at the Fanthrop Inn in Anderson.

12. Wolski, *American Impressions*, 165.

13. Wolski, *American Impressions*, 166.

14. Wolski, *American Impressions*, points out that it was considered a necessity to have a quantity of whisky or spirits and unhealthy to drink the water without mixing it with a small portion of some kind of spirits.

15. Savardan to his adopted children, June 9, 1855.

16. Savardan to his adopted children, June 9, 1855. His descriptions in *Naufrage au Texas* were less romantic.

17. Savardan to his adopted children, June 10, 1855, author's collection.

18. This is my assumption. The bottomlands of the Navasota were still heavily forested at this time and the most likely site for a Frenchman to become lost. Savardan only says that Barret became lost.

19. Savardan to his adopted children, June 7, 1855; *Bulletin*, August 6, 1855, 5.

20. Wolski, *American Impressions*, 177.

15. FIRST DAYS BUILDING

1. This settlement became Sowers and then Irving, Texas.

2. Issues of the *Bulletin*, New Orleans Customs Records, and letters.

3. Wolski, *American Impressions*, 177. Wolski's description is somewhat ambiguous: "Through the entire width of the house runs a wide vestibule. About the four walls outside are so-called 'Verandas'—wide balconies." In the Texas vernacular, this was likely an oversized dog-run house with the center hall open at both ends to attract the breeze.

4. See the long table and benches in the San Antonio Governor's Palace for an example of this table, handmade with axe and file, and a single piece of wrought iron pinned from top to stretcher to stabilize the legs, still clothed in their bark.

5. Wolski, *American Impressions*, 176.

6. Wolski, *American Impressions*, 178.

7. Wolski, *American Impressions*, 178.

8. Raisant's information about the railroad was wrong. It passed through the Réunion property, but only in 1872.

9. Raisant had not had time on this trip to be in Preston or Indian Territory. Did he make a previous trip to the States?

10. Raisant to Mon Ami, Bureau, April 22, 1855, at La Réunion, 10AS31(4), AN, has the first page of this letter (to the words "follow this example"); the remainder is printed verbatim in the *Bulletin*, August 6, 1855.

11. Wolski, *American Impressions*, 182.

12. Wolski, *American Impressions*, 182.

13. Coombes, *The Diary*, iv. Jane H. Heady married Leven G. Coombes.

14. Dallas County Deed Records, "Survey of an estate in Dallas County belonging to the European and American Society of Colonization."

15. Latimer may have sent Swindells to interview Cantagrel. However, Swindells was a much more confirmed southerner and likely would not have been as favorable as the article indicates, so it was most likely Latimer who interviewed Cantagrel, probably with Allen to translate.

16. Originally called the *Cedar Snag*, the newspaper changed its name in the early 1850s. No copies of any Dallas newspaper have been found before December 8, 1855.

17. Dallas City Directory, 1875, 64. Swindells became an associate of the *Dallas Herald* in March 1854 and managed the paper after Latimer's sudden death in 1859.

18. *Northern Standard*, about April 22, 1855.

16. CONFRONTING THE VISION

1. *Bulletin*, August 6, 1855, 5.

2. *Bulletin*, June 13, 1855, 1.

3. Savardan, *Un naufrage*, 180.

4. Godin to Considerant, who had heard that advice from Frederick Law Olmsted. Olmsted had recently been in San Antonio but not in North Texas. See Roper, *FLO*, 104.

5. Godin to Considerant, April 5, 1855, Laboratoire Psychologie, Sociologie, Sorbonne, 10AS38(13), AN.

6. Wolski, *American Impressions*, 183.

7. Ledger sheet, Considerant account, list of personnel, May 16, 1855. The letter X in the margin next to about twenty American names suggests the ones who were paid, perhaps drifted away, probably refused to join the later commune, or were later eliminated in favor of much cheaper European workers willing to put two-thirds of their wages into a deferred account. On an August 27 list, the last one I found, only Johnson was left.

8. *Bulletin*, August 6, 1855.

9. Considerant to Bureau, Paris, 1854, about his inviting Sauzeau.

10. Savardan, *Un naufrage*, 96.

11. The editor of the *Texas State Gazette*, John Marshall, had been a prior editor of a newspaper in Jackson, Mississippi.

12. *Texas State Times*, June 16, 1855.

13. Savardan, *Un naufrage*, 103, 104.

14. Savardan, *Un naufrage*, 195.

15. Daly, introduction.

16. Daly to James T. Fisher, March 31, 1855. This letter is the only direct expression of Daly's support for Fourierism after his arrival in the United States in 1855. The introduction to the *Revue générale de l'architecture et des travaux publics* 14 (1856) discusses his trip to America but includes only one sentence on Texas and not a single mention of his several months' stay at La Réunion and his time in Austin. In Austin he again championed the Fourierists' plea for land to the state legislature. Perhaps his declaration as being on commercial business, listed in the New York Customs Records, February 22, 1855, on his arrival in America, shows a reservation already felt.

17. Their land by letter patent #1465, May 31, 1855, attested by W. W. Peak, clerk, County Deed Records, 2:131, September 13, 1855.

18. The cemetery, located on Fish Trap Road, is the only land of La Réunion still extant.

19. It would be another twenty years before the railroads could import harder stone to the Dallas area for tombstones. Grave markers of this period have all decayed, with some being replaced after the arrival of the railroads.

20. Savardan, *Un naufrage*, 100.
21. *Bulletin*, October 8, 1855, 7.
22. Wolski, *American Impressions*, 185.
23. *Bulletin*, October 8, 1855, 7–8.

17. TRYING OUT LIFE

1. Savardan, *Un naufrage*, 245.
2. Savardan, *Un naufrage*, 80.
3. Savardan, *Un naufrage*, 82, 83.
4. Savardan, *Un naufrage*, 186.
5. Savardan, *Un naufrage*, 185.
6. Savardan, *Un naufrage*, 85.
7. Nécrologie, *Bulletin*, December 4, 1855, 7.
8. Savardan, *Un naufrage*, 132.
9. Savardan, *Un naufrage*, 133.
10. Savardan, *Un naufrage*, 186–88.
11. This may be the home sketched by Allyre Bureau in 1857 or 1858. A copy was given to me by Bureau's great-great-granddaughter.
12. Godin, *Documents*, 562.
13. Savardan, *Un naufrage*, 154.
14. Savardan, *Un naufrage*, 155.
15. Savardan, *Un naufrage*, 156.
16. Savardan, *Un naufrage*, 155.
17. Savardan, *Un naufrage*, 156.
18. Savardan, *Un naufrage*, 157.
19. Savardan, *Un naufrage*, 160.
20. *Galveston News*, August 17, 1855.
21. *Northern Standard*, August 25, 1855, 2.
22. *Bulletin*, December 18, 1855, 7.
23. See Texas History, *Texas State Gazette*.
24. Savardan, *Un naufrage*, 113.
25. Savardan, *Un naufrage*, 115.
26. Savardan, *Un naufrage*, 118.
27. It appeared on pages 154–74 of Joumet's *Documents apostoliques et prophéties* (Paris, 1858). However, it must have been circulated immediately on reaching France in October 1855, along with letters from major stockholder Jean Goetseels.
28. *Bulletin*, December 18, 1855, 3–4.
29. Savardan, *Un naufrage*, 107.

30. Savardan, *Un naufrage*, 108.
31. *Bulletin*, February 29, 1856, 7.
32. Savardan, *Un naufrage*, 112–13, 110.
33. Savardan, *Un naufrage*, 151.

18. CONSIDERANT AND TEXAS POLITICS

1. Simonin, Diary, November 26, 1855–June 12, 1856, quote from December 19, 1855, 4b.
2. Simonin, Diary, December 19, 1855, 5a.
3. Simonin, Diary, January 8, 1856, 45a–45b.
4. Simonin, Diary, January 1, 1856, 39a–40a.
5. *State Gazette Appendix* (Austin TX), Sixth Legislature, vol. 1, November 12, 1855.
6. Simonin, Diary, January 1, 1856, 38b, 39a.
7. Page, *The Old South*, 64–65.
8. Simonin, Diary, January 1, 1856, 39b.
9. Simonin, Diary, January 8, 1856, 45b.
10. Considerant to Julie, December 16, 1855, 10AS28(9), AN.
11. Brvt. Maj. H. W. Merrill (1814–92), born in Bryan, upstate New York, and known to Brisbane. Merrill led Fort Mason, Fort Worth, and Fort Belknap and had entertained Brisbane and Considerant at Fort Worth two years previously. He resigned his army commission in 1857.
12. Antoine Supervièle, one of two foreign-born persons in the legislature (the other a German also representing Bexar County) and one of only three born outside the South.
13. Simonin, Diary, December 21, 1855, 5b.
14. Simonin, Diary, December 21, 1855, 7b.
15. Simonin, Diary, December 22, 1855, 8a.
16. Moore, *The Life and Diary*, 25; and Uvalde County Deed Records, A 214–44, E 486. While this sentence encompassed a year and a quarter, it included the phrase "particularly in September and October, 1856."
17. Seen in the Frenchman's account records of headrights that he bought from the senator.
18. Simonin, Diary, December 25, 1855, 11a.
19. Simonin, Diary, December 22, 1855, 8a.
20. Simonin, Diary, December 25, 1855, 12a.
21. Simonin, Diary, December 25, 1855, 12a.
22. Simonin, Diary, 11a–11b.
23. Simonin, Diary, December 27, 1855, 12b.

24. Simonin, Diary, December 27, 1855, 13a.
25. Simonin, Diary, December 29, 1855, 14b.
26. Simonin, Diary, January 5, 1856, 44a.
27. Simonin, Diary, January 10, 1856, 46a.
28. Simonin, Diary, January 8, 1856, 45a–45b.
29. Simonin, Diary, January 16, 1856, 47a.
30. Simonin, Diary, January 25, 1856, 49b.
31. Simonin, Diary, January 10, 1856, 46b.
32. Simonin, Diary, January 16, 1856. 47a.
33. Simonin, Diary, January 21, 1856, 48a.
34. Simonin, Diary, January 23, 1856, 48b.
35. Simonin, Diary, January 23, 1856, 48b.
36. Simonin, Diary, January 23, 1856, 49a.
37. Simonin, Diary, January 23, 1856, 49a.
38. Simonin, Diary, January 23, 1856, 49a.
39. Simonin, Diary, January 23, 1856, 48b.
40. Simonin, Diary, January 28, 1856, 50a.
41. Simonin, Diary, January 28, 1856, 50a.
42. Simonin, Diary, n.d., 42b.
43. Simonin, Diary, January 2, 1856, 43a.
44. Simonin, Diary, January 2, 1856, 43a–43b.
45. Simonin, Diary, January 28, 1856, 50a.
46. Considerant to Julie.

19. DOWNWARD SLIDE

1. It was particularly bad because another boy of roughly the same age, Phillipe DeGuelles, was in bed with tuberculosis and near death.
2. Simonin, Diary, February 1, 1856, 50b.
3. Simonin, Diary, February 15, 1856, 51b.
4. Simonin, Diary, April 3, 1856, 55b.
5. Savardan, *Un naufrage*, 121–22.
6. *L'amie des sciences*, December 2, 1855.
7. Savardan, *Un naufrage*, 230.
8. Savardan, *Un naufrage*, 125.
9. Savardan, *Un naufrage*, 125.
10. Savardan, *Un naufrage*, 122.
11. Savardan, *Un naufrage*, 137–38.
12. Simonin, Diary, March 24, 1856, 53b.
13. Simonin, Diary, March 24, 1856, 53b.

14. Simonin, Diary, March 24, 1856, 53b.

15. Savardan, *Un naufrage*, 223.

16. Simonin, Diary, March 24, 1856, 53b.

17. Simonin, Diary, April 6, 1856, 57b.

18. Fourier's birthday, April 7, long had been celebrated by Fourierists in Europe. Savardan, *Un naufrage*, 225.

19. When the twenty-year corporate life ran out in 1874, Cantagrel, a man of principle, bought the corporation's remaining land resources and returned a portion of the small funds remaining to the original stockholders. Perhaps that is the reason there is a Cantagrel Street in East Dallas but not a Considerant Street.

20. Beecher, *Victor Considerant*, 338–39.

21. "The Fourth," *Dallas Herald*, July 5, 1856, 2.

20. DEMISE

1. Savardan, *Un naufrage*, 263.

2. Savardan, *Un naufrage*, 257.

3. Savardan, *Un naufrage*, 268.

4. Savardan, *Un naufrage*, 276.

5. Savardan, *Un naufrage*, 270.

6. Savardan, *Un naufrage*, 272.

7. Savardan, *Un naufrage*, 280.

8. Savardan, *Un naufrage*, 287–90.

9. Savardan, *Un naufrage*, 289–90.

10. Savardan, *Un naufrage*, 295.

11. Savardan, *Un naufrage*, 304.

12. Savardan, *Un naufrage*, 350.

13. Savardan, *Un naufrage*, 351.

21. ENDINGS AND NEW BEGINNING

1. Savardan, *Un naufrage*, 1.

2. Savardan, *Un naufrage*, 6.

3. Savardan, *Un naufrage*, 302.

AFTERWORD

1. William H. Gaston opened the first bank across from the courthouse square on Main at Jefferson in 1868.

2. Wolski, *American Impressions*, 180.

3. This information is taken from Pratt, "Our European Heritage."

4. Julien's niece by marriage commented to me in 1977 that the only place she had ever seen blooming and fruiting almonds was in her uncle Julien's garden.
5. Maximilien Reverchon's letter on the subject of farming, printed in the *Bulletin*, lays out his knowledge of the subject.
6. According to great-granddaughter Louise Dietrich, the French gave him a gold medal for the design of a plow, but his investments in Fourierism cost him some of his lands south of Lyon that he had pledged to the Sig commune.
7. Sibley, 100–101; and F. N. Hayes, RB, *Diary and Letters*, 1:256.
8. Photo illustration at the Dallas Historical Society.
9. In the two mounds left by the Tonkawas near the street where he resided and that was named for him, Rémond found many relics.

Bibliography

Some copies of documents or translated materials are unpublished but are located in the author's research papers for this book. Photocopies of original letters are organized in the author's collection by date with English summaries of content. Individual letters are cited in chapter notes.

PRIMARY SOURCES

Allen, John. *An Occasional Sermon Delivered before the Old Colony Association of Universalists*, May 6, 1841. Boston: Christian Freeman Office, 1841. Tract, 16 pp.

Anon. *Biographie de M. Cabet.* Paris: Imp. de P. Beaudoin, ca. 1840s. At Institut Français d'histoire sociale.

———. *Études sur le socialisme: Réponse à M. Thonissen.*

———. *Instructions pour les lecteurs des documents ci-joints relatifs à la Compagnie de la baie de Galveston et des terres du Texas.* New York, 1830; Paris: Imp. de L. E. Herban, 1835. Originally in English.

———. *La question sociale.* Louvain: Souvenirs contemporains de socialisme et d'histoire par un Louvainiste, 1886. At Bibliothèque Royale Albert 1er, Brussels.

———. *Le Phalanstère en Algérie, banquet du 7 avril 1848. Journée électorat du 9 avril. Plan d'organisation du travail.* (Statu de l'Union Agricole d'Afrique.) Algeria: Imp. A. Bouget, 1848. 56 pp. Union du Sig. At Institut Français d'histoire sociale.

——— ("un élève des Jésuites"). *Les Chrétiens et les socialistes et la bonne foi de M. Thonissen.*

———. *Les Phalanstériennes de Louvain et l'opinion publique.* Impr. Emile Lelong et Cie., 1849. 53 pp. At Bibliothèque Royale Albert 1er, Brussels.

———. *L'Université Catholique de Louvain et le christianisme ou Jésuitisme et Socialisme.* Louvain: Impr. Émile Lelong, 1850. 36 pp. At Bibliothèque nationale de France.

———. *Mélanges phalanstériennes, No. 1, Étrennes aux civilisés.* Brussels: Chez François Michel, ed., 1847. 15 pp. Product of the Louvain group.

Bar, Kaspar. *Heinrich Pestalozzi, sein Leben und Werken*. Zurich: Drell, Fussli, und Comp., 1845. At Stadtbibliothek Zurich.

Beeman, James J. "Memoirs of James J. Beeman." December 24, 1886. freepages .rootsweb.com/~bman/genealogy/vol1/p155to165.htm.

Bonnard, Dr. Arthur de. *Organisation du travail, organisation d'une Commune Sociétaire d'après la théorie de Charles Fourier*. Boudonville: L'auteur, 1845. xxxix–131 pp. At Bibliothèque nationale de France.

Brisbane, Albert. *The Social Destiny of Man*. Philadelphia, 1840. Also serialized in the *New York Tribune*, 1842.

Brisbane, Ridelia. *Albert Brisbane: A Mental Biography with a Character Study*. Boston: Arena Publishing Company, 1893.

Bureau, Alice. Diary. Gabrielle Cadier-Rey Collection. Private collection.

Cabet, Étienne. *Colonie ou République Icarienne dans les États-Unis d'Amérique* . . . 2nd ed. Paris: The author, 1854. 59 pp.

———. *Procès du Communisme a Toulouse, avec les portraits des 12 accusés et la vue de l'audience dessinés par Léon Soulie*. Paris: Au Bureau du Populaire, September 1843. 126 pp. At Bibliothèque nationale de France.

Caillet, Marie, and Joseph K. Mertzweiller, eds. *The Louisiana Iris: The History and Culture of Five Native American Species and Their Hybrids*. Waco: Texas Gardener Press, 1988.

Cobb, Sylvanus, D. D. *Autobiography of the First Forty-One Years of the Life of Sylvanus Cobb, D.D., to Which Is Added a Memoir by His Eldest Son, Sylvanus Cobb, Jr.* Boston: Universalist Publishing House, 1867. 552 pp.

Considerant, Victor. *Au Texas: Deuxième edition. Contenant 1er rapport a mes amis; 2e bases et statu de la Société de colonisation européo-américaine au Texas; 3e un chapitre final comprenant, sous le titre de "Convention provisoire," les bases d'une premier établissement sociétaire*. Brussels: Au Siège de la Société de Colonisation, 1854; Paris: Librairie Phalanstérienne, 1855. Repr., Philadelphia: Porcupine Press, 1975.

———. *Destinée sociale*. 3 vols. Vol. 1, Paris: Chez les Librairies du Palais-Royal, September 1834. Vol. 2, Paris: Bureau de la Phalange, 1838. Vol. 3, Paris: Librairie de l'École Sociétaire, 1844.

———. *Du Texas. Premier rapport a mes amis*. Paris: Librairie Sociétaire, 1857.

———. *European Colonization in Texas: An Address to the American People*. New York: Baker, Godwin, 1855.

———. *The Great West: A New Social and Industrial Life in Its Fertile Regions*. Translated by A. Brisbane. New York: Dewitt and Davenport, 1854.

———. *Ma justification*. Brussels: Librairie Rosez, 1854. At Bibliothèque de Musée Sociale.

———. *Son Compte.* 10AS31(4). At Archives nationales (France).

Discailles, Ernest. *Charles Rogier (1800–1885) d'après des documents inédits.* 3 vols. Brussels: J. Lebegue et Cie., 1894. At Bibliothèque Royale Albert 1ᵉʳ, Brussels.

Fisher, James T. Papers. Massachusetts Historical Society, Boston.

Fourier, Charles. *Traité de l'association domestique-agricole ou attraction industrielle.* Paris: Bossange, 1822.

Godin, Jean-Baptiste. *Social Solutions.* Translated by Marie Howland. New York: John W. Lovell Company, 1886.

Havland, Marie. *Papa's Own Girl; a Novel.* New York, 1874. 547 pp. Third edition published as *The Familistère, a Novel.* Boston, 1918.

Hutchins, Thomas. *An Historical Narrative and Topographical Description of Louisiana and West Florida.* Philadelphia: Published by the author, 1784.

Hymans, L. *Types et silhouettes.* Brussels: A. N. Lebegue et Cie., 1877. At Bibliothèque Royale Albert 1ᵉʳ, Brussels.

Laws, Frances Smith. Diary.

Lebrocquy, Guillaume. *Types et profiles parlementaires.* Brussels, 1873. At Bibliothèque Royale Albert 1ᵉʳ, Brussels.

Leray, Adolphe. *Poésies, précédées d'une preface.* Tournai: Vasseur-Delmee, 1878.

Milton, George Fort. *The Eve of Conflict: Stephen A. Douglass and the Needless War.* New York: Octagon Books, 1963.

Moore, Ike, ed. *The Life and Diary of Reading W. Black, a History of Early Uvalde.* Uvalde TX: El Progresso Club, 1934. At the Bibliothèque Royale Albert 1ᵉʳ, Brussels.

Mordecai, George W. Papers. Library of the University of North Carolina.

Nichols, Roy F. *Franklin Pierce: Young Hickory of the Granite State.* 2nd ed. Philadelphia: University of Pennsylvania Press, 1958.

Page, Thomas Nelson. *The Old South.* New York: Charles Scribner's Sons, 1911.

Rabaux, M. R. "En prélude à la commémoration d'un centenaire." In *Guise 80: Bulletin Officiel Municipal.*

Record of the Newton and Watertown Universalist Societies, 1826–58. Bound manuscript, bNS 235/1 (1). Andover-Harvard Theological Library, Harvard Divinity School, Cambridge MA.

Reverchon, Julien. Diary. Dallas Historical Society.

Rey, Gabrielle. *Le Fouriériste Allyre Bureau (1810–59).* Travaux et Mémoires no. 21. Aix-en-Provence: Publications des Annales de la Faculté des Lettres, 1962.

Roper, Laura Wood. *FLO: A Biography of Frederick Law Olmsted.* Baltimore MD: Johns Hopkins University Press, 1973.

Savardan, Auguste. *Asile rural d'enfants trouvés*. Paris: Librairie Sociétaire, 1846 or 1848.

———. *Avenir: Études d'économie sociale*. Paris: Librairie Sociétaire, 1866.

———. *Défense des enfants trouvés et de leur asile rural*. Paris: Librairie Sociétaire, 1849.

———. *De l'association appliquée aux communes rurales*. Le Mans: Monnyer, 1842.

———. *De l'organisation d'un service médical pour les pauvres des campagnes*.

———. *Dernier examen de conscience d'un médecin . . .* Paris: Librairie Sociétaire, 1849.

———. *L'extinction du paupérisme réalisée par les enfants . . .* Paris: Garnier-Frères, Librairies Éditeurs, 1860.

———. *Monseigneur l'évêque du mans et le phalanstère*. Paris: Librairie Sociétaire, 1846.

———. *Notice sur la vie et les écrits du Professeur Vaidy*. Saint-Calais: Peltier, 1839.

———. *Shipwreck in Texas, Observations and Impressions Collected during Two and a Half Years Spent in Texas and in Traveling through the United States*.

———. *Un naufrage au Texas*. Paris: Gamier, 1858. Translated by Eloise Santerre.

Saxon, Lyle. *Old Louisiana*. New Orleans: Crager & Company, 1950.

Simonin, Amédée. Diary. Interlinear translation by Alexandra Pratt.

———. Diary, 1855 and 1856. Library of Congress, Washington DC.

Thonissen, M. *Le socialisme et ses promesses*.

Vigoureux, Clarisse. *Parole de Providence*. Paris: Bossange, 1834. Reprinted with a preface by Jean Claude Dubos. Seyssel: Champ Vallon, 1993.

Wolski, Kalikst. *American Impressions*. Translated by Marion Coleman. Cheshire CT: Cherry Hill Books, 1968.

———. *Do Ameryki i w Ameryce: Pdroze, szkice obyczajowe i obrazki z zycia mieszkancow Ameryki* [To America and in America: Travels, sketches and pictures from the life of the inhabitants of America]. Lviv, Ukraine: J. P. Piller, 1876.

SECONDARY SOURCES

Agulhon, Maurice. *The Republican Experiment, 1848–1852*. Translated by Janet Lloyd. 1973; Cambridge: Cambridge University Press, 1983.

Andrews, Stephen Pearl. *"Love, Marriage, and Divorce" and "The Sovereignty of the Individual."* Weston MA: M&S Press, 1975.

Babson, John J. *History of the Town of Gloucester*. Gloucester: Procter Bros., 1860.

Bartier, John, et al. *1848, les Utopismes sociaux: Utopie et action à la veille des journées de février*. Preface by Maurice Agulhon. Paris: Editions C.d.U.-Sedes réunis, 1981.

Becherer, Richard John. "Between Science and Sentiment: Cesar Daly and the Formulation of Modern Architectural Theory." PhD diss., Cornell University, 1980.

Beecher, Jonathan. *Charles Fourier: The Visionary and His World*. Berkeley: University of California Press, 1986.

——— . "Une utopie manquée au Texas: Victor Considerant et Réunion." *Cahiers Charles Fourier* 4 (1993): 40–79.

——— . *Victor Considerant and the Rise and Fall of French Romantic Socialism*. Berkeley: University of California Press, 2001.

Beeman, William H. *Pioneer Tales of the West*. Kessinger Publishing, 2010.

Bestor, Arthur. "Albert Brisbane—Propagandist for Socialism in the 1840s." *New York History* 28 (April 1947): 128–58.

Bestor, Arthur Eugene, Jr. "American Phalanxes: A Study of Fourierist Socialism in the United States (with Special Reference to the Movement in Western New York)." 2 vols. PhD diss., Yale University, New Haven CT, 1938.

——— . "Victor Considerant, First Communitarian." Paper delivered at the annual meeting of the American Historical Association, December 28, 1948. Bestor Papers, University of Illinois.

Bourqin, Hubert. *Victor Considerant, son œuvre*. Lyon: Imprimeries Réunies, 1909.

Bowie, Ellen. *Gay as a Grig*. Austin: University of Texas Printing Division, 1963.

Brémand, Nathalie. "Auguste Savardan (1792–1867)." Les premiers socialismes—Bibliothèque virtuelle de l'Université de Poitiers. June 22, 2009. http://premierssocialismes.edel.univ-poitiers.fr/collection/augustesavardan.

Codman, John T. *Brook Farm*. Boston: Arena Publishing Co., 1894.

Coignet, Clarisse. *Victor Considerant, sa vie et son œuvre*. Paris: Felix Alcan, 1895.

Coleman, Marion Moore, ed. and trans. "Kalikst Wolski in Texas." *Texana* 5, no. 3 (Fall 1967): 203–14.

——— . "New Light on La Réunion: From the Pages of *Do Ameryki i w Ameryce* [The memoirs of Kalikst Wolski]." *Arizona and the West: A Quarterly Journal of History* 6, no. 1 (Spring 1964): 41–68; and 6, no. 2 (Summer 1964): 137–54.

————. "New Orleans and the Mississippi in 1855." *Polish American Studies* 24, no. 2 (July–December 1967): 65–83.

————. "A Visit to the North American Phalanx." *Proceedings of the New Jersey Historical Society* 83 (July 1965): 149–60.

Collard, Pierre. *Victor Considerant (1808–1893), sa vie, ses idées.* Dijon: Barbier, 1910.

Connor, Seymour V. *The Peters Colony of Texas: A History and Biographical Sketches of the Early Settlers.* Austin: Texas State Historical Association, 1959.

Coombes, Z. E. *The Diary of a Frontiersman, 1858–1859.* Edited by Barbara Neal Ledbetter. Newcastle TX: Ledbetter, 1962.

Daly, César. Introduction to *Revue générale de l'architecture et des travaux publics* 14 (1856): 1–10.

Davidson, Rondel Van. *Did We Think Victory Great? The Life and Ideas of Victor Considerant.* Lanham MD: University Press of America, 1988.

————. "Reform versus Revolution: Victor Considerant and the Communist Manifesto." *Social Science Quarterly* 58, no. 1 (June 1977): 74–85.

————. "Victor Considerant and the Failure of La Réunion." *Southwestern Historical Quarterly* 76, no. 3 (January 1973): 277–96.

Debenham, Ivor Spencer. *The Victor and the Spoils: A Life of William L. Marcy.* Providence RI: Brown University Press, 1959.

Discailles, Ernest. "Le socialiste français Victor Considerant en Belgique." *Bulletin de l'Académie royale des sciences, des lettres et des beaux-arts de Belgique*, 3rd ser., 29 (1895): 705–48.

Dommanget, Maurice. *Victor Considerant, sa vie, son œuvre.* Paris: Éditions Sociales Internationales, 1929.

Dubos, Jean-Claude. "Clarisse Vigoureux, grand honnête homme." In *Clarisse Vigoureux, parole de Providence.* Seyssel: Champ Vallon, 1993.

————. "Un cent-cinquantenaire oublié: Paroles de Providence, de Clarisse Vigoureux (1834)." *Le Jura Français* 185 (January–March 1985): 121–24.

Fuchs, Rachel G. *Abandoned Children: Foundlings and Child Welfare in Nineteenth-Century France.* SUNY Series in Modern European Social History. Albany NY: SUNY Press, 1984.

Gard, Wayne. "Trinity River." *Handbook of Texas Online.* Texas State Historical Association. http://www.tshaonline.org/handbook/online/articles/rnt02.

Gibbon, V. E., ed. "Lawrie's Trip to Northeast Texas (1854–5)." *Southwestern Historical Quarterly* 48, no. 2 (1944): 238–53.

Godin, Jean-Baptiste. Documents pour une biographie complète de Jean-Baptiste-André Godin, premier volume, Familistère de Guise (Aisne) (1897–1901).

Guarneri, Carl J. "Réunion, Texas, post scriptum ironique au fouriérisme américain." *Cahiers Charles Fourier* 4 (1993): 13–27.

———. *The Utopian Alternative: Fourierism in Nineteenth-Century America.* Ithaca NY: Cornell University Press, 1991.

Hammond, William J., and Margaret F. Hammond. *La Réunion: A French Settlement in Texas.* Dallas: Royal, 1958.

Hayden, Dolores. *Seven American Utopias: The Architecture of Communitarian Socialisme, 1790–1975.* Cambridge MA: MIT Press, 1976.

James, Marquis. *The Raven: A Biography of Sam Houston.* 1929.

Jones, Russell M. "Victor Considerant's American Experience (1852–1869)." *French-American Review* 1 (1976–77): 65–94, 124–50.

Klier, Betje Black. "Des Fourieristes au Texas: La famille Considerant à San Antonio." *French Review* 68, no. 6 (May 1995): 1035–50.

Marcy, R. B. *Thirty Years of Army Life on the Border.* New York: Harper's, 1866.

Miller, Russell M. *The Larger Hope: The First Century of the Universalist Church in America 1770–1870.* Vol. 1. Boston: Unitarian Universalist Association, 1979.

Moët, Marie. *Veuve.* Vol. 1, *Godin to Industry Employee.* January 21, 1855.

Morrison, John H. *History of American Steam Navigation.* New York: Stephen Daye, 1958.

Negley, Glenn. *Utopian Literature: A Bibliography.* Lawrence KS: Regents Press, 1977.

Nichols, Roy F. *Franklin Pierce: Young Hickory of the Granite State.* 2nd ed. Philadelphia: University of Pennsylvania Press, 1958.

Nicolas, Jean. "Essai sur la topographie physique et médicale du Champsaur." Thesis, Faculté de Médecine de Montpellier, December 24, 1824.

Noyes, John Humphrey. *History of American Socialisms.* 1870; New York: Hillary House, 1961. Repr. titled *Strange Cults and Utopias of 19th Century America.* New York: Dover, 1966.

Payne, Howard C., and Henry Grosshans. "The Exiled Revolutionaries and the French Political Police in the 1850s." *American Historical Review* 68, no. 4 (July 1963).

Pettit, Richard Norman, Jr. "Albert Brisbane: Apostle of Fourierism in the United States, 1834–1890." PhD diss., Miami University, Ohio, 1982.

Pratt, James. "Jeudi 22 décembre 1854: Les premiers fouriéristes foulent le sol du Texas." Translated into French by Michael Cordillot. *Cahiers Charles Fourier* 4 (1993): 28–29.

———. "Les femmes de Réunion." Translated into French by Gaston Bourdet. *Cahiers Charles Fourier* (2003).

——— . "Our European Heritage." *Legacies* 1, no. 2 (Fall 1989): 14–17.

——— . "Secret Saboteur." *Legacies* 21, no. 2 (Fall 2009).

Prieur, Vincent. "Un syncrétisme utopie: Le cas du Fouriérisme américaine." In *1848, les utopismes sociaux: Utopie et action à la veille des journées de février,* by John Bartier et al. Paris: Editions C.d.U.-Sedes réunis, 1981. See the translation by James Pratt.

Reynolds, David S. *Beneath the American Renaissance: The Subversive Imagination in the Age of Emerson and Melville.* Cambridge MA: Harvard University Press, 1988.

Rozwenc, Edwin. *Cooperatives Come to America: A History of the Protective Union Stall Movement 1847–1865.* Mount Vernon, 1947.

Saint-Ferreol, Amédée. *Les proscrits français en Belgique, ou la Belgique contemporaine vue a travers l'exil.* 2 vols. Brussels: Librairie Européenne C. Muquardt, Henry Merzbach, Successeur, 1870–71.

Santerre, Eloïse. "Reunion, a Translation of Dr. Savardan's *Un naufrage au Texas,* with an Introduction to Reunion and a Biographical Dictionary of the Settlers." MA thesis, Southern Methodist University, Dallas, 1936.

Santerre, George H. *White Cliffs of Dallas: The Story of La Réunion, the Old French Colony.* Dallas: Book Craft, 1955.

Schama, Simon. *Citizens: A Chronicle of the French Revolution.* New York: Alfred A. Knopf, 1989.

Smith, Eugene W. *Passenger Ships of the World.* Boston: G. H. Dean Co., 1963.

Swift, Lindsay. *Brook Farm, Its Members, Scholars, and Visitors.* New York: Macmillan, 1900.

Verlet, Bruno. "Les Fourieristes au Texas: Du rêve à la réalité." *Cahiers Charles Fourier* 4 (1993): 80–101.

Zeldin, Theodore. *France 1848–1945.* Vol. 1, *Ambition, Love and Politics.* Oxford: Clarendon Press, 1973.

Index

Page numbers in italics indicate illustrations.